RIGHTS OF JUVENILES:

The Juvenile Justice System

CRIMINAL LAW SERIES

Searches & Seizures, Arrests and Confessions
by William E. Ringel

Eye-Witness Identification: Legal and Practical Problems
by Nathan R. Sobel

New York Criminal Practice Under the CPL
by Robert M. Pitler

Prisoners' Rights Sourcebook: Theory•Litigation•Practice
edited by Michele G. Hermann
and Marilyn G. Haft

Political Criminal Trials: How to Defend Them
by John M. Sink

Plea Bargaining and Guilty Pleas
by James E. Bond

Representation of Witnesses Before Federal Grand Juries
by National Lawyers Guild

The Law of Electronic Surveillance
by James G. Carr

RIGHTS OF JUVENILES:

THE JUVENILE JUSTICE SYSTEM

by

SAMUEL M. DAVIS

Clark Boardman Company, Ltd.
New York, New York
1974

To Carolyn

FOREWORD

More and more lawyers are called upon to make appearances in juvenile courts. For most of them, representing a client in juvenile court is a strange and confusing experience. The atmosphere is likely to be quite informal, yet the issues litigated are governed by constitutional principles and legal rules. An attorney often feels uncertain about his role. Is he or she to serve as a traditional advocate, as a help to the court, as one who provides assistance to the parents, or as a guardian for the youngster, taking only those legal positions which the attorney believes will benefit the child?

In my view, a lawyer in a juvenile court who has been engaged to represent the respondent child has *that child* as the client—not the parents or the court. The child is entitled to all the legal advantages provided under the law. If a child's confession has been taken unlawfully or if illegally obtained evidence is offered to support an adjudication of delinquency, the evidence should be suppressed if the child wishes to defeat the allegation of the petition. Of course, a litigant can in most cases waive constitutional rights. The difficulty in respect to children is that, generally speaking, they are not completely free to make their own judgments. Yet I submit that a lawyer is not a happy choice for a guardian's role. Parents, or others more skilled in judging the real needs of children, can perform the role better.

In short, I think a lawyer in the juvenile court best
serves as a lawyer, not as a "dutch uncle" counsel to the
child, or as a wise friend. It is too easy for these roles to be
confused and conflicting. There is, of course, a great deal
of controversy respecting such views. However that may
be, Professor Davis' excellent volume is a great gift to any
lawyer who need appear in a juvenile court—no matter
how that lawyer perceives the professional role.

Professor Davis introduces counsel to the traditional "juvenile court philosophy," *i.e.*, that the court exists to help, not to punish; to exercise the state's powers
parens patriae. Those who established the juvenile court
sought to create a tribunal which would open the doors of
help for the child. The state's resources for the salvation of
youth would be made available by the court's adjudication. Nevertheless, Professor Davis goes on and reminds
all of us of the limitations of that dream and the new
constitutional limits on the operation of the child-saving
apparatus. This book is heavily researched. A lawyer in
any state will find much here that is of direct relevance at
home. More importantly, the great issues of the juvenile
court are explored in an articulate and careful fashion:
How should one define delinquency? Should the juvenile
courts exercise power over children who have committed
no crime but merely are involved as "ungovernables,"
"beyond the control of parents," or children in-the-need-
of-supervision? Professor Davis gives careful attention to
the scope of the constitutional limitations. He presents a
rich discussion of the application of the Fourth and Fifth
Amendments to the court's proceedings as well as of the
Sixth Amendment's right to counsel. He explores the problems of waiver of juvenile cases to criminal court and also
the question of when a child can choose not to exercise his
constitutional rights.

Set forth in full is the Uniform Juvenile Court Act

which has had a great impact throughout the country (also useful for the explanatory notes to each section, which illuminate the legal issues involved in the proposed draft).

Professor Davis has done the legal profession a great service. Those who appear in juvenile court at any time will find this book indispensable.

Monrad G. Paulsen
John B. Minor Professor and
Dean, University of Virginia
Law School

Charlottesville, Virginia
July, 1974

INTRODUCTION

In *In re Gault*, 387 U.S. 1 (1967), the United States Supreme Court in a single move set in motion forces that have brought about a reexamination of the entire breadth of the relationship between children and the state. The result of this inquiry has been accommodation of constitutional due process standards in juvenile proceedings. The purpose of this book is to present a current view of the impact of the *Gault* case and its *progeny* on the juvenile process. Toward this purpose it is written for a general audience with hope that it will prove useful to juvenile court judges, lawyers, law students, and nonlawyers who have an interest in the juvenile justice process.

I would be remiss if I did not take this opportunity to acknowledge my appreciation to the many people whose assistance made this book possible. First of all, I wish to thank several students, present and former, of the University of Georgia School of Law whose research assistance and contributions were invaluable. They are: Darrell Begnaud, James L. Gale, William V. Hearnberg, Lettie Elizabeth Lane, Richard W. Littlefield, James F. Martin, Thomas L. Martin, Phyllis P. McSheain, and the students in my Juvenile Courts Seminar. Secondly, I would like to thank the secretaries at the University of Georgia School of Law who assisted from time to time in typing and proofreading the manuscript. Special thanks is offered to my secretaries, who did most of the typing: Joyce Looney and

Judi Pitts. Thirdly, I am grateful to the School of Law for the research time generously given to assist me in completing the manuscript. I am especially grateful to my colleagues for their encouragement as I undertook this project, and for their understanding during the time I worked on it. Also, appreciation is expressed to the Duke Law Journal for permission to use portions of my article, "Justice for the Juvenile: The Decision to Arrest and Due Process," published in 1971 Duke Law Journal 913, and to the North Carolina Law Review for permission to use in this book portions of my article, "The Jurisdictional Dilemma of the Juvenile Court," published at 51 North Carolina Law Review 195 (1972). Finally, I wish to acknowledge, with deep appreciation and affection, the long-suffering but untiring patience and understanding of my wife, whose strength enabled our relationship to withstand the heavy demands of an undertaking such as this one.

Samuel M. Davis

Athens, Georgia
May, 1974

TABLE OF CONTENTS

Chapter 1

Philosophy of the Juvenile Court

Chapter 2

Jurisdiction

Chapter 3

The Pre-Judicial Process: Police Investigation

I. Taking Into Custody

II Search and Seizure

III. Post-Custody Release

IV. Police Interrogation

Chapter 4

Waiver of Jurisdiction

Chapter 5

The Adjudicatory Process

Chapter 6

The Dispositional Process

Chapter 7

Future Direction of The Juvenile Court

Chapter 1

PHILOSOPHY OF THE JUVENILE COURT

§ 1.01. Origin in the United States
§ 1.02. Philosophical Underpinnings
§ 1.03. The Philosophy Today

§ 1.01. Origin in the United States.

The establishment of the first juvenile court in Cook County, Illinois, on July 1, 1899, was a milestone as an innovative procedural concept for the treatment and handling of juveniles separately from adults, but it was not the first attempt to reform the laws relating to children.

The first reform efforts date to the early part of the nineteenth century, characterized by its religious and moral awakening. Early concern, however, was not directed toward massive procedural change in all stages of the state's relationship with children, but rather toward the dispositional stage, particularly toward protection of wayward children (orphans, paupers, and juveniles convicted of offenses in criminal courts). As an outgrowth of this concern, houses of refuge were established in a number of cities by well-meaning reformists anxious to keep youthful offenders separate from adult criminals. H.

1

Lou, *Juvenile Courts in the United States* 13-19 (1927). For an historical account of the houses of refuge and other early efforts toward juvenile reform, *see* R. Mennel, *Origins of the Juvenile Court: Changing Perspectives on the Legal Rights of Juvenile Delinquents*, 18 Crime & Delinq. 68 (1972).

Judged in terms of the impact of the later juvenile court movement, these were modest reforms. They were designed to mollify the harshness of certain phases of the existing system, particularly the correctional phase. In other respects, the procedures for handling juveniles were identical in form and application to those employed in dealing with adults — in essence, penal in nature. What was still lacking was a completely new concept of an independent but parallel system for processing juveniles, a concept that would redefine the relationship between the juvenile and the state.

§ 1.02. Philosophical Underpinnings.

Establishment of a juvenile court in Cook County, Illinois, in 1899 marked the first implementation of a separate judicial framework whose sole concern was directed to problems and misconduct of youth. The juvenile court was designed to be more than a court for children, however. It marked a conceptual change in the nature of the child's conduct, the child's responsibility for its conduct, and the state's role in dealing with that conduct.

The redefinition of the state's relationship to the child was not really an innovation but rather was based on the old English concept of *parens patriae*, whereby a court of equity, exercising the Crown's paternal prerogative, could declare a child a ward of the Crown when the parents had failed to maintain the child's welfare. The *parens patriae* principle was central to the juvenile court concept, because it altered not only the state's role but altered as well the state's perception of the child and the child's conduct. Children were no longer to be dealt with as criminals, but rather through the *parens patriae* power of the state were to be treated as wards of the state, not fully responsible for their conduct and capable of being rehabilitated. J. Mack, *The Juvenile Court*, 23 Harv. L. Rev. 104, 109 (1909). This gave rise to the designation of youthful offenders as delinquents rather than criminals. S. Breckinridge, and E. Abbott, *The Delinquent Child and the Home* 247 (1970).

The juvenile court was a by-product of the sociological jurisprudence movement, the major thrust of which was that the law was simply a means for attaining certain social ends. A tenet of sociological jurisprudence was that law ought to be infused with the social sciences. Logically, since delinquency was regarded as primarily a social phenomenon, reclamation of children was to occur through application of the tools of the social sciences rather than the familiar paraphernalia of the criminal process. Acceptance of this sociological premise represented the most striking change in the process. Lawyers and prosecutors were replaced by social workers, probation officers, psychologists, psychiatrists, and physicians whose role was to produce information about the child and its background and environment that would be helpful in assessing and treating the child's problem.

The proceeding was thus nonadversary, presided over by a judge — a father-figure — who represented at once the interests of the child and the interests of the state. H. Lou, *Juvenile Courts in the United States* 1-2 (1927).

Because the juvenile court was geared to protection, not punishment, the juvenile proceeding was conceptualized as a civil and not a criminal proceeding. *See Ex parte Sharp*, 15 Idaho 120, 96 P. 563 (1908). Indeed, the juvenile court was regarded as dispensing a higher form of justice than that obtainable in the criminal courts. P. Alexander, *Constitutional Rights in the Juvenile Court*, in *Justice for the Child* 82, 84-85 (M. Rosenheim ed. 1962).

§ 1.03. The Philosophy Today.

Few voices have been heard to decry the very existence of the juvenile court or to question seriously its underlying premises. *But see* J. Wigmore, *Juvenile Court vs. Criminal Court*, 21 Ill. L. Rev. 375 (1926). Most of the objections that have been articulated are in derogation of what the juvenile court has *become*, since its procedures have been altered to conform to requirements of the Constitution. *See, e.g., In re Winship*, 397 U.S. 358, 375-76 (1970) (Burger, C.J., dissenting); *In re Gault*, 387 U.S. 1, 78-81 (1967) (Stewart, J., dissenting). *See also* P. Alexander, *Constitutional Rights in the Juvenile Court*, in *Justice for the Child* 82, 92 (M. Rosenheim ed. 1962).

These modern critics have urged that, through application of constitutional due process standards, the juvenile process has been endowed with all the trappings of the criminal process and has lost its informal, nonadversary character. What the critics overlook, perhaps, is that the advent of the juvenile court can be viewed in different perspectives. At the same time that the juvenile court established a benevolent, protective, nonadversary relationship between the child and the state, it also effected a loss of procedural rights upon children, a loss that was obscured and forgotten for over half a century in the glow and promise of a system that purported to serve the best interests of the child. *See* S. Fox, *The Reform of Juvenile Justice: An Historical Perspective*, 22 Stanford L. Rev. 1187 (1970).

Thus, throughout the history of the juvenile court movement, courts denied children procedural rights that

they had previously enjoyed, on the basis that the proceeding was civil and not criminal, that it was a nonadversary proceeding, and that the juvenile court was able to
protect the interests of the child as well as serve the interests of society, those interests being identical. *See, e.g.,*
Application of Gault, 99 Ariz. 181, 407 P.2d 760 (1965), *rev'd*,
367 U.S. 1 (1967).

What in principle was the product of the highest
motives and enlightened benevolence, however, in practice often led to procedural arbitrariness. This sacrifice of
substantive rights for the sake of procedural informality
was condemned by the United States Supreme Court in *In
re Gault*, 387 U.S. 1 (1967). The Court pointed out earlier in
Kent v. United States, 383 U.S. 541, 556 (1966), that a child
likely receives the worst of both worlds, that he receives
"neither the protections accorded to adults nor the solici-
tous care and regenerative treatment postulated for children."

Procedural reforms, while altering the most visible
part of the juvenile process — the procedural setting —
have not prevented the juvenile court from attaining its
basically ameliorative purposes, particularly at the dispositional stage. The protective philosophy has endured, and
the juvenile court continues to perform its function of
tailoring justice to meet the needs of the child as those
needs are determined by the social services staff. Only by
assuring a child of procedural fairness will a court that
purports to represent that child's interests impart to him
an unjaundiced view of a system of justice that is fair and
benevolent. This goal, after all, was one of the original
purposes sought to be achieved by application of the principle of *parens patriae.*

Chapter 2

JURISDICTION

§ 2.01. Age Jurisdiction: Maximum Age.

Two principal factors determine the jurisdiction of the juvenile court: age and conduct.

7

The outer limit for exercise of the juvenile court's jurisdiction is determined by establishing a maximum age, below which children are deemed subject to the ameliorative processes of the court. Indeed, "child" is generally defined as a person under the maximum age establishing the court's jurisdiction.

The jurisdictional age is generally the same for all children and for all forms of conduct. A few states set the jurisdictional age at sixteen. *See, e.g.*, Ala. Code tit. 13, § 350 (1959). Some states prescribe seventeen as the jurisdictional age. *See, e.g.*, La. Rev. Stat. Ann. § 13:1569(3) (1968); Mass. Gen. Laws Ann. ch. 119, § 52 (1969). By far the most common maximum jurisdictional age is eighteen, which is accepted as the jurisdictional age in slightly more than two-thirds of the states and the District of Columbia. *See, e.g.*, Alaska Stat. § 47.10.010 (1971); Cal. Welf. & Inst'ns Code §§ 600-602 (1972); Minn. Stat. Ann. § 260.015(2) (1971); Va. Code Ann. § 16.1-141(3) (Supp. 1973); Wyo. Stat. Ann. § 14-115.2(e) (Supp. 1973). *See* Appendix B, *infra*, for all the state jurisdictional ages.

Although a maximum age jurisdiction is generally prescribed, there are occasionally other factors that alter the court's maximum age jurisdiction. For example, some states by statute provide that the juvenile court may acquire jurisdiction over children who are actually over the jurisdictional age of the juvenile court. Jurisdiction over this older group of children is acquired upon transfer from the criminal court; the juvenile court may not initially take jurisdiction over such a child. In Alabama, for example, the maximum age for original juvenile court jurisdiction is sixteen, but the criminal court has discretion to transfer to juvenile court a person who has reached his sixteenth birthday but who is under eighteen years of age. Ala. Code tit. 13, § 363 (1959). *See also* Mich. Compiled Laws Ann. § 712A.2(d) (Supp. 1974); Vt. Stat. Ann. tit. 33, § 635(b) (Supp. 1973).

The maximum jurisdictional age may vary depending on the kind of conduct that is the basis for the petition. Some states establish one jurisdictional age limit for purposes of dealing with truant, incorrigible or runaway children, but set a lower jurisdictional age for purposes of dealing with children who have violated the criminal code. N.H. Rev. Stat. Ann. § 169.2(III) (Supp. 1971); N.C. Gen. Stat. § 7A-278(1) (Supp. 1973); Vt. Stat. Ann. tit. 33, § 632(a) (1) (Supp. 1973).

Some states have a lower jurisdictional age limit for the more urban areas than that applicable in the rest of the state. S.C. Code Ann. § 15-1103(1), (7) (1962). A similar statutory scheme in Maryland was declared to be an unconstitutional denial of due process of law and equal protection of the laws in *Long v. Robinson*, 316 F. Supp. 22 (D. Md. 1970), *aff'd*, 436 F.2d 1116 (4th Cir. 1971).

Some states formerly prescribed different jurisdictional ages for males and females. Upholding the validity of an Oklahoma statute setting sixteen as the jurisdictional age for males and eighteen for females, the Oklahoma Supreme Court stated: "As we view the situation, the statute exemplifies the legislative judgment of the Oklahoma State Legislature, *premised upon the demonstrated facts of life*; and we refuse to interfere with that judgment." (emphasis added). *Lamb v. State*, 475 P.2d 829, 830 (Okla. 1970).

However, the United States Court of Appeals for the Tenth Circuit disagreed, holding the Oklahoma statute unconstitutional on equal protection grounds:

> "The 'demonstrated facts' which the Court relied upon are not spelled out. They are not obvious or apparent. We therefore cannot weigh them to determine if they 'might suffice to characterize the classification as reasonable rather than arbitrary and invidious'. [citation omitted]

> "... Because the purpose of the disparity in the
> age classification between 16-18 year old males
> and 16-18 year old females has not been demon-
> strated, we hold that 10 Okl. Stat. Ann. § 1101(a)
> is violative of the equal protection clause." *Lamb
> v. Brown*, 456 F.2d 18, 20 (10th Cir. 1972).

See also Patricia A. v. City of New York, 31 N.Y.2d 83, 286 N.E.2d 432, 335 N.Y.S.2d 33 (1972), which reached a substantially similar result regarding a New York statute that differentiated between males and females on the basis of age. On the question of sexual bias in juvenile court laws generally, *see* S. Davis, and S. Chaires, *Equal Protection for Juveniles: The Present Status of Sex-Based Discrimination in Juvenile Court Laws*, 7 Ga. L. Rev. 494 (1973).

All of the above matters, to the extent they alter the juvenile court's jurisdiction, are treated in § 2.07, *infra*, as limitations on the jurisdiction of the juvenile court.

§ 2.02. Age Jurisdiction: Minimum Age.

Statutes describing juvenile court jurisdiction generally do not address the problem of a minimum jurisdictional age. The problem, of course, arises out of the common law presumption that a child under the age of seven is deemed incapable of committing a criminal offense. Does this presumption operate in a juvenile proceeding in which the basis of a delinquency allegation is the commission of a criminal offense? If so, then a child under the statutory age of criminal responsibility is entitled to the same defense of incapacity available in a criminal proceeding.

Some states have made it clear that there *is* a minimum age below which the juvenile court is powerless to act, below which the child is not to be held accountable for criminal conduct, in either a juvenile or a criminal proceeding. Massachusetts law, for example, defines "child" as a person who is under seventeen years of age but over the age of seven years, using the common law age of seven years as a terminal of juvenile court jurisdiction. Mass. Gen. Laws Ann. ch. 119, § 52 (1969); see also Tex. Fam. Code Ann. § 51.02(1) (A) (1973) (child is person ten years of age or older and less than seventeen years of age). Under the provisions of a Colorado statute describing criminal accountability, a child under the age of ten is not responsible for his acts in juvenile or criminal court. Colo. Rev. Stat. Ann. § 22-1-3(17) (a) (Supp. 1967).

Moreover, in a recent California case, the California Supreme Court held that in a juvenile proceeding the court must determine whether the child appreciated the wrongfulness of her act in deciding whether the child should be adjudicated a ward of the state (the child was under the age of fourteen, which is California's age of presumptive incapacity). *In re Gladys R.*, 1 Cal.3d 855, 464 P.2d 127, 83 Cal. Rptr. 671 (1970). Thus California takes the view that the age of accountability is a relevant factor in a juvenile proceeding as well as a criminal proceeding.

Other states do not accord the age of criminal responsibility any relevance in a juvenile proceeding, which by its nature is a civil and not a criminal proceeding. In Georgia, for example, the notes following the statute setting thirteen as the age of criminal responsibility suggest that in a criminal proceeding a child under thirteen would have an absolute defense of incapacity, but nevertheless could be proceeded against as a juvenile in a juvenile proceeding. Ga. Code Ann. § 26-701, Committee Notes (1972). This seems to reflect the view that a child may be incapable of committing a *crime* but is not incapable for reasons of age of committing a delinquent act, since capacity is not a consideration in a juvenile proceeding. *K.M.S. v. State*, 129 Ga. App. 683, 200 S.E.2d 916 (1973).

Likewise, the Model Penal Code's provision setting forth juvenile court age jurisdiction was designed to emasculate the legal issue of criminal capacity and to hold a person under sixteen accountable only in juvenile court, where the traditional concept of incapacity has no application. *See* Model Penal Code § 4.10, Comment (Tent. Draft No. 7, 1957). The Model Penal Code formulation indicates that an age of criminal responsibility was made an archaic concept by enactment of juvenile court laws, which were unknown to the common law.

Having an age of accountability is neither helpful nor appropriate in light of juvenile court jurisdictional age limits and waiver procedures. This view would render capacity an irrelevant concept in a juvenile proceeding, since diminished capacity was one of the justifications for having a juvenile court at all.

Oklahoma law includes accountability as one of the criteria considered during the waiver process. Before the juvenile court may waive jurisdiction over a child and transfer the case to criminal court, the court must first find that the child is capable of discerning right from wrong and is accountable for its acts. Okla. Stat. Ann. tit. 10, § 1112(b) (Supp. 1974). To the same effect is a decision of the Mississippi Supreme Court that a child under the age of 18 (the juvenile court's jurisdictional age) is not criminally accountable unless the juvenile court waives jurisdiction and transfers the case for adjudication to the criminal court. *Wheeler v. Shoemake*, 213 Miss. 374, 399, 57 So.2d 267, 279 (1952). *See also State ex rel. Slatton v. Boles*, 147 W. Va. 674, 683-85, 130 S.E.2d 192, 198-99 (1963). These decisions and statutory provisions indicate, of course, that capacity to commit crime does not become a consideration in the juvenile court unless that court is contemplating waiving jurisdiction and transferring the case to criminal court.

The problem of the age factor in juvenile court jurisdiction has been treated in S. Davis, *The Jurisdictional Dilemma of the Juvenile Court*, 51 N.C.L. Rev. 195, 219-29 (1972).

§ 2.03. Determination of Age Jurisdiction.

For purposes of establishing juvenile court jurisdiction, a fundamental question is whether the child's age should be determined as of the time the offense was committed or as of the time the proceeding is instituted.

Suppose a child commits an offense while he is within the range of juvenile age jurisdiction, but a petition is not filed against him until after he is beyond the jurisdictional age limit. What should be done with him? The draftsmen of the Model Penal Code suggest that the age at the time of commission of the offense is most relevant because of the child's diminished capacity at that time to commit the wrong. Why, they ask, should the mere passage of time operate to deny the juvenile court initial jurisdiction over the case? Model Penal Code § 4.10, Comment (Tent. Draft No. 7, 1957).

Most jurisdictions ostensibly take the approach suggested in the Model Penal Code. *See, e.g.*, Cal. Welf. & Inst'ns Code § 604(a) (1972); Fla. Stat. Ann. § 39.02(3) (1961); Ga. Code Ann. §§ 24A-401 (c), 24A-901 (Supp. 1973) (jurisdiction over older youths allowed only in narrow instance where youth is already under court's supervision and is charged with act committed before becoming seventeen); Hawaii Rev. Stat. § 571-12 (1968), § 571-11(1) (Supp. 1972); Ind. Ann. Stat. § 9-3213 (1956); La. Rev. Stat. Ann. §§ 13:1570(B), 13:1571 (1968); Md. Ann. Code, Cts. & Jud. Proc. § 3-814(a) (1974); Mass. Gen. Laws Ann. ch. 119, § 72A (1965); Minn. Stat. Ann. § 260.115 (1971); Mo. Ann. Stat. § 211.061(2) (1962); Mont. Rev. Codes Ann. §§

10-603(b), 10-610 (Supp. 1973); Neb. Rev. Stat. § 43-211 (1968); Nev. Rev. Stat. § 62.050 (1973); N.H. Rev. Stat. Ann. § 169.2(III) (Supp. 1971); N.J. Stat. Ann. § 2A:4-20 (1952); N.M. Stat. Ann. § 13-14-11 (Supp. 1973); N.Y. Fam. Ct. Act § 714(a) (McKinney 1963); N.D. Cent. Code §§ 27-20-02(1) (b), 27-20-09 (1974); Okla. Stat. Ann. tit. 10, § 1112(a) (Supp. 1974); Pa. Stat. Ann. tit. 11, § 50-102(1) (Supp. 1974); R.I. Gen. Laws Ann. § 14-1-28 (1970); Tex. Fam. Code Ann. § 51.02(1) (1973); Utah Code Ann. § 55-10-79 (Supp. 1973); Vt. Stat. Ann. tit. 33, § 635(a) (Supp. 1973); Va. Code Ann. § 16.1-175 (1960); W. Va. Code Ann. § 49-5-3 (1966); Wyo. Stat. Ann. § 14-115.4 (a) (ii) (Supp. 1973).

Other jurisdictions, however, seem to favor determination of jurisdiction according to the age of the person at the time proceedings are commenced. The statutes generally require transfer of a child to the juvenile court if it appears to the transferring court that he is a child or is at that time below the jurisdictional age of the juvenile court. No reference is made to the age of the child at the time the act was allegedly committed. *See, e.g.*, Ala. Code tit. 13, § 363 (1959); Conn. Gen. Stat. Ann. § 17-65 (1960); Iowa Code Ann. § 232.64 (1969); Ohio Rev. Code Ann. § 2151.25 (1971); Ore. Rev. Stat. § 419.478 (1971); S.C. Code Ann. § 15-1188 (1962); Tenn. Code Ann. § 37-209 (Supp. 1973).

In still other instances the intent is unclear. For example, one Michigan statute provides that if during pendency of a criminal proceeding in another court, the court learns that the defendant is under seventeen years of age, the case must be transferred to the juvenile court. Mich. Compiled Laws Ann. § 764.27 (Supp. 1974). This would suggest that jurisdiction is determined as of the time of the hearing. However, the Code elsewhere provides for transfer if it appears to the transferring court that the person was under seventeen years of age at the time the act was committed. *Id.* § 712A.3 (Supp. 1974).

The draftsmen of the Model Penal Code suggest that when the statutes are silent the courts tend to favor determination of age jurisdiction as of the time of the proceeding. Model Penal Code § 4.10, Comment (Tent. Draft No. 7, 1957). They show the following as favoring this interpretation: *Davis v. State*, 259 Ala. 212, 66 So. 2d 714 (1953); *Burrows v. State*, 38 Ariz. 99, 297 P. 1029 (1931); *People v. Ross*, 235 Mich. 433, 209 N.W. 663 (1926); *Farr v. State*, 199 Miss. 637, 24 So. 2d 186 (1946); *State v. Adams*, 316 Mo. 157, 289 S.W. 948 (1926); *Ex parte Albiniano*, 62 R.I. 429, 6 A.2d 554 (1939); *Smith v. State*, 99 Tex. Crim. 432, 269 S.W. 793 (1925); *State v. Melvin*, 144 Wash. 687, 258 P. 859 (1927). The following are listed as *contra* this interpretation: *United States v. Fotto*, 103 F. Supp. 430 (S.D.N.Y. 1952); *White v. Commonwealth*, 242 Ky. 736, 47 S.W.2d 548 (1932); *State v. Cable*, 181 N.C. 554, 107 S.E. 132 (1921); *Sams v. State*, 133 Tenn. 188, 180 S.W. 173 (1915). Of course, in some instances the statutes are no longer silent.

The difficulty with the solution proposed by the Model Penal Code is that, while commission of the act may have been reflective of the child's capacity at the time the act was committed, reality suggests that he may no longer be amenable to the rehabilitative processes of the juvenile court because of his present age. The decision has correctional implications. Not only may this child not be responsive, but he may pose a problem to effective treatment of other, younger children. M. Paulsen, *The Delinquency, Neglect, and Dependency Jurisdiction of the Juvenile Court*, in *Justice for the Child* 44, 58-59 (M. Rosenheim ed. 1962).

It may seem unfair to decide on the issue of jurisdiction without considering factors other than age. Age, after all, is only one of many elements considered in waiver of jurisdiction. (*See* § 4.03, *infra*, for discussion of other factors.) For this reason, the best approach would be to authorize the juvenile court to assume original jurisdiction over all youths between the maximum age limit and twenty-one years of age (or the age of majority), in cases in which the offense occurred before the youth reached the maximum age limit. The juvenile court probably would waive jurisdiction over most of these cases and transfer them to criminal court, but an examination of considerations in addition to age may, in some cases, indicate that a youth would be responsive to treatment as a juvenile. Of course, if such person is beyond the age of majority at the time he appears before the criminal court, such court has proper jurisdiction in any event. *See, e.g., State v. Dehler*, 257 Minn. 549, 555, 102 N.W.2d 696, 702 (1960); *State ex rel. Pett v. Jackson*, 252 Minn. 418, 422, 90 N.W.2d 219, 222, (1958); *State ex rel. Knutson v. Jackson*, 249 Minn. 246, 253, 82 N.W.2d 234, 239 (1957).

§ 2.04. Jurisdiction Over Conduct: Neglect, Deprivation.

The second factor determining juvenile court jurisdiction is conduct. The juvenile court has jurisdiction over a number of different kinds of conduct, ranging from the rather passive status of neglect or abandonment (i.e., non-conduct) to the intentional commission of criminal acts.

There is a great deal of diversity in the classification and description of conduct, especially with regard to the "status" forms of conduct. A child who has been abandoned, abused, or is without adequate parental care or supervision is variously referred to as a "dependent child," Fla. Stat. Ann. § 39.01(10) (Supp. 1973), a "deprived child," Ga. Code Ann. § 24A-401(h) (Supp. 1973); N.D. Cent. Code § 27-20-02(5) (1974), or, more commonly, a "neglected child." D.C. Code Ann. § 16-2301(9) (1973); Ill. Ann. Stat. ch. 37, § 702-4 (1972); La. Rev. Stat. Ann. § 13:1569(16) (Supp. 1974); Ohio Rev. Code Ann. § 2151.03

(1971); Vt. Stat. Ann. tit.33, § 632(12) (Supp. 1973); Wyo. Stat. Ann. § 14-115.2(o) (Supp. 1973).

A few jurisdictions use both the "neglected" and "dependent" classifications and attach different meanings to each. Nebraska law, for example, describes a "dependent" child as one who, *inter alia*, is homeless or destitute through no fault of the parent, and describes a "neglected" child as one who is abandoned or who lacks adequate parental care through some failure on the part of the parent. Neb. Rev. Stat. § 43-201(2)-(3) (1968).

In similar fashion North Carolina law describes a "dependent" child as one who is without a parent or other person responsible for its care, and a "neglected" child as one who lacks proper parental care and supervision or who has been abandoned. N.C. Gen. Stat. § 7A-278(3)-(4) (1969).

At least one jurisdiction uses the term "dependent child" in a very broad sense to include not only abandoned children and children without proper parental care and guidance but also truants, incorrigibles, runaways, etc. Wash. Rev. Code Ann. § 13.04.010 (1962). The latter forms of conduct are usually grouped under a separate heading.

§ 2.05. Jurisdiction Over Conduct: Children in Need of Supervision.

The juvenile court also has jurisdiction over other kinds of conduct that at times can be very difficult to describe in precise statutory language. Some forms, such as truancy, incorrigibility (disobedience to parents or school officials), and running away from home are easily described, and children committing such acts are usually grouped under a single classification. Such children are variously described as "unmanageable," Vt. Stat. Ann. tit. 33, § 632(18) (Supp. 1973), "undisciplined," N.C. Gen.

Stat. § 7A-278(5) (1969), "unruly," Ga. Code Ann. § 24A-401(g) (Supp. 1973); N.D. Cent. Code § 27-20-02(4) (1974); Ohio Rev. Code Ann. § 2151.022 (1971); Tenn. Code Ann. § 37-202(5) (Supp. 1973), and perhaps more commonly as "children (or persons) in need of supervision." D.C. Code Ann. § 16-2301(8) (1973); Fla. Stat. Ann. § 39.01(12) (Supp. 1973); Ill. Ann. Stat. ch. 37, § 702-03 (1972); Neb. Rev. Stat. § 43-201(5) (1968); N.Y. Fam. Ct. Act § 712(b) (McKinney Supp. 1973); S.D. Compiled Laws Ann. § 26-8-7.1 (Supp. 1973); Wyo. Stat. Ann. § 14-115.2(n) (Supp. 1973).

The classification "children in need of supervision" also may include forms of conduct or status that are less precise, certainly difficult to ascertain, and considerably difficult to describe in statutory language. California law, for example, provides that a child may be made a ward of the court "who from any cause is in danger of leading an idle, dissolute, lewd, or immoral life . . . ." Cal. Welf. & Inst'ns Code § 601 (1972). This statute and others similar to it have been subjected to constitutional challenge on vagueness grounds. The question of vagueness is discussed in § 2.07, *infra*.

§ 2.06. Jurisdiction Over Conduct: Delinquency.

Perhaps the most significant part of the juvenile court's jurisdiction over conduct is its jurisdiction over delinquent conduct. This form of conduct presents some classification problems also. Most modern juvenile court codes, in an attempt to destigmatize noncriminal conduct, limit the classification of "delinquency" to acts that are in violation of state or federal law or local ordinance. Ariz. Rev. Stat. Ann. § 8-201(8) (Supp. 1973); Cal. Welf. & Inst'ns Code § 602 (Supp. 1973); Colo. Rev. Stat. Ann. § 22-1-3(17) (a) (Supp. 1967); D.C. Code Ann. § 16-2301(7) (1973); Fla.

Stat. Ann. § 39.01(11) (Supp. 1973); Ga. Code Ann. § 24A-401(e) (1) (Supp. 1973); Ill. Ann. Stat. ch. 37, § 702-2 (1972); Kan. Stat. Ann. § 38-802(b) (1973) (but also includes child who has been adjudicated a miscreant child three or more times); La. Rev. Stat. Ann. § 13:1569(14) (Supp. 1974); Md. Ann. Code, Cts. & Jud. Proc. § 3-801(j) (1974); Mass. Gen. Laws Ann. ch. 119, § 52 (1965); Neb. Rev. Stat. § 43-201(4) (1968); Nev. Stat. Ann. § 62.040(1) (c) (1973); N.M. Stat. Ann. § 13-14-4(N) (Supp. 1973); N.Y. Fam. Ct. Act § 712(a) (McKinney 1963); N.C. Gen. Stat. § 7A-278(2) (1969); N.D. Cent. Code § 27-20-02(2) (1974); Ohio Rev. Code Ann. § 2151.02 (1971); Okla. Stat. Ann. tit. 10, § 1101(b) (Supp. 1974); R.I. Gen. Laws Ann. § 14-1-3(F) (1970); S.D. Compiled Laws Ann. § 26-8-7 (Supp. 1973); Tenn. Code Ann. § 37-202(3) (Supp. 1973); Tex. Fam. Code Ann. § 51.03(a) (1973); Vt. Stat. Ann. tit. 33, § 632(a) (3) (Supp. 1973); Wash. Rev. Code Ann. § 13.04.010 (1962); Wis. Stat. Ann. § 48.12(1) (Supp. 1973); Wyo. Stat. Ann. § 14-115.2(l) (Supp. 1973).

The old formulations, however, typically include in the classification of "delinquency" not only what would otherwise be criminal conduct, but also conduct that normally would be grouped under the classification of "child in need of supervision," *e.g.*, truancy, incorrigibility, running away from home, and any number of other kinds of conduct relating to the child's physical, mental and moral well-being. Ala. Code tit. 13, § 350(3) (1959); Ark. Stat. Ann. § 45-204 (Supp. 1973); Conn. Gen. Stat. Ann. § 17-53 (Supp. 1973); Del. Code Ann. tit. 10, § 1101 (1953); Ind. Ann. Stat. § 9-3204 (Supp. 1972); Iowa Code Ann. § 232.2(13) (1969); Minn. Stat. Ann. § 260.015(5) (1971); Miss. Code Ann. § 43-21-5(g) (1972); Mont. Rev. Codes Ann. § 10-602(2) (Supp. 1973); N.H. Rev. Stat. Ann. § 169:2(II) (Supp. 1971); N.J. Stat. Ann. §2A:4-14 (1952); Pa. Stat. Ann. tit. 11, § 50-102(2) (Supp. 1974); S.C. Code Ann. § 15-1103(9) (1962); W. Va. Code Ann. § 49-1-4 (1966).

The remaining jurisdictions do not attempt to classify conduct as "delinquent" or otherwise, but rather list all forms of conduct subject to juvenile court jurisdiction in one general category. Alaska Stat. § 47.10.010(a) (1971); Hawaii Rev. Stat. § 571-11 (Supp. 1972); Idaho Code § 16-1803 (Supp. 1973); Ky. Rev. Stat. Ann. § 208.020(1) (1969); Me. Rev. Stat. Ann. tit. 15, § 2552 (1964); Mich. Compiled Laws Ann. § 712A.2 (Supp. 1974); Mo. Ann. Stat. § 211.031 (1962); Ore. Rev. Stat. § 419.476(1) (1971); Utah Code Ann. § 55-10-77(1)-(2) (Supp. 1973); Va. Code Ann. § 16.1-158 (Supp. 1973).

§ 2.07. Jurisdiction Over Conduct: The Vagueness Problem.

As noted, the conduct jurisdiction of the juvenile court is quite broad. Section 16 of the Standard Juvenile Court Act, for example, provides that a child may be taken into custody when he violates a law in the presence of an officer, when there are reasonable grounds to believe that he has committed an act that if committed by an adult would be a felony, when he is "seriously endangered in his surroundings," and when there are reasonable grounds to believe that he has run away from home. Exactly what circumstances would indicate to a police officer that a child is "seriously endangered in his surroundings" are not at all clear.

A California statute (referred to in § 2.05, *supra*) provides that a child under the age of eighteen who habitually disobeys the proper orders of his parents or guardian, or who is a truant, or "who from any cause is in danger of leading an idle, dissolute, lewd, or immoral life," is within the jurisdiction of the court. Cal. Welf. & Inst'ns Code § 601 (1972).

A former Texas statute described a child who "habitually so deports himself as to injure or endanger the morals or health of himself or others" as a delinquent child. Ch. 204, § 3(f) [1943] Tex. Laws 48th Sess. 313. If any situation is more tenuous than one in which a youth is "seriously in danger of his surroundings," it is one in which the youth is "in danger of leading an idle, dissolute, lewd, or immoral life," or "habitually so deports himself as to injure or endanger the morals or health of himself or others." These statutory expressions of concern, even though founded on the worthy desire to protect the young from themselves, take in a wide range of conduct. Indeed, a major problem is the difficulty of determining exactly what conduct is included.

The California and Texas provisions and a number of others like them have invited challenge on the ground that they are unconstitutionally vague. In California, a three-judge federal panel declared unconstitutionally vague the above provision of the California Welfare and Institutions Code permitting a child "in danger of leading an idle, dissolute, lewd, or immoral life" to be declared a ward of the court. *Gonzalez v. Mailliard*, No. 50424 (N.D. Cal., Feb. 9, 1971), *excerpted in* 5 Clearinghouse Rev. 45 (1971). In subsequent action, the United States Supreme Court by per curiam order summarily vacated judgment in the California case, apparently on the basis that the injunctive relief granted was inappropriate and that declaratory relief should be granted instead. *Mailliard v. Gonzalez*, U.S. (1974). *See also In re E.M.B.*, 13 Crim. L. Rep. 2328 (D.C. Super. Ct., Fam. Div., 6/14/73) (statute allowing court to adjudicate as children in need of supervision, children "habitually disobedient and ungovernable and in need of rehabilitation" declared unconstitutionally vague).

The former Texas statute, however, was upheld as being within the protective purposes of the broad grant of jurisdiction to the juvenile court. *E.S.G. v. State*, 447

S.W.2d 225 (Tex. Civ. App. 1969). The Texas provision was repealed when Texas enacted a new Family Code. Ch. 544, § 3 [1973] Tex. Laws 63rd Sess. 1485. The old provision does not appear in the new Family Code.

Most courts that have considered the question have concluded that these statutes are *not* unconstitutionally vague. In addition to the Texas decision, *see State v. Mattielo*, 4 Conn. Cir. 55, 225 A.2d 507 (1966); *S.S. v. State*, 299 A.2d 560 (Me. 1973); *Patricia A. v. City of New York*, 31 N.Y.2d 83, 286 N.E.2d 432, 335 N.Y.S.2d 33 (1972); *People v. Salisbury*, 18 N.Y.2d 899, 223 N.E.2d 43, 276 N.Y.S.2d 634 (1966); *In re L.N.*, 109 N.J. Super. 278, 263 A.2d 150, *aff'd*, 57 N.J. 165, 270 A.2d 409 (1970).

Vagueness challenges to such statutes will probably continue to mount. It has been suggested, however, that the descriptions contained in the statutes are imprecise because the kind of behavior they seek to define is itself vague, and the standard for measuring such conduct or status therefore "does not admit of a more certain formulation." M. Paulsen, *The Delinquency, Neglect, and Dependency Jurisdiction of the Juvenile Court*, in *Justice for the Child* 44, 50 (M. Rosenheim ed. 1962). *See also* N. Dorsen, and D. Rezneck, *In re Gault and the Future of Juvenile Law*, 1 Fam. L.Q. 1, 33 (Dec. 1967).

§ 2.08. Exclusion of Certain Conduct from Jurisdiction.

There are indications that many states have never fully accepted the notion of specialized treatment of juveniles who have violated the criminal code. The juvenile court, after all, deals with truants, incorrigibles, runaways, children in danger of moral dissolution and other "wayward" children. From the very inception of the juvenile court until the present time, most states have treated the latter conduct with a great deal of solicitude and benevolence, and in doing so have paid proper respect to the philosophical aims of the *parens patriae* theory. The function of the juvenile court, however, involves more than teaching manners to impudent children; its primary function relates to law enforcement — *i.e.*, the administration of criminal justice to children. O. Ketcham, *Guidelines from Gault: Revolutionary Requirements and Reappraisal*, 53 Va. L. Rev. 1700, 1701 (1967). It is precisely in the exercise of this law enforcement function that many states are reluctant to rely upon the rehabilitative powers of the juvenile court and to remit to its protective processes cases of a more serious nature.

Some jurisdictions, for example, exclude capital offenses from the jurisdiction of the juvenile court. Del. Code Ann. tit. 10, § 1159 (1953); La. Rev. Stat. Ann. § 13:1570(A) (5) (1968); N.C. Gen. Stat. § 7A-280 (1969); W. Va. Code Ann. § 49-1-4(2) (1966).

Other states exclude offenses punishable by death *or* life imprisonment, usually when committed by an older group of children. Colo. Rev. Stat. Ann. § 22-1-3(17)(b) (Supp. 1969) (fourteen or older); Miss. Code Ann. § 43-21-31 (1972) (thirteen or older); S.C. Code Ann. § 15-1103(9) (a) (1962) (no age limitation).

Still other jurisdictions exclude certain enumerated offenses from the juvenile court's jurisdiction. D.C. Code Ann. § 16-2301(3)(A) (1973) (excludes enumerated offenses when committed by children sixteen years of age or older); La. Rev. Stat. Ann. § 13:1570(A)(5) (1968) (in addition to all capital offenses, excludes attempted aggravated rape when committed by child fifteen years of age or older).

In addition, one state excludes crimes punishable by death or life imprisonment committed by children fourteen years of age or older, and also the crime of robbery with a deadly weapon when committed by a child sixteen years of age or older, unless the case has been transferred from the criminal court to the juvenile court as provided. Md. Ann. Code, Cts. & Jud. Proc. § 3-808(1), (4) (1974).

One explanation for such exclusionary statutes is that the community may be outraged at the commission of the more serious offenses, whether the offender is an adult or a child, and it may feel a need to express its social and moral condemnation through the harsh medium of the criminal process. *See* M. Paulsen, *The Delinquency, Neglect, and Dependency Jurisdiction of the Juvenile Court*, in *Justice for the Child* 44, 62 (N. Rosenheim ed. 1962).

If the community's rage in response to the crime itself overcomes its sense of purpose in dealing with youthful offenders, this represents an abandonment, or at least a suspension in certain cases, of the commitment to the rehabilitative ideal and a return to the purely retributive concepts prevalent in the nineteenth century. *See* 2 J. Stephens, *A History of the Criminal Law of England* 81-82 (1883) for an expression of purely punitive philosophy. A better approach (discussed in § 2.14, *infra*) would be to give the juvenile court exclusive jurisdiction over all offenses committed by children, with discretion to waive jurisdiction and transfer the case to the criminal court. There may well be cases in which the gravity of the offense suggests that the child is not amenable to the rehabilitative processes of the juvenile court and should instead be treated as an adult. It seems rather harsh and unrealistic, however, to exclude arbitrarily *all* cases on the basis of the seriousness of the offense alone. This factor, after all, is only one among several criteria that are considered in the waiver process. *See* Chapter 4, *infra*, on waiver.

§ 2.09. Other Limitations on Jurisdiction: Prosecutorial Discretion.

In addition to the exclusion of certain offenses from the juvenile court's jurisdiction, there are other limitations that have affected the juvenile court's jurisdictional autonomy. For example, some jurisdictions confer upon the criminal court or the prosecutor authority to decide in which court — juvenile or criminal — the case should be commenced. See Wyo. Stat. Ann. § 14-115.12 (Supp. 1973), which empowers the prosecutor to make this decision when a juvenile is charged with commission of an offense. See also Md. Ann. Code art. 27, § 594A (1971), which grants the criminal court discretion, in cases in which a child fourteen years of age or older is charged with a crime punishable by death or life imprisonment, to transfer the case to the juvenile court or retain jurisdiction and try it as a criminal matter.

§ 2.10. Other Limitations on Jurisdiction: Discretionary Transfer from Criminal Court.

Other jurisdictions grant the criminal court discretion to transfer to the juvenile court for treatment an older group of children beyond the juvenile court's age jurisdiction, rather than giving the juvenile court initial jurisdiction over such persons with discretion to transfer them to the criminal court. See Ala. Code tit. 13, § 363 (1959) (maximum age limit for original juvenile court jurisdiction is sixteen; criminal court has discretion to transfer to juvenile court a person who has reached his sixteenth birthday but who is under eighteen years of age); Vt. Stat. Ann. tit. 33, § 635(b) (Supp. 1973) (maximum age limit for original juvenile court jurisdiction over delinquent child is sixteen; criminal court has discretion to transfer to juvenile court a child who was over sixteen but under eighteen years of age at time offense was committed). See also Mich. Compiled Laws Ann. § 712A.2(d) (Supp. 1974) (maximum age limit for original juvenile court jurisdiction generally is seventeen; juvenile court and criminal court have concurrent jurisdiction over children between seventeen and eighteen years of age charged with certain enumerated offenses or conduct). This problem is also discussed in § 2.01, *supra*, which deals with age jurisdiction.

§ 2.11. Other Limitations on Jurisdiction: Differential Age Jurisdiction.

A further device to limit the jurisdiction of the juvenile court over offenses committed by children is the practice of setting a lower jurisdictional age limit for delinquent children than the age limit establishing age jurisdiction for other kinds of conduct. *See* N.H. Rev. Stat. Ann. § 169:2 (III) (Supp. 1971) (seventeen is maximum age limit for jurisdiction over children alleged to be delinquent on the basis of violations of law, but eighteen is the maximum jurisdictional age for children alleged to be delinquent on the basis of incorrigible behavior or a wayward status); Vt. Stat. Ann. tit. 33, § 632(a) (1) (Supp. 1973) (sixteen is the maximum age limit for exercising jurisdiction over delinquent children, but a maximum age limit of eighteen is prescribed in the case of neglected and unmanageable children).

Oklahoma formerly prescribed a lower jurisdictional age for delinquent conduct, at least for male offenders, but its statutory scheme was held violative of fourteenth amendment equal protection, because it provided for differential treatment of males and females according to age. *Lamb v. Brown*, 456 F.2d 18 (10th Cir. 1972). Differential age jurisdiction based on conduct is discussed also in § 2.01, *supra*.

In a slightly different vein, some jurisdictions set a lower jurisdictional age limit for the more urban areas than that prescribed for other areas.

For example, South Carolina law provides that the jurisdictional age is sixteen in counties containing a city with a population over 70,000 according to the official U.S.

Census, but seventeen in counties containing a city with a population between 60,000 and 70,000 according to the U.S. Census of 1940. S.C. Code Ann. § 15-1103(1), (7) (1962).

A similar statutory scheme in Maryland, prescribing a jurisdictional age of eighteen, except in the City of Baltimore, where, until July 1, 1971, the jurisdictional age was to be sixteen years of age, was held unconstitutional on the basis of the equal protection and due process clauses of the fourteenth amendment to the United States Constitution. *Long v. Robinson*, 316 F. Supp. 22 (D. Md. 1970), *aff'd*, 436 F.2d 1116 (4th Cir. 1971). As a problem of age jurisdiction, this problem was mentioned in § 2.01, *supra*.

§ 2.12. Concurrent Jurisdiction: Legislation.

Perhaps the most invidious limitation on the juvenile court's jurisdiction is the failure of some states to confer upon the juvenile court exclusive jurisdiction. Instead they provide that in some cases the jurisdiction of the juvenile court is concurrent with that of another court (referred to here as the criminal court, although it might actually be designated the district court, superior court, etc.).

Concurrent jurisdiction comes in many forms and degrees. In some instances the juvenile and criminal courts are expressly given concurrent jurisdiction over all children within the jurisdictional age limit of the juvenile court. In others concurrent jurisdiction exists only with respect to a particular age group, usually older children. In still others concurrent jurisdiction is authorized only with respect to a child charged with a certain offense or one of a class of offenses, for example, felony or capital offenses. Concurrent jurisdiction also may occur on the basis of some combination of the above factors.

In whatever form the following states provide by statute for some degree of concurrent jurisdiction between the juvenile and criminal courts: *Arkansas*, Ark. Stat. Ann. §§ 45-224, 45-241 (1964); *Delaware*, Del. Code Ann. tit. 11, §§ 2711, 2712 (Supp. 1970); *Florida*, Fla. Stat. Ann. § 39.02(6) (c) (Supp. 1973); Ga. Code Ann. § 24A-301(b) (Supp. 1973); *Idaho*, Idaho Code § 16-1806(1) (a)-(b) (Supp. 1973); *Illinois*, Ill. Ann. Stat. ch. 37, § 702-7(3) (1972); *Indiana*, Ind. Ann. Stat. § 9-3213 (1956); *Michigan*, Mich. Compiled Laws Ann. § 712A.2(d) (Supp. 1974); *Nevada*, Nev. Rev. Stat. § 62.050 (1973); *Pennsylvania*, Pa. Stat. Ann. tit. 11, § 50-303 (Supp. 1974); *South Dakota*, S.D. Compiled Laws Ann. § 26-11-3 (1967); *Virginia*, Va. Code Ann. §§ 16.1-175 (1960), § 16.1-176(a) (Supp. 1973); *Wyoming*, Wyo. Stat. Ann. §§ 14-115.4(c), 14-115.12 (Supp. 1973).

Generally, however, legislatures have conferred upon the juvenile court exclusive jurisdiction over children alleged to be delinquent on the basis of criminal conduct. Ala. Code tit. 13, § 351 (1959); Conn. Gen. Stat. Ann. § 17-59 (Supp. 1973); Hawaii Rev. Stat. § 571-11(1) (Supp. 1972); Kan. Stat. Ann. § 38-806(a) (1) (Supp. 1971); Me. Rev. Stat. Ann. tit. 15, §§ 2551, 2552 (1964); Mich. Compiled Laws Ann. § 712A.2(a) (Supp. 1974) (included here because while concurrent jurisdiction is authorized, it is permitted only with respect to a group of persons *over* the exclusive jurisdictional age of the juvenile court); Minn. Stat. Ann. § 260.111(1) (1971); Mo. Ann. Stat. § 211.031 (1962); Mont. Rev. Codes Ann. § 10-603 (Supp. 1973); N.H. Rev. Stat. Ann. § 169.29 (1964); N.J. Stat. Ann. § 2A:4-14 (1952); N.M. Stat. Ann. § 13-14-9(A) (Supp. 1973); N.Y. Fam. Ct. Act § 713 (McKinney 1963); N.D. Cent. Code § 27-20-03(1) (1974); Ohio Rev. Code Ann. § 2151.23(A) (1971); Ore. Rev. Stat. § 419.476(1) (1971); R.I. Gen. Laws Ann. § 14-1-5 (1970); Tenn. Code Ann. §

37-203(a) (1) (Supp. 1973); Tex. Fam. Code Ann. § 51.04(a) (1973); Utah Code Ann. § 55-10-77 (Supp. 1973); Vt. Stat. Ann. tit. 33, § 633(a) (Supp. 1973); Wash Rev. Code Ann. § 13.04.030 (1962); Wis. Stat. Ann. § 48.12(1) (Supp. 1973).

To the latter states can be added a number of others that exclude certain offenses from the juvenile court's jurisdiction but grant it exclusive jurisdiction in all other cases. This is not true concurrent jurisdiction. Depending on the offense charged, the juvenile court or the criminal court will have exclusive jurisdiction, but in no event will they share jurisdiction. *See* Colo. Rev. Stat. Ann. §§ 22-1-4(1) (a)-(b) (Supp. 1967) (juvenile court has exclusive jurisdiction except over children fourteen and older charged with crimes of violence); Fla. Stat. Ann. § 39.02(1) (a) (Supp. 1973) (juvenile court has exclusive jurisdiction except over children charged by indictment with any offense punishable by death or life imprisonment); La. Rev. Stat. Ann. § 13:1570(A) (5) (1968) (juvenile court has exclusive jurisdiction except over children fifteen or older charged with a capital offense or attempted aggravated rape); Md. Ann. Code, Cts. & Jud. Proc. § 3-808(1), (4) (1974) (juvenile court has exclusive jurisdiction except over children fourteen or older charged with a crime punishable by death or life imprisonment and children sixteen or older charged with robbery with a deadly weapon); Miss. Code Ann. §§ 43-21-7, 43-21-31 (1972) (juvenile court has exclusive jurisdiction except over children thirteen or older charged with a crime punishable by death or life imprisonment); N.C. Gen. Stat. § 7A-279 (1969) (juvenile court has exclusive jurisdiction except over children charged with a capital offense); S.C. Code Ann. §§ 15-1103(9) (a), 15-1171 (1962) (juvenile court has exclusive jurisdiction except over children charged with offenses punishable by death or life imprisonment); W.Va. Code Ann. § 49-5-3 (1966) (juvenile court has exclu-

sive jurisdiction except over children charged with a capital offense).

As a further means of assuring the exclusive jurisdiction of the juvenile court, most legislatures have added
provisions compelling any other court before which a
child charged with a criminal offense might appear to
transfer the case to the juvenile court for further proceedings. Ala. Code tit. 13, § 363 (1959); Cal. Welf. & Inst'ns
Code § 604(a) (1972); Conn. Gen. Stat. Ann. § 17-65 (1960);
Fla. Stat. Ann. § 39.02(3) (1961); Hawaii Rev. Stat. § 571-12
(1968); Idaho Code § 16-1804 (Supp. 1973) (except where
child is sixteen or older and is charged with a felony
offense, or eighteen or older and charged with any offense
committed before becoming eighteen); Ind. Ann. Stat. §
9-3213 (1956) (except where child is over sixteen and
charged with a capital offense); Iowa Code Ann. § 232.64
(1969); La. Rev. Stat. Ann. § 13:1571 (1968) (except where
child fifteen or older is charged with a capital offense or
attempted aggravated rape); Mich. Compiled Laws Ann.
§§ 712A.3, 764.27 (Supp. 1974); Minn. Stat. Ann. § 260.115
(1971); Mo. Ann. Stat. § 211.061(2) (1962); Mont. Rev.
Codes Ann. § 10-610 (Supp. 1973); Neb. Rev. Stat. § 43-211
(1968); Nev. Rev. Stat. § 62.050 (1973) (except where charge
is a capital offense); N.J. Stat. Ann. § 2A:4-20 (1952); N.M.
Stat. Ann. § 13-14-11 (Supp. 1973); N.D. Cent. Code §
27-20-09 (1974); Ohio Rev. Code Ann. § 2151.25 (1971);
Okla. Stat. Ann. tit. 10, § 1112(a) (Supp. 1974); Ore. Rev.
Stat. § 419.478 (1971); Pa. Stat. Ann. tit. 11, § 50-303 (Supp.
1974) (except where child is charged with murder; also,
transfer of child over sixteen but under eighteen is discretionary); R.I. Gen. Laws Ann. § 14-1-28 (1970); S.C.
Code Ann. § 15-1188 (1962) (except where child is charged
with offense punishable by death or life imprisonment as
provided elsewhere in Code); Tenn. Code Ann. § 37-209
(Supp. 1973); Tex. Fam. Code Ann. § 51.08 (1973); Utah

Code Ann. § 55-10-79 (Supp. 1973); Vt. Stat. Ann. tit. 33, § 635(a) (Supp. 1973); Va. Code Ann. § 16.1-175 (1960) (however, if court is a court of record it may, after investigation prescribed in § 16.1-176(b), proceed with trial of case); W. Va. Code Ann. § 49-5-3 (1966) (except where child is charged with a capital offense).

§ 2.13. Concurrent Jurisdiction: Judicial Construction.

While legislatures generally have seen fit to confer exclusive jurisdiction on the juvenile court, in a few instances courts have viewed such measures as attempts to remove criminal jurisdiction from another court. The usual case calls for constitutional interpretation. The state's constitution typically empowers a court of general jurisdiction to try "all criminal cases," "all offenses punishable by death or life imprisonment," or the like. The juvenile court, however, by statute is granted exclusive jurisdiction to deal with children charged with delinquent acts, which generally include all criminal offenses. Confronted with what appears to be a jurisdictional conflict, some courts have concluded that statutory grants of exclusive jurisdiction to the juvenile court are in violation of constitutional grants of jurisdiction to another court to try criminal cases; consequently, the juvenile court and criminal court have concurrent jurisdiction in certain criminal cases. *See, e.g., Jackson v. Balkcom*, 210 Ga. 412, 80 S.E.2d 319 (1954); *State v. Lindsey*, 78 Idaho 241, 300 P.2d 491 (1956); *State v. McCoy*, 145 Neb. 750, 18 N.W.2d 101 (1945).

In most cases in which the question has been raised, however, the courts have concluded that the juvenile court has exclusive jurisdiction in cases in which juveniles are charged with criminal conduct. *See, e.g., People ex rel. Terrell v. District Court*, 164 Colo. 437, 435

P.2d 763 (1967); *Mallory v. Paradise*, 173 N.W.2d 264 (Iowa 1969); *Commonwealth v. Franks*, 164 Ky. 239, 175 S.W. 349 (1915); *State v. Connally*, 190 La. 175, 182 So. 318 (1938) (except over children fifteen or older charged with capital offenses or attempted aggravated rape, as provided by statute); *State ex rel. Knutson v. Jackson*, 249 Minn. 246, 82 N.W.2d 234 (1957); *Wheeler v. Shoemake*, 213 Miss. 374, 57 So. 2d 267 (1952); *State ex rel. Boyd v. Rutledge*, 321 Mo. 1090, 13 S.W.2d 1061 (1929); *State v. Monahan*, 15 N.J. 34, 104 A.2d 21 (1954); *State ex rel. Slatton v. Boles*, 147 W. Va. 674, 130 S.E.2d 192 (1963) (except over children charged with capital offenses, as provided by statute); *Gibson v. State*, 47 Wis. 2d 810, 177 N.W.2d 912 (1970).

The latter cases seem to represent the soundest view. Statutes granting exclusive jurisdiction to the juvenile court in delinquency cases where the delinquency is based on criminal conduct are not attempts to *remove* jurisdiction from another court.

In the first place, such statutes do not deprive another court of its constitutionally granted criminal jurisdiction but simply furnish procedures (*i.e.*, waiver procedures) that must be followed before the criminal jurisdiction of the other court attaches. *See State ex rel. Knutson v. Jackson*, 249 Minn. 246, 250-51, 82 N.W.2d 234, 237-38 (1957). *See also State v. Dehler*, 257 Minn. 549, 102 N.W.2d 696 (1960); *State ex rel. Pett v. Jackson*, 252 Minn. 418, 90 N.W.2d 219 (1958).

Secondly, such statutes do not operate to divest another court of its criminal jurisdiction because by definition the grants of jurisdiction to the other court usually refer to *criminal* cases; a delinquency proceeding, however, is a civil and not a criminal case, even when the allegation of delinquency rests upon conduct that if committed by an adult would be felonious. By definition, the conduct complained of is not a crime at all. Based on this qualitative distinction, granting the juvenile court exclusive jurisdiction over delinquent conduct does not divest another court of its jurisdiction over criminal cases. *See People ex rel. Rodello v. District Court*, 164 Colo. 530, 535, 436 P.2d 672, 675 (1968); *State ex rel. Slatton v. Boles*, 147 W. Va. 674, 683-85, 130 S.E.2d 192, 198-99 (1963). In accord, Minnesota law specifically provides that a violation of law by a child under the age of eighteen is not a crime unless jurisdiction is waived as provided by statute and the case is transferred for prosecution as a criminal matter. Minn. Stat. Ann. § 260.215(1) (1971). Far from being merely argumentative or semantic, the distinction is valid, realistic, and fundamental to the rehabilitative purposes of the juvenile court. *See People ex rel. Terrell v. District Court*, 164 Colo. 437, 444-45, 435 P.2d 763, 766 (1967).

§ 2.14 Concurrent Jurisdiction: An Assessment.

Concurrent jurisdiction between the juvenile and criminal courts is at best an awkward arrangement. The tendency is for the criminal court to take the more infamous cases. *Jackson v. Balkcom*, 210 Ga. 412, 80 S.E.2d 319 (1954), involved a black youth convicted of raping a white woman. He was sentenced to death by electrocution; the sentence was duly carried out. An additional Nebraska case upholding concurrent jurisdiction is *Fugate v. Ronin*, 167 Neb. 70, 91 N.W.2d 240 (1958), which involved sensational mass murders that created widespread public reaction across the country at the time.

Even less sensational examples, if a serious crime has been committed, evoke a very strong emotional reaction from the public, which in turn produces a substantial skepticism of the ability of the juvenile court to deal with serious, especially older, offenders. Certainly the juvenile court's role as a law enforcement agency is called into question. It is rather viewed as a social agency whose function is to deal with truants, orphans, runaways, and other misguided waifs, and occasionally to adjust minor difficulties between the child and the law. This function is often viewed as inadequate to satisfy the apparent need of the community to express its disapproval of antisocial conduct through the traditional processes of the criminal law.

Likewise, all other limitations on juvenile court jurisdiction (discussed in §§ 2.08-2.13, *supra*) manifest a basic mistrust of the juvenile court and represent the absence of a firm commitment to the juvenile court's rehabilitative philosophy. This mistrust of the juvenile court's capacity to deal with youthful offenders is unfounded. Just as arbitrary exclusion of certain conduct (such as commission of specific enumerated offenses or commission of felony or capital offenses) from juvenile court jurisdiction is unjustified, concurrent jurisdiction over certain conduct or certain age groups is not supportable by logic or reason. To decide otherwise is to overlook the most basic premise of a sound concept of juvenile court jurisdiction. The premise is that once a jurisdictional age is established, *all* children under that age, regardless of the offense committed, should be entitled to treatment as juveniles unless some reason exists to indicate otherwise. Certainly the same sociological and correctional principles that support the existence of the juvenile court apply with equal force whether the conduct alleged is truancy, petty theft, or a serious offense.

If a child is to be tried in a criminal court, a statutory scheme generally exists whereby the juvenile court can waive jurisdiction over the child and transfer him to criminal court. The juvenile court has the staff and expertise to make such a decision, whereas the criminal court and prosecutor do not. Moreover, in determining how a given case should be handled, the juvenile court represents the interests of the community as well as those of the child, and the decision is made following a hearing at which both of those interests are considered. (Waiver of jurisdiction by the juvenile court is discussed in Chapter 4, *infra*).

For these reasons, it is important that the case originate in juvenile court. If, following the waiver hearing, that court is of the opinion that the child is not amenable to treatment and rehabilitation, only then should the criminal court acquire jurisdiction over the child. It is no doubt true, as the United States Court of Appeals for the District of Columbia Circuit stated in *Black v. United States*, 355 F.2d 104, 105 (D.C. Cir. 1965), that "[t]reatment as a juvenile is not a statutory bounty which can be withdrawn lightly."

Chapter 3

THE PRE-JUDICIAL PROCESS: POLICE INVESTIGATION

I. TAKING INTO CUSTODY.

§ 3.01. Applicability of the Law of Arrest.

The decision to invoke the criminal process by arresting someone is not simply a mechanical procedure, but rather involves a complicated, though informal and perhaps unconscious, policy-making process. The police officer must assimilate — often quickly and under pressure — the nature of the conduct and the seriousness of the incident, and respond appropriately. The complexity of the process is compounded when dealing with juveniles, since to the existing morass is added a great deal of uncertainty on the part of law enforcement officers concerning their proper role in handling juveniles. The President's

Commission on Law Enforcement and the Administration of Justice, *Task Force Report: The Police* 13-14 (1967).

One role of law enforcement is perhaps reflected in the historical development of the juvenile court. Historically court decisions have emphasized the protective rather than the punitive nature of the juvenile process. *See, e.g., Ex parte Sharp*, 15 Idaho 120, 126-28, 96 P. 563, 564-65 (1908); *State v. Monahan*, 15 N.J. 34, 38, 104 A.2d 21, 23 (1954); *Application of Gault*, 99 Ariz. 181, 192, 407 P.2d 760, 768 (1965). The same emphasis is also seen in statutory affirmation of the civil nature of the proceedings, *see, e.g.,* Colo. Rev. Stat. Ann. § 22-1-9 (Supp. 1967); Mass. Gen. Laws Ann. ch. 119, § 53 (1969), and in statutes describing the protective function of the juvenile court. *See, e.g.,* Ga. Code Ann. § 24A-101 (Supp. 1973); N.J. Stat. Ann. § 2A:4-2 (1952). But the majority of jurisdictions in this country make no special provisions for handling juveniles. M. Luger, *The Youthful Offender*, in The President's Commission on Law Enforcement and the Administration of Justice, *Task Force Report: Juvenile Delinquency and Youth Crime* 119, 121 (1967).

This has perhaps led law enforcement authorities to believe that traditional limitations placed on their dealing with adults suspected of crime — in particular, that the arresting officer possess knowledge sufficient to justify his interference — do not apply in handling juveniles. Rather the concern seems to be to "protect" the youth and to instill in him respect for law and its processes. *See* F. Remington, *Criminal Justice Administration* 959 (1967).

Gault, after all, specifically did not apply to the prejudicial stages of juvenile proceedings. 387 U.S. at 13. All constitutional rights accorded adults in criminal proceedings are not necessarily applicable in juvenile proceedings; if a particular right is to be applicable, its applicability must rest on a finding that it is required in order to assure fundamental fairness in the proceeding as determined by due process standards of the fourteenth amendment. (*See* discussion in Chapter 7, *infra*.) It is no doubt in reliance on the failure of the courts, in particular the Supreme Court, to deal with the issue of arrest that has led officers to conclude that the constitutional safeguards attending an arrest do not necessarily apply with full force to taking a juvenile into custody.

The idea that the law of arrest does not apply to juveniles in fact has been fostered in the courts. *In re James L., Jr.*, 25 Ohio Op. 2d 369, 194 N.E.2d 797 (Juv. Ct., Cuyahoga Co. 1963). It also finds potential support in the legislative position that taking a juvenile into custody does not amount to an arrest. *See, e.g.*, Ill. Ann. Stat. ch. 37, § 703-1(3) (1972); Minn. Stat. Ann. § 260.165(2) (1971); Standard Juvenile Court Act § 16 (6th ed. 1959). *See also* E. Ferster, and T. Courtless, *The Beginning of Juvenile Justice, Police Practices, and the Juvenile Offender*, 22 Vand. L. Rev. 567, 583-89 (1969).

It is perhaps significant that some statutes provide that taking a juvenile into custody is not deemed an arrest "except for the purpose of determining its validity under the Constitution of this State or of the United States." Georgia Code Ann. § 24A-1301(b) (Supp. 1973); Tenn. Code Ann. § 37-213(b) (Supp. 1973); *see* Ohio Rev. Code Ann. § 2151.31 (1971). This clearly indicates that the law of arrest applies to juveniles in the same manner in which it is applicable to adults. Moreover, with the extension of *Gault's* mandate into the investigatory stages of juvenile proceedings, *vis-a-vis* the *Miranda* (see §§ 3.12 - 3.13, *infra*) and search and seizure (*see* §§ 3.06 - 3.09, *infra*) requirements, law enforcement officers apparently will apply to juveniles the same standards relating to arrest that are now applied in the case of adults.

The most that can be said now is that police are

uncertain about what is required of them in taking a juvenile into custody. One thing is clear, however: because juvenile proceedings are not regarded as criminal in nature, the police exercise considerably more discretion in dealing with juveniles than they exercise in dealing with adults. J. Wilson, *The Police and the Delinquent in Two Cities,* in *Controlling Delinquents* 9, 10 (S. Wheeler ed. 1968); Ferster and Courtless, *supra,* at 575-83.

§ 3.02. Broadness of Jurisdiction to Take into Custody.

Traditionally, too little attention has been paid to the relationship between state power and individual liberty where the juvenile is concerned. But this relationship is critical because, given the protective role of the juvenile court, when authority is exercised to do something *for* a youth, it generally begins by doing something *to* him as well. M. Paulsen, *The Expanding Horizons of Legal Services – II,* 67 W. Va. L. Rev. 267, 269 (1965). *See also* J. Kenny, and D. Pursuit, *Police Work with Juveniles* 47 (3d ed. 1965).

One of the characteristics of the juvenile justice system is that the scope of its jurisdiction, derived from the original scheme of the juvenile court concept, is very broad, taking in all youths in need of help for whatever reason. After all, this sweeping approach represents a continuation of the philosophy that spawned the juvenile court movement in the last century. The concern for the welfare of children prevalent from the early through the latter part of the century produced a juvenile court that was protective in nature, designed to function *in loco parentis* for orphans, runaways, and all sorts of wayward children. By nature its embrace was all-encompassing (*see* Chapter 1, *supra*).

Discarding momentarily the area of neglect and dependency jurisdiction, the broad jurisdictional scope of the juvenile court includes not only conduct that if committed by an adult would be criminal, but also a rather large area of other, more general, youthful misbehavior. The intake of a typical juvenile court includes all sorts of youths who are in trouble, although the "trouble" may consist simply of truancy, youthful criminality — *i.e.*, conduct that society deems unlawful when engaged in by youth, but not when committed by adults — or something less serious.

Such an approach seeks to enforce the criminal code as well as a more general code of juvenile conduct embracing duties owed by children both to parents and school authorities. Enforcement of a more general code of behavior was marked by the advent of the "incorrigibility" status. Endemic to youth, the incorrigibility status means that if a child exhibits such an attitude of defiance that he cannot be controlled by his parents or school authorities, the juvenile court may intervene in situations amounting to something less than the violation of criminal laws. The President's Commission on Law Enforcement and Administration of Justice, *Task Force Report: Juvenile Delinquency and Youth Crime* 22 (1967).

"Incorrigibility" (or "unruly," "unmanageable," "ungovernable") statutes vary somewhat in scope, but many are similar to Georgia's:

"(g) 'Unruly child' means a child who:
"(1) while subject to compulsory school attendance is habitually and without justification truant from school; or
"(2) is habitually disobedient of the reasonable and lawful commands of his parent, guardian or other custodian, and is ungovernable; or
"(3) has committed an offense applicable only to a child; or
"(4) without just cause and without the consent

of his parent or legal custodian deserts his home
or place of abode; or
"(5) wanders or loiters about the streets of any
city, or in or about any highway or any public
place, between the hours of 12:00 o'clock midnight and 5:00 o'clock a.m.; and
"(6) in any of the foregoing, is in need of supervision, treatment or rehabilitation, or
"(7) has committed a delinquent act or is in
need of supervision but not of treatment or rehabilitation. ..." Ga. Code Ann. § 24A-401(g)
(Supp. 1973).

Perhaps the powers of police to intervene in the
conduct of juveniles *ought* to be broader than it is in the
case of adults. Perhaps an officer should be able to take a
juvenile into custody when he reasonably believes that the
child is delinquent or in need of help or supervision for
whatever reason; otherwise, the police may be powerless
to act in situations where their knowledge indicates that a
child is "in trouble" but falls short of knowledge sufficient
to show a violation of law. Viewed in this light, broad
authority is necessary for the protection of youth and is not
necessarily a means of abrogating their rights. However,
even if the police should have this power, the circumstances under which a youth is taken into custody in the
first place should be a major area of concern, particularly in
light of the fact that most officers probably feel that limitations placed on their dealings with adults are not applicable when handling juveniles.

Indeed, the broad power granted to police and the
great degree of discretion entrusted to them are consistent
with the notion that a juvenile is not "arrested," but is
"taken into custody," which implies a protective and not a
punitive form of detention. *See, e.g.*, Ga. Code Ann. §
24A-1301(b) (Supp. 1973); Ill. Ann. Stat. ch. 37, § 703-1(3)
(1972); Minn. Stat. Ann. § 260.165(2) (1971); Ohio Rev.

Code Ann. § 2151.31 (1971); Wis. Stat. Ann. § 48.28(2) (1957). A recent study indicated that some thirty-six jurisdictions employ the substituted phraseology. E. Ferster, and T. Courtless, *The Beginning of Juvenile Justice, Police Practices, and the Juvenile Offender*, 22 Vand. L. Rev. 567, 583-84 & n.76 (1969). Of these thirty-six, fifteen specifically state that taking a juvenile into custody does not constitute an arrest. *Id.* at 584 & n.77.

On the one hand, the euphemism "taking into custody" may be viewed as an attempt to mollify the harshness of the criminal system, to free the child from the stigma of arrest or to enable him to state on employment questionnaires, for example, that he has never been "arrested." On the other hand, avoidance of the term "arrest" may be read as an attempt to avoid the traditional limitations on the arrest powers of the police.

Another example may suffice to illustrate the potential abuse inherent in the broad jurisdictional power to take a child into custody, specifically in situations involving noncriminal conduct. In *In re Daniel R.*, 274 Cal. App.2d 749, 79 Cal. Rptr. 247 (1969), a California appellate court was called upon to review the decision of a juvenile court that a sixteen-year old boy who admitted to selling marijuana was in danger of leading a "dissolute life." Although the decision was reversed for lack of sufficient evidence, the appellate court expressed no concern over the fact that the juvenile had been taken into custody with neither warrant nor probable cause. 274 Cal. App.2d at 754, 79 Cal. Rptr. at 250. There was thus *some* indication of criminal conduct in the case; in fact, this conduct furnished the basis for the adjudication. But the juvenile was not adjudicated a ward of the court on an allegation that he violated a criminal law, but rather on an allegation that he was in danger of leading an idle, dissolute, lewd, or immoral life, supported by *some* evidence, however slight (in fact, insufficient), that he had engaged in criminal conduct. This suggests that the police, in the absence of probable cause to believe that the youth had committed a criminal offense, relied instead on the much broader "protective" jurisdiction that permits a youth to be taken into custody where he is "seriously endangered in his surroundings" or is "in danger of leading an idle, dissolute, lewd, or immoral life." It should also be noted that particularly in a case where the evidence is weak, an incorrigibility adjudication can be sought for what amounts to criminal (or delinquent) conduct, since the standard of proof required to establish incorrigibility is less than that required to establish an act of delinquency (*see* § 5.03, *infra*, for discussion of standard of proof).

In re Daniel R., *supra*, illustrates that the broad jurisdictional power allows police officers to take juveniles into custody for criminal law violations under circumstances in which they would not be permitted to arrest adults. This is not to say that the broad grant of jurisdiction is improper *per se*. Many young people are in need of help for reasons that fall short of criminal behavior, and their problems ought to be brought to the attention of the juvenile authorities. But the broad jurisdictional power should not be abused by using it as a subterfuge to avoid, for example, the requirements of probable cause or other constitutional rights where a child is taken into custody for what amounts to criminal conduct. Suggested limitations on the power of police to take juveniles into custody are discussed in § 3.03, *infra*.

§ 3.03. Taking into Custody Without Warrant.

The problem of taking youth into custody is compounded by the fact that most of them are undoubtedly taken into custody without a warrant — normally when they are caught in the act of committing an offense or when an officer observes circumstances that seem to require such action. F. Sussman, and F. Baum, *Law of Juvenile Delinquency* 33 (3d ed. 1968).

Because the decision to take a youth into custody is primarily a police decision, the disparity between the handling of adults and juveniles is perhaps greatest at this point. In the criminal process, for example, despite the fact that most arrests are made without a warrant, the law has a clear preference for the detached judgment of a magistrate rather than the subjective judgment of the policeman on the beat. *See Giordenello v. United States*, 357 U.S. 480, 486-87 (1958). This is not to say that arresting without a warrant is improper or for that matter a practice to be discouraged. It simply suggests that whenever the circumstances permit a choice to be made, a warrant should be obtained, issuance of which is based on a magistrate's impartial, objective judgment. *See Wong Sun v. United States*, 371 U.S. 471, 479-80 (1963). After all, the requirement of a warrant is a safeguard that is bypassed whenever a warrantless arrest is made. *Beck v. Ohio*, 379 U.S. 89, 96 (1964).

Admittedly, a police officer ought to possess the flexibility of authority to take an individual — adult or juvenile — into custody without warrant when he has a reasonable belief that the person has violated a law. In fact, most jurisdictions provide by statute that a juvenile may be taken into custody pursuant to the laws of arrest. *See, e.g.*, Ga. Code Ann. § 24A-1301(a) (2) (Supp. 1973); N.Y. Fam. Ct. Act. § 721 (McKinney Supp. 1972); Ohio Rev. Code Ann. § 2151.31(B) (1971); Tenn. Code Ann. § 37-213(a) (2) (Supp. 1973).

The authority of the police to arrest persons for violations of law is not questioned at all, nor is there any reason why their power to arrest for law violations should be limited when dealing with juveniles. The real question is whether a police officer should have the same power in cases involving noncriminal conduct, where more subtle decisions are to be made — such as whether a child is "in danger of leading an idle, dissolute, lewd, or immoral life."

Most states grant very broad authority to police officers to take juveniles into custody in situations involving noncriminal conduct, under circumstances in which they are, in the broadest sense, endangered by their surroundings. See Calif. Welf. & Inst'ns Code § 601 (1972); Minn. Stat. Ann. § 260.165(1) (c) (1971); Ohio Rev. Code Ann. § 2151.31(C) (1971); Wis. Stat. Ann. § 48.28(1) (c) (1957). These statutes indicate, as has already been acknowledged, that the decision to take a youth into custody is regarded primarily as a police decision. However, should it be solely a police decision when the broad jurisdictional power is invoked to take into custody a youth who is *not* charged with a criminal violation but rather, for example, is "in danger of leading a dissolute life"? Police officers generally are poorly equipped to make this sort of decision, and the possibility of abuse is too hazardous to allow them to exercise it unchecked. To be sure, juveniles "in trouble" should receive help, but someone other than the officer in the street ought to assume the *primary* responsibility in the decision-making process.

New York's juvenile jurisdiction statute furnishes a sensible solution to the dilemma. The statute provides that a person under the age of sixteen may be taken into custody without a warrant only when he is committing an act that if performed by an adult would justify an arrest. N.Y. Fam. Ct. Act. § 721 (McKinney Supp. 1972). Thus, the statute does not authorize taking a juvenile into custody on the ground that he is in need of supervision, because in such situations "there is no such urgency that the matter may not be dealt with by summons." *Id*. Committee Comment.

Under this statutory scheme if a juvenile violates a criminal law he can be taken into custody on the same basis that an adult can be arrested. If the juvenile's conduct or surroundings indicate something less than criminal behavior, New York law does not authorize taking him into custody; rather, one may make application to a judicial officer for issuance of a summons, presumably upon presenting the magistrate with facts supporting the belief that the minor requires supervision.

As the Committee Comment following section 721 explains, no situation in which a youth requires supervision is so compelling that it cannot be handled through use of a summons. This provides a practical, workable approach, removing the decision from the policeman on the beat and lodging it with the juvenile court judge, who understands more about youth, youth problems, and the realities of the juvenile justice system, and is better able to assimilate this knowledge and place it in proper context. The criminal justice system, by preferring the procurement of a warrant wherever practicable, deemphasizes the competence of the police to weigh evidence and make the on-the-street decision to arrest. The juvenile process should operate on no less precise a standard. Requiring a summons to issue whenever protective jurisdiction is to be invoked seems to be reasonable in light of the gravity and far reaching effects of the decision to be made.

Cases may arise, of course, in which the child's immediate safety is in peril, and in such cases the officer may need to act immediately to prevent harm from coming to the child. For example, in *State v. Hunt*, 2 Ariz. App. 6, 406 P.2d 208 (1965), an officer responded to the call of a babysitter who had discovered a five-year old child lying on the floor of a furnace room, her hands tied behind her back, her head under the hot water heater, and blood on her face from what appeared to be strap marks. Certainly in a situation such as this one, a police officer should be able to act quickly to remove the child from immediate risk of harm. New York has a statute that permits emergency removal in such a case. N.Y. Fam. Ct. Act § 1024 (McKinney Supp. 1973). In these instances the officer is acting solely out of concern for the child's welfare. There may be other situations that would evoke the same concern and demand the same immediate response. What is involved is a matter of degree, and the officer is charged initially with determining the degree and electing a course of action. Whenever circumstances permit, however, he ought to obtain a warrant or summons, and the impartial judicial officer ought to be the one who determines the course of action to be taken.

§ 3.04. The Decision to Take into Custody: The Criteria.

Encounters between youth and the police are a critical stage of the juvenile process. A minor's initial contact with the juvenile justice system is with the police, and it sets in motion forces of informal decision-making that may determine whether he is to be ensnared in the juvenile process. In many cases he is caught violating the law or is being sought in connection with a particular offense, but it frequently occurs that no particular act has been committed — i.e., the police officer surmises through means other than actual observation that something is amiss. The President's Commisssion on Law Enforcement and the Administration of Justice, The Challenge of Crime in a Free Society 78 (1967); see R. MacIver, The Prevention and Control of Delinquency 139 (1966). In such instances the officer can respond in a number of ways. He can do nothing; he can stop the juveniles and ask their names, their addresses, and their destination; he can search and order them to disperse; he can send or take them home and warn their parents to keep them off the street; or, he can take them to the station for further questioning or checking. The President's Commission on Law Enforcement and the Administration of Justice, *The Challenge of Crime in a Free Society* 78 (1967).

Police response to on-the-street juvenile situations varies greatly from one department to the next. L. Swanson, *Police and Children*, in *Readings in Juvenile Delinquency* 361 (R. Cavan ed. 1969). The degree of discretion exercised depends to a large extent on the characterization of the department in terms of departmental policy, attitudes, and philosophy. A comparison of two departments — one a large eastern department characterized as a "fraternal" department, the other a large western department characterized as a "professional" department — revealed that the highly professional department exercised less discretion and responded to juvenile problems with greater formality (*i.e.*, more "arrests" and referrals to juvenile court), than the fraternal department which exercised great discretion and tended to dispose of many juvenile matters without any further official action or referral to juvenile court or any other agency. The professional department was described as "one governed by values derived from general, impersonal rules which bind all members of the organization and whose relevance is independent of circumstances of time, place or personality". On the other hand, the fraternal department was described as one that "relies to a greater extent on particularistic judgments — that is, judgments based on the significance to a particular person of his particular relations to particular others". Further distinguishing characteristics were that the professional department recruited officers from the general population and promoted officers on the basis of merit, whereas the fraternal department tended to recruit officers from the neighborhoods in which they would work and based promotions on tenure. J. Wilson, *The Police and the Delinquent in Two Cities*, in *Controlling Delinquents* 10-12 (S. Wheeler ed. 1968); *see* J. Wilson, *Varieties of Police Behavior: The Management of Law and Order in Eight Communities* 111-18, 217-18 (1968).

Thus, an officer's response to a street situation may be regulated to a significant degree by departmental practice, whether expressly or tacitly understood. But his judgment is also affected by more subtle factors. Suspecting that something has happened or is about to happen, but with nothing concrete upon which to select a course of action, he may be guided by his subjective attitudes toward, for example, members of a particular race, length of hair, style of clothes, or other qualities of appearance, as well as the reaction and attitude of the juvenile himself — whether he is cooperative and respectful or impudent, defiant or indifferent. The President's Commission on Law Enforcement and the Administration of Justice, *The Challenge of Crime in a Free Society* 78 (1967); E. Ferster, and T. Courtless, *The Beginning of Juvenile Justice, Police Practices and the Juvenile Offender*, 22 Vand. L. Rev. 567, 578-79 (1969). *See generally* Comment, *Socio-Legal Aspects of Racially Motivated Police Misconduct*, 1971 Duke L.J. 751. In the absence of any "legal" basis, reticence or equivocation on the part of the youth may well be the basis of his being taken into custody. The President's Commission on Law Enforcement and the Administration of Justice, *Task Force Report: The Police* 186 (1967).

§ 3.05. The Decision to Take into Custody: The Respective Views.

In street encounters there may be a convergence of conflicting attitudes. Police officers, for example, view as essential to effective law enforcement the power to stop persons on the street, ask questions, and if the occasion seems to require it, detain them for further questioning. *See Terry v. Ohio*, 392 U.S. 1 (1968); *Sibron v. New York*, 392 U.S. 40 (1969). This is no less true in dealing with juveniles. *See In re Lang*, 44 Misc.2d 900, 255 N.Y.S.2d 987 (Fam. Ct., New York Co. 1965).

Further, the officer on the street exercises an authoritative function, setting the tone of law enforcement on his beat and maintaining order and the established routine. Anything that appears to be a departure from the routine gives cause for suspicion and presents strong likelihood that the officer will intervene. P. Chevigny, *Police Power: Abuses in New York City* 276 (1969); Swanson, *Police and Children*, in *Readings in Juvenile Delinquency* 362 (R. Cavan ed. 1969). If the officer's authority is questioned, this may appear menacing to him and may in his view manifest another departure from the routine and a threat to established order. Such a challenge to the exercise of his authoritative function is likely to be regarded as a serious matter and may be met with a rather severe (*i.e.*, official) response. P. Chevigny, *supra; see* J. Wilson, *Varieties of Police Behavior: The Management of Law and Order in Eight Communities* 217 (1968).

A youth usually has preexisting attitudes toward the police that, depending on the officer's handling of the situation, will be confirmed or changed by his initial encounter with a police officer. Therefore, much may depend upon the attitude of the officer himself — whether it evokes respect or antagonism. The interaction of these attitudes may in fact determine whether the child will be taken into custody or released. National Council on Crime and Delinquency, *Standards and Guides for the Detention of Children and Youth* 23 (1961).

Juveniles possess unique characteristics that demand a specialized form of handling. Youth are very impressionable, and when they first encounter the juvenile justice system they may feel all alone and view the police, as well as other forms of authority, as demanding, judgmental and hostile. O. Ketcham, *Legal Renaissance in the Juvenile Court*, 60 Nw. U.L. Rev. 585, 595 (1965).

There is evidence to suggest, in fact, that despite efforts to shield children, on a child's level of understanding and experience, a juvenile proceeding carries the same stigmatizing effect as a criminal prosecution. P. Tappan, *Unofficial Delinquency*, 29 Neb. L. Rev. 547, 548 (1950); *see generally*, M. Baum, and S. Wheeler, *Becoming an Inmate*, in *Controlling Delinquents* 153 (S. Wheeler ed. 1968); B. Maher, *The Delinquent's Perception of the Law and the Community*, in *Controlling Delinquents* 187 (S. Wheeler ed. 1968).

The young, because they are especially vulnerable to influence, however slight, must be handled with a great deal more circumspection and understanding than adult offenders. It is important that the impression of the administration of justice that a minor perceives at this point be one of fairness, for if this impression is formed, the process of rehabilitation has already commenced. M. Paulsen, *Fairness to the Juvenile Offender*, 41 Minn. L. Rev. 547, 551 (1957). *See also* R. MacIver, *The Prevention and Control of Delinquency* 139 (1966). Otherwise, he may be imbued with a disrespect for lawful authority and a sense of bitter resentment for the form of justice he sees. S. Wheeler, and L. Cottrell, *Juvenile Delinquency* 33 (1966). *See also* The President's Commission on Law Enforcement and the Administration of Justice, *The Challenge of Crime in a Free Society* 79 (1967). The concern for the consequences flowing from the encounter between the youth and police is thus justified. Implicit in this concern, however, is the officer's view of himself as a vital, functioning part of the rehabilitative process. F. Remington, *Criminal Justice Administration* 959 (1969).

II. SEARCH AND SEIZURE.

§ 3.06. Applicability of the Fourth Amendment.

The Supreme Court in *In re Gault*, 387 U.S. 1 (1967), made it clear at the outset of its opinion that the due process requirements announced in its ruling were directed toward the adjudicatory stage of juvenile proceedings only, and that it specifically was not addressing itself to the applicability of constitutional rights to the prejudicial stages of the proceedings. 387 U.S. at 13.

Moreover, the Court reiterated with added emphasis its earlier statement in *Kent v. United States*, 383 U.S. 541, 562 (1966), that the purpose of its decision was not to require in the juvenile process all of the constitutional rights now mandatory in the criminal or even administrative process, but rather simply to require in adjudicatory hearings those rights required by notions of fundamental fairness and due process *under the fourteenth amendment*, in the context of the case before it. 387 U.S. at 30-31.

In other contexts, applying the same approach, the Court found additional, *but not all*, guarantees of the criminal process applicable to the juvenile process. *See In re Winship*, 397 U.S. 358 (1970) ("beyond reasonable doubt" standard required in delinquency proceeding where child is charged with act that if committed by adult would be a crime); *McKeiver v. Pennsylvania*, 403 U.S. 528 (1971) (right to jury trial is not constitutionally required in delinquency proceedings).

The question remaining after *Gault* was to what extent its mandate logically extended to other stages of the juvenile process, particularly the police investigatory process. In the case of any ruling of such profound significance, the tendency is to extend the rule to its logical conclusion. *Krulewitch v. United States*, 336 U.S. 440, 445 (1949) (Jackson, J., concurring); *Hudson County Water Company v. McCarter*, 209 U.S. 349, 355 (1908); W. Schaefer, *The Suspect and Society* 27 (1967); B. Cardozo, *The Nature of the Judicial Process* 51 (1921). *Gault* has proved to be no exception. Just as the applicability of *Gault* has been extended to cover police interrogation of juveniles (*see* §§ 3.12-3.13, *infra*) and lineups (*see* § 3.15, *infra*), it has been read as well to require application of the fourth amendment and the exclusionary rule to the juvenile process.

All courts that have specifically considered the question of the applicability of the fourth amendment to the juvenile process have held in favor of its applicability, or more correctly, no court considering the question has held the fourth amendment to be inapplicable to juvenile proceedings. *See, e.g., In re Marsh*, 40 Ill.2d 53, 237 N.E.2d 529 (1968); *State v. Lowry*, 95 N.J. Super. 307, 230 A.2d 907 (1967); *In re Harvey*, 222 Pa. Super. 222, 295 A.2d 93 (1972).

The decisions vary a great deal, but at the outset it is safe to say that before evidence is excluded in a juvenile proceeding the court must find that (1) the prohibition of the fourth amendment and its exclusionary rule are applicable to juveniles; (2) the search and seizure complained of were unreasonable; (3) the search was conducted or instigated by a state (government) agent; and (4) there were no circumstances present such as consent or waiver to suspend operation of the exclusionary rule.

In many cases the courts assume, without actually stating, that the first requirement is met, *i.e.*, that the fourth amendment is applicable to juvenile proceedings, and proceed to resolve the fourth amendment issue in the case on the basis of one of the other requirements, *i.e.*, whether the search was or was not reasonable, or whether a valid consent or waiver was present, etc. *See, e.g., In re Joseph A.*, 30 Cal. App.3d 880, 106 Cal. Rptr. 729 (1973); *In re Robert T.*, 8 Cal. App.3d 990, 88 Cal. Rptr. 37 (1970); *In re J.R.M.*, 487 S.W.2d 502 (Mo. 1972); *In re Ronny*, 40 Misc.2d 194, 242 N.Y.S.2d 844 (Fam. Ct., Queens Co. 1963); *In re Baker*, 18 Ohio App.2d 276, 248 N.E.2d 620 (1969).

Courts have employed various rationales in handling, or in some cases evading, the question of the fourth amendment's application. A number of federal cases, for example, indicate a trend toward holding the provisions of the Bill of Rights directly applicable in federal juvenile proceedings, rather than utilizing the due process analysis of *Gault. See Nieves v. United States*, 280 F. Supp. 994, 999-1000, 1004-05 (S.D.N.Y. 1968); *see also Trimble v. Stone*, 187 F. Supp. 483 (D.D.C. 1960). On this basis, the fourth amendment would seem to be directly applicable in federal juvenile proceedings. *See Brown v. Fauntleroy*, 442 F.2d 838 (D.C. Cir. 1971); *Cooley v. Stone*, 414 F.2d 1213 (D.C. Cir. 1969).

Indeed, some state courts have expressed the view that the provisions of the fourth amendment are applicable to juveniles in the same way and for the same reason they are applicable to adults, *i.e.*, by virtue of the decision in *Mapp v. Ohio*, 367 U.S. 643 (1961), rather than by virtue of a due process and fair treatment analysis. *See, e.g., State v. Lowry*, 95 N.J. Super. 307, 313, 230 A.2d 907, 909-10 (1967). Since the exclusionary rule is not necessarily limited to criminal cases, this approach is taken apparently to negate the argument that certain constitutional rights guaranteed in criminal proceedings are inapplicable to juvenile proceedings because of their civil nature.

Most of the state courts that have dealt with the applicability of the fourth amendment to juvenile proceedings have relied on the traditional due process and fair treatment analysis that existed prior to *Gault,* or in some post-*Gault* cases, have relied on constitutional due process standards announced in *Gault* to extend to juveniles the same protections afforded adults in the criminal process. In each instance the courts have concluded that the fourth amendment is applicable to juvenile proceedings. *See, e.g., In re Williams,* 49 Misc.2d 154, 169-70, 267 N.Y.S.2d 91, 109-10 (Fam. Ct., Ulster Co. 1966); *State v. Lowry,* 95 N.J. Super. 307, 313-17, 230 A.2d 907, 910-12 (1967) (although court also held, as mentioned *supra,* that fourth amendment is applicable without resort to due process analysis); *In re Morris,* 29 Ohio Misc. 71, 278 N.E.2d 701 (Ct. Com. Pleas, Juv. Div., Columbiana Co. 1971); *In re Harvey,* 222 Pa. Super. 222, 229, 295 A.2d 93, 96-97 (1972); *Ciulla v. State,* 434 S.W.2d 948, 950 (Tex. Civ. App. 1968).

A number of other state courts, however, hold the fourth amendment applicable to juvenile proceedings, either expressly or by implication, without stating the basis or rationale for doing so. This often occurs where the court overlooks the fundamental question of the applicability of the fourth amendment, and assuming or conceding its applicability, resolves the search and seizure issue on some other basis — for example, that the search was conducted with the child's consent, *see, e.g., In re Ronny,* 40 Misc.2d 194, 242 N.Y.S.2d 844 (Fam. Ct., Queens Co. 1963); or that the parties did not have a reasonable expectation of privacy, *see, e.g., In re Joseph A.,* 30 Cal. App.3d 880, 106 Cal. Rptr. 729 (1973); or that the child waived the right to object to the illegal search and seizure, *see, e.g., In re Baker,* 18 Ohio App.2d 276, 248 N.E.2d 620 (1969).

In addition, a number of other courts have held the fourth amendment applicable to juveniles without stating an underlying rationale, or have tacitly assumed the fourth amendment's applicability. *See In re Robert T.,* 8 Cal. App.3d 990, 88 Cal. Rptr. 37 (1970); *In re Marsh,* 40 Ill.2d 53,

237 N.E.2d 529 (1968); *In re Urbasek*, 76 Ill. App.2d 375, 222 N.E.2d 233 (1966), *rev'd on other grounds*, 38 Ill.2d 535, 232 N.E.2d 716 (1968); *In re J.R.M.*, 487 S.W.2d 502 (Mo. 1972); *In re Robert P.*, 40 App. Div.2d 638, 336 N.Y.S.2d 212 (1972).

These decisions indicate that courts are applying the fourth amendment to children in juvenile proceedings in precisely the same way it is applicable to adults in criminal proceedings. Thus, the issues of consent and waiver are treated in juvenile proceedings in precisely the same as they are treated in criminal cases. *See In re Ronny*, 40 Misc.2d 194, 242 N.Y.S.2d 844 (Fam. Ct., Queens Co. 1963) (consent); *In re Baker*, 18 Ohio App.2d 276, 248 N.E.2d 620 (1969) (waiver).

As in criminal proceedings, a search without a warrant is lawful only where it occurs incident to a lawful arrest. *See In re Marsh*, 40 Ill.2d 53, 237 N.E.2d 529 (1968). Stop and frisk procedures are applicable to juveniles in the same way they are applicable to adults. *See In re Lang*, 44 Misc.2d 900, 255 N.Y.S.2d 987 (Fam. Ct., New York Co. 1965) (note that this case actually precedes *Terry v. Ohio*, 392 U.S. 1 (1968), which gave police officers limited authority to stop persons and conduct a limited search for weapons). The law relating to searches of automobiles is applicable to juvenile proceedings as well as criminal proceedings. *See In re J.R.M.*, 487 S.W.2d 502 (Mo. 1972), which contains an excellent fourth amendment analysis in a case involving a juvenile, just as if the case were a criminal case. All of the cases suggest in the strongest terms that the fourth amendment is equally applicable to all persons regardless of age, and is fully applicable in juvenile proceedings, regardless of the civil nature of the proceedings. *See especially State v. Lowry*, 95 N.J. Super. 307, 313, 230 A.2d 907, 909-10 (1967).

In addition to judicial decisions that have held the

fourth amendment applicable to juvenile proceedings, several states have incorporated the exclusionary rule safeguard into their juvenile codes in the form of a provision stating that evidence illegally seized shall be inadmissible in any hearing in the juvenile court. *See, e.g.*, Ga. Code Ann. § 24A-2002(b) (Supp. 1973); N.M. Stat. Ann. § 13-14-25(C) (2) (Supp. 1973); N.D. Cent. Code § 27-20-27(2) (1974); Pa. Stat. Ann. tit. 11, § 50-318(b) (Supp. 1974); Tenn. Code Ann. § 37-227(b) (Supp. 1973); Tex. Fam. Code Ann. § 54.03(e) (1973); Vt. Stat. Ann. tit. 33, § 652 (Supp. 1973); *see also* Cal. Welf. & Inst'ns Code § 701 (1972) (evidence is admissible that would be "legally admissible in the trial of criminal cases"); Ill. Ann. Stat. ch. 37, § 704-6 (1972) (applicable rules of evidence in juvenile proceedings are those prescribed for criminal cases); Miss. Code Ann. § 43-21-17 (Supp. 1973) (adjudicatory hearing conducted in accordance with such rules of evidence "as may comply with applicable constitutional standards").

§ 3.07. School Searches.

(a) Private Citizen-State Agent Distinction.

Searches of students and students' lockers on school property present problems that are unique for juveniles. Generally, where the search is conducted by a school official, the validity of such searches centers on whether the school official was acting as a private individual or as a government agent, whether the official was authorized to make the search on the basis of his *in loco parentis* relationship to the child, and whether the search was reasonable.

The Supreme Court has long since held that the fourth amendment does not protect the individual against searches and seizures conducted by private persons not acting on behalf of the government. *Burdeau v. McDowell*,

256 U.S. 465 (1921). Even in jurisdictions applying the exclusionary rule to juveniles, courts frequently have taken the view that school officials conducting searches on their own initiative are acting as private citizens and for that reason are not subject to the limitations of the fourth amendment. In *In re Donaldson*, 269 Cal. App.2d 509, 75 Cal. Rptr. 220 (1969), for example, the vice-principal of a high school, acting alone, conducted a search of a student's locker and discovered marijuana. The court held the evidence admissible on the basis that the principal was acting as a private citizen whose conduct was not governed by the fourth admendment. 269 Cal. App.2d at 510-11, 75 Cal. Rptr. at 222.

Likewise, in *People v. Stewart*, 63 Misc.2d 601, 313 N.Y.S.2d 253 (Crim. Ct., New York Co. 1970), a New York court held that a high school dean of boys who conducted a search of the person of a student was acting as a private person for purposes of determining admissibility of evidence seized as a result of the search. 63 Misc.2d at 603-04, 313 N.Y.S.2d at 256-57. In a more recent decision, however, a New York court held that a high school disciplinary officer who conducted a search prior to the arrival of police was acting as a government agent. *People v. Jackson*, 65 Misc.2d 909, 319 N.Y.S.2d 731 (Sup. Ct. 1971), *aff'd* 30 N.Y.2d 734, 284 N.E.2d 153, 333 N.Y.S.2d 167 (1972).

In still another decision, *Mercer v. State*, 450 S.W.2d 715 (Tex. Civ. App. 1970), the court determined that a search by a high school principal was not an action by a government agent but an action by a private citizen not controlled by the fourth amendment. Thus, there is at least some support for the notion that a school official, acting on his own in conducting a search, is regarded as a private citizen, not a government agent.

Whether or not the school official is regarded as acting under state authority often depends on two factors:

whether police officers were also involved in the search, and the purpose for which the search was conducted. When the school official does not act alone in conducting the challenged search but acts together with law enforcement officers, the search loses its private characterization and becomes a search conducted under state authority, subject to the protections of the fourth amendment. *See, e.g., Piazzola v. Watkins,* 316 F. Supp. 624, 626-27 (M.D. Ala. 1970), *aff'd,* 442 F.2d 284 (5th Cir. 1971); *see also In re Donaldson,* 269 Cal. App.2d 509, 510-11, 75 Cal. Rptr. 220, 222 (1969), *citing Stapleton v. Superior Court,* 70 Cal.2d 97, 447 P.2d 967, 73 Cal. Rptr. 575 (1969); *People v. Stewart,* 63 Misc.2d 601, 603-04, 313 N.Y.S.2d 253, 256-57 (Crim. Ct., New York Co. 1970).

Some courts have held that a school official, even when not acting in concert with police in conducting a search, is regarded as a government agent for purposes of application of the fourth amendment to school-related searches. *See, e.g., State v. Baccino,* 282 A.2d 869, 870-71 (Dela. 1971).

Similarly, in most cases in which courts have considered whether the official was acting as a government official, they have inquired into the purpose of the search. Specifically, the inquiry has centered on whether the search was conducted for the purpose of meeting legitimate school objectives, such as maintaining order and discipline, or for the purpose of gathering evidence for a criminal prosecution. *See, e.g., Piazzola v. Watkins,* 316 F. Supp. 624, 626-27 (M.D. Ala. 1970), *aff'd,* 442 F.2d 284 (5th Cir. 1971); *In re Donaldson,* 269 Cal. App.2d 509, 511-12, 75 Cal. Rptr. 220, 222 (1969).

The latter point raises an alternative ground that several courts have employed to hold school searches outside the operation of the fourth amendment — the *in loco parentis* doctrine.

(b) In Loco Parentis Doctrine.

The philosophy of *in loco parentis* is that school officials take the place of parents with regard to the education and protection of children while they are at school. In assuming the parental role, school officials (including principals, teachers, and other school officials) are vested with the powers of control, restraint, and discipline over the students to achieve the goals of education. *See Mercer v. State,* 450 S.W.2d 715, 717 (Tex. Civ. App. 1970).

The rationale behind allowing a school official to search a student's locker without consent, arrest, or search warrant is that the official must move quickly to deal with a student who will likely jeopardize the educational process or the health and morals of other students. The high school is not equipped to afford each child suspected of a crime the procedural safeguards assured in a criminal court. Under the *in loco parentis* doctrine, school officials may have not only the right but perhaps the duty to inspect students' lockers or to consent to searches by police officers. *See* D. Donoghoe, *Emerging First and Fourth Amendment Rights of the Student,* 1 J. Law & Educ. 449, 451 (1972).

In *In re Donaldson,* 269 Cal. App.2d 509, 75 Cal. Rptr. 220 (1969), for example, the court upheld a search of a student's locker by the vice-principal of a school on the alternative theory that the vice-principal was acting *in loco parentis.* To support the existence of an affirmative duty on the part of school officials, the court emphasized statutes that imposed upon school officials the duty to give diligent care to the health and physical development of the students, and that granted school officials the authority to expel students who threatened the welfare of fellow students by such activities as possessing, using, or selling drugs. 269 Cal. App.2d at 512, 75 Cal. Rptr. at 222-23.

Similarly, in *People v. Overton*, 20 N.Y.2d 360, 229 N.E.2d 596, 283 N.Y.S.2d 22 (1967), the court invoked, as an alternative basis for its holding, the *in loco parentis* doctrine.

In the *Overton* case police detectives had procured a search warrant to search the lockers of two students, and the vice-principal gave his permission for the search. Even though the search warrant later turned out to be defective, the court upheld the search of the lockers and admitted into evidence the marijuana found therein. The court maintained that the supervisory powers of school officials, made necessary by the duty to maintain order and discipline in the school, gave the vice-principal authority to consent to the search. Because parents were naturally concerned about the emerging drug culture in high schools, the school officials, *standing in the place of the parents*, had an affirmative duty to investigate charges of drug use among students. 20 N.Y.2d at 363, 229 N.E.2d at 597-98, 283 N.Y.S.2d at 24-25.

On occasion, however, school officials seem to have powers, rights, and duties even greater than those of parents. In *Mercer v. State*, 450 S.W.2d 715 (Tex. Civ. App. 1970), a high school student complied with a principal's demand that he empty his pockets. Police were immediately notified when search of the juvenile produced marijuana. The court ruled that the principal acted *in loco parentis* and not as an arm of the government. In a dissenting opinion, however, Justice Hughes was of the view that the court had enlarged the *in loco parentis* doctrine beyond its permissible scope. He pointed out that a parent conducting a similar search could remain silent as to the results of the search without incurring criminal liability, whereas a school official does not have the same right or privilege. He argued that few parents of teenage children would knowingly transfer to school authorities their right to determine whether incriminating evidence should be ignored or used against their children. 450 S.W.2d at 720-21 (Hughes, J., dissenting).

(c) Proprietary Interest Theory.

Some courts have upheld the right of school officials to search students' lockers, not on the distinction between private and state action, but on the basis that the students' possession of lockers is exclusive only in relation to other students.

In *In re Donaldson*, 269 Cal. App.2d 509, 75 Cal. Rptr. 220 (1969), for example, the court ruled that the student's locker was not under his exclusive control but was jointly controlled by school officials. In such a case the focus often is on the existence or absence of school customs or regulations allowing inspections by school officials. In *Donaldson* the vice-principal testified that it was the custom of school authorities to search student lockers in a great variety of situations, such as bomb threats, or when contraband such as drugs, liquor, stolen goods, or weapons were suspected of being hidden therein. 269 Cal. App.2d at 512-13, 75 Cal. Rptr. at 222-23.

Similarly, in *People v. Overton*, 20 N.Y.2d 360, 229 N.E.2d 596, 283 N.Y.S.2d 22 (1967), the court held that the school maintained a proprietary interest in students' lockers even though assigned for their exclusive use. Not only did the school keep a list of the combinations of the lockers but had promulgated specific rules and regulations regarding what could and could not be kept in them, subject to periodic spot checks. In fact, the vice-principal on a number of occasions had inspected students' lockers prior to the search in question. 20 N.Y.2d at 363, 229 N.E.2d at 598, 283 N.Y.S.2d at 25. The state court's rationale was upheld in a subsequent decision in a federal habeas corpus action by the student whose locker was searched. *Overton v. Rieger*, 311 F. Supp. 1035 (S.D.N.Y. 1970).

Jurisdictions that take this view reason that school authorities, who are in a quasi-parental relationship to the student, have the right and possibly a duty to inspect lockers for disciplinary purposes. Thus, school officials may themselves inspect lockers or consent to such an inspection by law enforcement officers. *See, e.g., In re Donaldson, supra* (school officials stand *in loco parentis* to the student and share the parent's right to use moderate force to obtain obedience); *State v. Stein*, 203 Kan. 638, 456 P.2d 1, *cert. denied*, 397 U.S. 947 (1969) (school has joint control of student lockers; therefore, high school principal has an inherent right to inspect school lockers); *People v. Overton, supra* (vice-principal of high school has power to consent to a search of students' lockers by police detectives).

(d) Reasonableness of Search.

The usual inquiry into the application of the fourth amendment to a search on school property might be expected to begin with a determination of whether the school official conducting the search acted as a private citizen or as a government agent. If it determines that the school official acted as an individual, the court need inquire no further into the applicability of the fourth amendment. If, on the other hand, the court determines that the school official acted under state authority, then it must inquire into the reasonableness of the search. Occasionally, however, courts begin their analysis of the fourth amendment issue by first examining the reasonableness of the search, deciding *sub silentio* that the school official acted under state authority, or else by ignoring the distinction altogether. *See, e.g., In re Thomas G.*, 11 Cal. App.3d

1193, 90 Cal. Rptr. 361 (1970); *People v. Jackson*, 65 Misc.2d 909, 319 N.Y.S.2d 731 (Sup. Ct. 1971).

In any event, if the search is found to have been reasonable, the search is valid regardless of the status of the school official. Thus, the court can resolve the issue along more familiar lines of analysis applicable in criminal cases, without getting into the troublesome issue of whether the school official was functioning as a private citizen or government agent in conducting the search. *See People v. Lanthier*, 5 Cal.3d 751, 755, 488 P.2d 625, 627-28, 97 Cal. Rptr. 297, 299-300 (1971).

A search is generally "reasonable" if it bears a reasonable relationship to a legitimate educational interest which the school official was pursuing in conducting the search. *See, e.g., State v. Baccino*, 282 A.2d 869, 872 (Del. Super. Ct. 1971); *People v. Jackson*, 65 Misc.2d 909, 910-12, 319 N.Y.S.2d 731, 734 (Sup. Ct. 1971).

However, in determining what is reasonable under the fourth amendment, courts frequently have used a less demanding standard than the probable cause standard. For example, in *In re Thomas G.*, 11 Cal. App.3d 1193, 90 Cal. Rptr. 361 (1970), the court felt that a lesser standard, such as a "reasonable suspicion" standard, would satisfy fourth amendment requirements in cases involving school searches because of the duty imposed on school officials to care for the health and welfare of the students. *Accord: In re Fred C.*, 26 Cal. App.3d 320, 102 Cal. Rptr. 682 (1972); *State v. Baccino, supra; People v. Jackson, supra*. In *In re Fred C., supra*, the courts stated that a search of a high school student by a school official "is not measured by the rules authorizing the search of an adult by the police." 26 Cal. App.3d at 324, 102 Cal. Rptr. at 684. In this crucial respect, the fourth amendment's application to children differs from its application to adults.

§ 3.08. Consent and Waiver.

A search of a juvenile may be conducted with the juvenile's consent, as is the case with an adult; further, if the juvenile's consent is found to be valid, the usual requirement of a warrant is excused.

In *In re Ronny*, 40 Misc.2d 194, 242 N.Y.S.2d 844 (Fam. Ct., Queens Co. 1963), for example, an officer observed the respondent, a fifteen-year old boy, pass an unseen object to another youth in exchange for money. Suspicious of the transaction, the officer followed the respondent, who was walking very unsteadily and, in the opinion of the officer, was obviously under the influence of an intoxicant. When the officer finally approached the boy and questioned him, the boy emptied his pockets, which contained illegal drugs and the money he had received from the other youth. As he produced these items, the youth confessed to the sale of illegal drugs. Noting the lack of objection by the boy, his physical cooperation and his voluntary confession, the court held that the search was conducted with his consent and therefore was lawful under the fourth amendment.

Just as in a criminal investigation, other parties may consent to a search of premises jointly occupied with the juvenile or in which the juvenile and the consenting party share a proprietary interest. The most common example occurs when a school official consents to the search of a juvenile's locker by the police. A number of courts have held that a school locker is not within the exclusive control of the student, except as against other students, but rather that the school has joint control over the locker. Perhaps the leading, as well as the most controversial case in this area is *People v. Overton*, 20 N.Y.2d 360, 229 N.E.2d 596, 283 N.Y.S.2d 22 (1967), in which the vice-principal of a high school permitted police detectives to search a student's locker after being shown a search warrant that later proved to be defective. The defendant student objected to the search because of the defective warrant, but the court held that the vice-principal properly consented to the search, since the school has joint control over student lockers. The court also rejected the argument that the consent was invalid because it was given under compulsion of the defective warrant. Emphasizing the vice-principal's testimony that he always personally conducted a search when he received a report from *any person* that an illicit article was in a locker, the court concluded that consent would have been given regardless of the defective warrant. 20 N.Y.2d at 362, 229 N.E.2d at 597, 283 N.Y.S.2d at 24.

The case was subsequently appealed to the United States Supreme Court, which vacated and remanded, 393 U.S. 85 (1968), for further consideration in light of *Bumper v. North Carolina*, 391 U.S. 543 (1968). On remand, the New York Court of Appeals again affirmed defendant's conviction, emphasizing that despite the invalid search warrant, a school official has not only a right but an obligation to investigate the reported presence of illegal material in a student's locker. *People v. Overton*, 24 N.Y.2d 522, 526, 249 N.E.2d 366, 368, 301 N.Y.S.2d 479, 482 (1969). For the same reasons, a federal district court subsequently rejected defendant's claim for post-conviction relief. *Overton v. Rieger*, 311 F. Supp. 1035, 1038 (S.D.N.Y. 1970).

Nevertheless, a strong dissent was registered by Judge Bergan of the New York Court of Appeals in the first *Overton* decision and renewed in the second *Overton* decision. In the first decision, he stated: "There can be no doubt, reading this record, that the principal opened the door, not because he was exercising a free supervisory control over the locker in the interest of the school program, but because he felt the invalid search warrant compelled him to do so." 20 N.Y.2d at 364, 229 N.E.2d at 598, 283 N.Y.S.2d at 25-26. Judge Bergan likewise would have found present, in the second *Overton* decision, the element of coercion prohibited by *Bumper v. North Carolina*, since the "consent" of the vice-principal was given only in reliance on the defective warrant. 24 N.Y.2d at 527, 249 N.E.2d at 368-69, 301 N.Y.S.2d at 483.

Similarly, in a dissent in *Mercer v. State*, 450 S.W.2d 715 (Tex. Civ. App. 1970), Justice Hughes pointed out that, since a principal who had conducted a search of a student's person persuaded the boy that he was *obligated* to empty his pockets, this amounted to the kind of coercion that vitiates consent, in accordance with *Bumper v. North Carolina*. 450 S.W.2d at 719n.1.

Although a child generally is viewed as lacking capacity to consent on the parent's behalf to a search of the home, see, e.g., *May v. State*, 199 So.2d 635 (Miss. 1967), a parent generally may consent on behalf of the child to a search of the child's quarters, on the theory that the consenting party (usually the head of the household) has a proprietary interest in the premises or is in immediate control of the premises. *See, e.g., United States v. Stone*, 401 F.2d 32 (7th Cir. 1968); *Tolbert v. State*, 224 Ga. 291, 161 S.E.2d 279 (1968). Some courts have adopted a more qualified approach. For example, in *People v. Bunker*, 22 Mich. App. 396, 177 N.W.2d 644 (1970), the court stated that homeowning parents may consent to a search of the premises for items that may incriminate a child who is living at home, *provided that the search is limited to an area commonly accessible to all members of the family*. 22 Mich. App. at 403, 177 N.W.2d at 648 (search of basement area, open to all members of family, was reasonable). Thus, it has been held that a sister lacks authority to consent to a search of a bedroom occupied by her brother, but may consent only to a search of areas occupied in common with other tenants.

Beach v. Superior Court, 11 Cal. App.3d 1032, 1035, 90 Cal. Rptr. 200, 201-02 (1970).

Curiously, slightly over a month after the Michigan Court of Appeals decided *People v. Bunker, supra*, it decided another case in which it purported to deal with the authority of a parent to consent to a search of a child's room as a question of first impression, without mentioning its earlier decision in *People v. Bunker. People v. Flowers*, 23 Mich. App. 523, 179 N.W.2d 56 (1970). In *People v. Flowers* the court held that consent to search is a personal right that can not be waived by a parent having "no personal or punishable involvement in the crime suspected or charged." 23 Mich. App. at 527, 179 N.W.2d at 58. The *Bunker* and *Flowers* cases are perhaps distinguishable on the basis that in *Bunker* the parent consented to a search of an area open to all members of the family, whereas in *Flowers* the parent consented to a search of the child's own room. *See People v. Simmons*, 49 Mich. App. 80, 84, 211 N.W.2d 247, 249-50 (1973).

As pointed out in *Bumper v. North Carolina*, 391 U.S. 543 (1968), if entry is gained through trickery or misrepresentation by police officers, consent is negated. The same rule applies in juvenile proceedings. For instance, in *In re Robert T.*, 8 Cal. App.3d 990, 88 Cal. Rptr. 37 (1970), a plainclothes policeman, accompanied by the landlord of an apartment building, gained entrance to the juvenile's apartment on the landlord's statement that he just wanted to come in and check the apartment. The policeman was not identified as a police officer, but rather as the landlord's "friend Joe." The court held that entry was not gained by consent, since consent was given based on the landlord's assertion that his companion was simply his friend, an assertion that the policeman did not correct. Use of this deception vitiated consent.

Presumably, the same rule would apply where deception is employed to obtain the consent of a parent or other occupant in control of the premises, to search a child's room or property.

Consent itself is a form of waiver of fourth amendment rights. Waiver can occur in a variety of other ways. In *In re Baker*, 18 Ohio App.2d 276, 248 N.E.2d 620 (1969), the court held that the failure of a juvenile or his attorney to object to an alleged unlawful search and seizure, where the grounds for objection were known prior to the hearing, constituted a waiver of the right to object to use of the evidence against him.

On the other hand, an Illinois court has concluded that to find a waiver in such a case would be inappropriate in a delinquency proceeding, because of the fundamental nature of the fourth amendment protection, and because loss of the right by waiver in the case of a minor would be "contrary to the spirit of the 'laudable purposes of Juvenile Courts'." *In re Urbasek*, 76 Ill. App.2d 375, 385, 222 N.E.2d 233, 238 (1966), *rev'd on other grounds*, 38 Ill. 2d 535, 232 N.E.2d 716 (1968). The view expressed by the Illinois court is highly protective of a juvenile's rights, since in the *Urbasek* case the juvenile was represented by counsel at the delinquency hearing.

III. POST-CUSTODY RELEASE.

§ 3.09. Notice and Release.

In terms of protecting a juvenile's rights, the decision making process that begins immediately after he is taken into custody is perhaps an area of even greater concern than the decision to take into custody. *See* M. Paulsen, *Fairness to the Juvenile Offender*, 41 Minn. L. Rev. 547, 551 (1957).

The custodial stage of the juvenile process, includ-

ing detention, if any, and police investigation and interrogation, is confusing to children and parents alike, and
their reaction is frequently one of bewilderment and won-
der. E. Studt, *The Client's Image of the Juvenile Court,* in
Justice for the Child 200, 204-05 (M. Rosenheim ed. 1962).

As already noted (§3.03, *supra*) most youths are
taken into custody without warrant or summons. The
most immediate problem is what to do with the child —
whether to release him into the custody of his parents,
hold him for further investigation and questioning, or
place him in confinement.

Because children are often held at police stations on
suspicion or for investigation for indefinite periods of
time, a number of states have attempted to alleviate the
potential harm of unnecessary detention by following the
examples set forth in model juvenile court acts.

The Standard Juvenile Court Act, for example, provides that if a child is taken into custody, with or without
warrant, his parents or guardian shall be notified immediately. The Act further provides that unless there is
some compelling reason why he should not be released,
the youth shall be released in parental custody upon a
written promise to produce him in court at the designated
time. Standard Juvenile Court Act § 16 (6th ed. 1959). *See
also* Uniform Juvenile Court Act § 15 (1968); National
Council on Crime and Delinquency, *Standards and Guides
for the Detention of Children and Youth* 23 (1961).

Following this example, New York's statute provides as follows:

> "(a) If a peace officer takes into custody under
> section seven hundred twenty-one or if a person
> is delivered to him under section seven hundred
> twenty-three, the peace officer shall im-
> mediately notify the parent or other person leg-
> ally responsible for his care, or the person with

whom he is domiciled, that he has been taken into custody.

"(b) After making every reasonable effort to give notice under paragraph (a), the peace officer shall

"(i) release the child to the custody of his parent or other person legally responsible for his care upon the written promise, without security, of the person to whose custody the child is released that he will produce the child before the family court in that county at a time and place specified in writing; or

"(ii) forthwith and with all reasonable speed take the child directly, and without his first being taken to the police station house, to the family court located in the county in which the act occasioning the taking into custody allegedly was done...; or

"(iii) take the child to a place designated by rules of court as a juvenile detention facility for the reception of children.

"(c) In the absence of special circumstances, the peace officer shall release the child in accordance with paragraph (b) (i)." N.Y. Fam. Ct. Act § 724 (McKinney Supp. 1973). *See also* Ill. Ann. Stat. ch. 37, § 703-2 (1972); Minn. Stat. Ann. § 260.171 (1971); Wis. Stat. Ann. § 48.29 (1957).

The statutory duty to notify the child's parents or guardian that he has been taken into custody is fairly typical, as is the preference that the child be released into the custody of his parents or other custodian. If a child is to be detained, however, on what grounds is continued custody warranted? The Uniform Juvenile Court Act sets forth several factors that may require holding the child in custody. Section 14 of the Act states that a child shall *not* be detained *unless*:

"(1) his detention or care is required to protect the person or property of others or of the child or

> (2) because the child may abscond or be re-
> moved from the jurisdiction of the court or (3)
> because he has no parent, guardian, or custo-
> dian or other person able to provide supervision
> and care for him and return him to the court
> when required, or (4) an order for his detention
> or shelter care has been made by the court pur-
> suant to this Act." Uniform Juvenile Court Act §
> 14 (1968). *See also* Md. Ann. Code, Cts. & Jud.
> Proc. § 3-823(a)-(b) (1974); N.M. Stat. Ann. §
> 13-14-22 (Supp. 1973).

These considerations might very well require that the child be held in custody rather than released outright to a parent, guardian, or other custodian, although continued custody ought to be the rare exception rather than the rule. The presumption in most such statutes, after all, is that the child should be released unless some good reason appears to indicate otherwise, rather than the reverse. If the child is to be detained on one of these infrequent occasions, however, a more poignant question arises. Does the child have the same right to release on bail that an adult would have if charged with the same offense in a criminal proceeding?

§ 3.10. Release on Bail.

As a practical matter, with these special release provisions for juveniles and the emphasis on releasing them into parental custody, bail for juveniles has not been a question of paramount concern, in terms of litigation over the right to bail for children.

In *In re William M.*, 3 Cal.3d 16, 473 P.2d 737, 89 Cal. Rptr. 33 (1970), the California Supreme Court pointed out that the release provisions of the California juvenile laws — properly administered — were an adequate alternative to the bail system, in effect rendering moot the question of a right to bail for juveniles.

A number of states have expressly determined that juveniles do not have a right to release on bail. *See, e.g.,* Hawaii Rev. Stat. § 571-32(f) (1968); Ore. Rev. Stat. § 419.583 (1971); *Cinque v. Boyd,* 99 Conn. 70, 121 A. 678 (1923) (despite statutory provision that appears to grant discretionary release on bail, Conn. Gen. Stat. Ann. § 17-63 (1958)); *A.N.E. v. State,* 156 So.2d 525 (Fla. Dist. Ct. App. 1963); *Ex parte Newkosky,* 94 N.J.L. 314, 116 A. 716 (N.J. Sup. Ct. 1920); *State ex. rel. Peaks v. Allaman,* 66 Ohio L. Abs. 403, 115 N.E.2d 849 (Dist. Ct. App. 1952); *Ex parte Espinosa,* 144 Tex. 121, 188 S.W.2d 576 (1945); *Estes v. Hopp,* 73 Wash.2d 263, 438 P.2d 205 (1968) (despite statutory provision that implies availability of bail to juveniles, Wash. Rev. Code Ann. § 13.04.115 (1962)).

Several states, while not granting a right to bail, do authorize release on bail as a matter within the discretion of the judge before whom the child is brought. *See, e.g.,* Me. Rev. Stat. Ann. tit. 15, § 2608 (1965); Minn. Stat. Ann. § 260.171 (1971); Neb. Rev. Stat. § 43-205.03 (1968); S.C. Code Ann. § 15-1185 (1962); Tenn. Code Ann. § 37-217(d) (Supp. 1973); Vt. Stat. Ann. tit. 33, § 641(c) (Supp. 1973); Va. Code Ann. § 16.1-197 (1960).

Significantly, however, a number of other states and at least one federal court have secured for juveniles the same right to bail that adults enjoy in criminal proceedings. *See, e.g.,* Ala. Code tit. 13, § 368 (1960); Ark. Stat. Ann. § 45-227 (1964); Colo. Rev. Stat. Ann. § 22-8-7(3) (1964); Ga. Code Ann. § 24A-1402(c) (Supp. 1973); Mass. Gen. Laws Ann. tit. 119, § 67 (Supp. 1973); Okla. Stat. Ann. tit. 10, § 1112(c) (Supp. 1974); S.D. Compiled Laws Ann. § 26-8-21 (1967); W. Va. Code Ann. § 49-5-3 (1966); *Trimble v. Stone,* 187 F. Supp. 483 (D.D.C. 1960); *State v. Franklin,* 202 La. 439, 12 So.2d 211 (1943).

Undoubtedly, most juveniles within the jurisdiction of the juvenile court who are taken into custody for violations of law are released into the custody of their parents under the liberal release provisions applicable to juveniles. This accounts for the paucity of court decisions, particularly in the post-*Gault* era, elaborating on the right to bail, or absence thereof, for juveniles. Thus, bail has simply not been an issue meriting great concern, except in the abstract.

On the one hand, the expanding constitutionalization of the juvenile process might very well include the right to release on bail to the extent it is presently enjoyed by adults. Arguably, however, bail should not be accorded a child as a matter of right, not due to characterization of a juvenile proceeding as civil rather than criminal in nature, but because the child may be in need of care, supervision, or protection that might be denied him without proper inquiry into the conditions and environment into which he will be released. For example, if released on bail as a matter of right, he might be returned to the very same environment that caused him to be referred to the juvenile court in the first place. M. Paulsen, *Fairness to the Juvenile Offender*, 41 Minn. L. Rev. 547, 552 (1957).

The California case cited earlier, *In re William M.*, 3 Cal.3d 16, 473 P.2d 737, 89 Cal. Rptr. 33 (1970), contains a penetrating discussion on the question of release of juveniles and concludes that the liberal release provisions of the juvenile court act, when correctly administered, offer an adequate system of release from custody without reaching the bail question. One of the provisions to which the court referred indicates a preference that a child be released rather than detained, following his being taken into custody. Cal. Welf. & Inst'ns Code § 626 (1972). Another indicates that if the child is not released immediately following his being taken into custody, a petition must be filed against him and a detention hearing must be held within one judicial day. *Id.* § 632. A third provision states the responsibility of the court at the detention hearing:

> "The court will examine such minor, his parent, guardian, or other person having relevant knowledge, hear such relevant evidence as the minor, his parent or guardian or their counsel desires to present, and, *unless it appears* that such minor has violated an order of the juvenile court or has escaped from the commitment of the juvenile court or *that it is a matter of immediate and urgent necessity for the protection of such minor or the person or property of another that he be detained or that such minor is likely to flee the jurisdiction of the court, the court shall make its order releasing such minor from custody.*" Cal. Welf. & Inst'ns Code § 635 (1972) (emphasis added).

The child who was taken into custody for an alleged sale of marijuana was not initially released into the custody of his parents, and a detention hearing was held in accordance with the statute. At the hearing, the juvenile's counsel offered evidence favoring his release, but the court refused to hear the evidence, stating instead that it was the policy of the court automatically to detain all children charged with this particular offense. The court stated, "The Legislature must have thought it was serious, it is five years to life if he were an adult," to which counsel replied, "If he were an adult, he would be out on bail at this very moment." The court's response to this challenge was, "If you want to have him handled as an adult, I will certify him to adult court and you can bail him out." 3 Cal.3d at 21-22, 473 P.2d at 740, 89 Cal. Rptr. at 36.

The California Supreme Court vigorously disapproved of this abuse of the procedures set up for release of juveniles. The court indicated that detention should be the exception, not the rule, and that in cases where the juvenile is not released initially by the police officer or probation officer, and a detention hearing is thereafter held, the probation officer bears the burden of presenting sufficient evidence to support detention. This includes proof of a prima facie case that the alleged offense was committed by the child to demonstrate the "immediate and urgent necessity" for detention required by the statute. 3 Cal.3d at 26-28 & n.20, 473 P.2d at 744-75 & n.20, 89 Cal. Rptr. at 40-41 & n.20.

The California provisions outlined in the above statutes set forth sufficient safeguards to protect the rights of the child and his parents, if as the court points out, they are properly administered. The police officer who first takes the child into custody may release the child on his own or release him to his parents. His one and only alternative is to refer the child immediately to a probation officer. The probation officer in turn is authorized to release the child into the custody of the parents. It is expected that by this point most children will have been released. In the event the probation officer feels detention is required, however, a detention hearing must be held within one judicial day, and the child should be released unless good cause is shown to indicate otherwise. The probation officer bears the responsibility of demonstrating that the child falls within one of the exceptions authorizing further detention. *See also* Tex. Fam. Code Ann. § 54.01 (1973).

In re Gault, 387 U.S. 1 (1967) did not announce that *all* procedural rights guaranteed to adults in criminal proceedings were perforce applicable to children in juvenile proceedings. It only requires that procedures in juvenile court be measured according to the essentials of fairness and due process under fourteenth amendment standards. The Supreme Court might find, just as it did in *McKeiver v.*

Pennsylvania, 403 U.S. 528 (1971) (denying to juveniles a constitutional right to a jury trial), that fairness and due process do not necessarily require that juveniles be accorded a constitutional right to bail. Such a finding might well be warranted in evaluating a system of release like California's, for it could be sustained on the ground that a system so replete with safeguards affords an adequate alternative to release on bail.

No doubt such a conclusion would acknowledge that the juvenile court still exercises a protective function, consistent with constitutional notions of due process. The protective function of the juvenile court requires that it exercise a special responsibility toward children that is not necessary or appropriate in the case of adults. While exercise of this responsibility normally means that a child should be, and is, released in the custody of his parents, it also demands that the court conduct an investigation into the circumstances and surroundings into which a child will be released. It sometimes happens that those circumstances warrant his detention. Indeed, such an approach, *properly administered*, might be required by standards of fairness and due process.

IV. POLICE INTERROGATION.

§ 3.11. General Background.

(a) The Voluntariness Test.

To understand fully the limitations placed on police during questioning of juveniles, it is necessary briefly to examine the development of constitutional limitations placed on police in dealing with adults.

The first limitation placed on state officials was that police procedures during interrogation of a suspect had to comport with traditional notions of fairness and due process under standards of the fourteenth amendment. Thus, in *Brown v. Mississippi*, 297 U.S. 278 (1936), a confession extracted through use of brutal physical coercion was held inadmissible. The test employed in *Brown v. Mississippi* and in a long line of subsequent cases was that of voluntariness. In fact, the Court quoted with approval language from an opinion by a dissenting minority of the Mississippi Supreme Court, employing the voluntariness test. 297 U.S. at 283, *quoting Brown v. State*, 173 Miss. 542, 574-75, 161 So. 465, 471 (1935) (Griffith, J., dissenting).

To determine whether a confession or statement was freely and voluntarily given, the Supreme Court always conducted an inquiry into the totality of the circumstances surrounding the giving of the statements. Thus, in *Brown v. Mississippi* the presence of physical coercion rendered the confession involuntary and therefore inadmissible. Other factors rendering confessions involuntary have been fatigue on the part of the defendant and duration of intensive questioning, *Ashcraft v. Tennessee*, 322 U.S. 143 (1944) (thirty-six hours of continuous questioning without rest or interruption); persistent interrogation over an extended period of time, *Chambers v. Florida*, 309 U.S. 227 (1940) (seven days of sustained questioning and all night vigil on the last day); isolation from the outside world, *Haynes v. Washington*, 373 U.S. 503 (1963) (defendant's repeated requests to see his wife or a lawyer denied until he agreed to confess); and psychological pressure, *Spano v. New York*, 360 U.S. 315 (1959) (eight hours of incommunicado interrogation, plus sympathy falsely aroused by policeman who was boyhood friend of suspect). All of these cases, of course, were decided prior to *Miranda v. Arizona*, 384 U.S. 436 (1966). In limited situations the Court has continued to apply the voluntariness test in determining the admissibility of statements given to the police. *See* § 3.11(c), *infra*.

The voluntariness and totality of the circumstances standards have been applied to test the admissibility of statements obtained from juveniles as well.

In two significant cases, *Haley v. Ohio*, 332 U.S. 596 (1948), and *Gallegos v. Colorado*, 370 U.S. 49 (1962), both of which concerned juveniles who were convicted of criminal offenses in adult court, the Supreme Court held statements inadmissible which were obtained in violation of fourteenth amendment due process standards. The age of the defendants (fifteen in *Haley* and fourteen in *Gallegos*), plus incommunicado custody without the presence of a parent, attorney, or other friendly adult (three days in *Haley*, which included a five-hour period of intensive questioning from midnight until 5:00 a.m. the next morning, and five days in *Gallegos*) were the circumstances that persuaded the Court of the involuntary character of the statements.

Particularly in *Haley*, the first case considered by the Court, the age factor was highly persuasive to the Court in reaching its decision. Acknowledging that the facts of the case "would make us pause for careful inquiry if a mature man were involved," Justice Douglas, announcing the judgment of the Court, added a significant note: "And when, as here, a mere child—an easy victim of the law—is before us, *special care* in scrutinizing the record must be used." 332 U.S. at 599 (emphasis added). Addressing himself also to the incommunicado nature of the proceedings, Justice Douglas went on to say:

> "No friend stood at the side of this 15-year old boy as the police, working in relays, questioned him hour after hour, from midnight until dawn.
> No lawyer stood guard to make sure that the police went so far and no further, to see to it that they stopped short of the point where he became the victim of coercion. No counsel or friend was

called during the critical hours of questioning."
332 U.S. at 600.

Perhaps significantly, this is the precise language from *Haley* quoted by the Supreme Court in the momentous case in *In re Gault*, 387 U.S. 1 (1967), in holding the privilege against self-incrimination applicable to juveniles under the requirements of the fourteenth amendment. 387 U.S. at 45-46.

(b) The Fifth and Sixth Amendment Tests.

Following its long-standing application of the voluntariness test as dictated by due process standards of the fourteenth amendment, the Court suddenly turned toward reliance on the fifth and sixth amendments to test the voluntariness and admissibility of statements taken from an accused.

The fifth amendment's privilege against self-incrimination had been the basis for exclusion of illegally obtained confessions in federal courts for some time. *Bram v. United States*, 168 U.S. 532 (1897). The fifth amendment privilege was made applicable to the states via the due process clause of the fourteenth amendment in *Malloy v. Hogan*, 378 U.S. 1 (1964). This step, however, was only the first toward incorporation of the fifth amendment privilege against self-incrimination in a new test for determining admissibility of confessions. Before this occurred, however, the Court began exploring application of the sixth amendment right to counsel to custodial interrogation situations.

In *Spano v. New York*, 360 U.S. 315 (1959), although the defendant's conviction was reversed because under the totality of the circumstances his confession was involuntary, the Supreme Court did not reach the defendant's sixth amendment right to counsel argument.

Four of the justices who concurred in the Court's judgment, however, were of the opinion that the defendant's conviction should have been reversed on the sole ground that his confession was inadmissible—due to the fact that it was taken at a time when he was without, but clearly entitled to receive, assistance of counsel.

Later, in *Massiah v. United States*, 377 U.S. 201 (1964), a federal prosecution, the sixth amendment was directly applicable. The Court not only reached the sixth amendment argument avoided in *Spano v. New York* but, citing with approval the concurring opinions in *Spano*, held that the guarantee of assistance of counsel contained in the sixth amendment was denied the defendant where incriminating statements were taken from him in the absence of counsel at a time—following indictment—when he was entitled to it.

Almost simultaneously, the Court in *Escobedo v. Illinois*, 378 U.S. 478 (1964) (involving a state proceeding), relied on the sixth amendment right to counsel in creating a qualified formula, applicable only in specific factual situations, to determine the admissibility of confessions. The Court listed specific circumstances that would call for exclusion of any statement given by the suspect, on the ground of denial of the sixth amendment right to counsel as made applicable to the states under the fourteenth amendment. The circumstances calling for exclusion of the statement on sixth amendment grounds were set forth by the Court as follows:

(1) The investigation is no longer a general inquiry into an unsolved crime but has begun to focus on a particular suspect.

(2) The suspect has been taken into police custody.

(3) The police carry out a process of interrogation that lends itself to eliciting incriminating statements.

(4) The suspect has requested and been denied an opportunity to consult with his lawyer.

(5) The police have not effectively warned him of his absolute constitutional right to remain silent. 378 U.S. at 490-91.

The Court held that if all of these factors are present, the accused has been denied the right to counsel guaranteed to defendants in state proceedings in *Gideon v. Wainwright*, 372 U.S. 335 (1963), and any statements so obtained are inadmissible against him in a criminal proceeding. 378 U.S. at 491.

Two years later, in *Miranda v. Arizona*, 384 U.S. 436 (1966), the Court relied on the fifth amendment to forge a new test of admissibility of confessions. The new test demanded that every accused person in a setting involving custodial interrogation be warned:

(1) He has a right to remain silent.

(2) Any statement he makes may be used against him in a court proceeding.

(3) He has a right to be represented by counsel and to have counsel present during any questioning.

(4) If he cannot afford counsel, the court will appoint counsel to represent him.

(5) He may invoke the right to remain silent at any time, which means that if at any time prior to or during questioning he indicates that he wishes to remain silent, the questioning must stop. 384 U.S. at 444, 467-74.

The Court clearly indicated that since the warnings were so simple to give, it expected the mandatory requirement to be observed strictly. 384 U.S. at 468-69.

(c) Post-Miranda Standards for Judging Pre-Miranda Confessions.

Significantly, the *Escobedo* and *Miranda* decisions did not completely abolish the voluntariness test. In *Johnson v. New Jersey*, 384 U.S. 719 (1966), the Supreme Court ruled that *Escobedo* and *Miranda* would only apply prospectively, that is, only to trials commenced after the respective date of each decision.

The Court's reason for so holding was that in the case of trials occurring prior to *Escobedo* or *Miranda*, petitioners had an existing standard—voluntariness—by which the admissibility of any statements given the police were to be tested. The Court then added that a person whose trial commenced prior to the date of the *Escobedo* or *Miranda* decisions could include *as a part of his involuntariness claim* the failure of the police to observe the safeguards announced in the two decisions. 384 U.S. at 730.

On the same day it decided *Johnson v. New Jersey*, the Court decided *Davis v. North Carolina*, 384 U.S. 737 (1966), in which the defendant, in accordance with *Johnson v. New Jersey*, argued the absence of *Miranda* safeguards as a part of his involuntariness claim. Applying the voluntariness test and looking at the totality of the circumstances, the Court concluded that the defendant's confession was involuntarily given and therefore inadmissible.

The Court has continued to employ this same analysis in subsequent cases—*i.e.*, although the *Miranda* requirements are not directly applicable to cases tried before its date of decision, the presence or absence of *Miranda* warnings is relevant to the voluntariness determination. *See Darwin v. Connecticut*, 391 U.S. 346 (1968); *Greenwald v. Wisconsin*, 390 U.S. 519 (1968); *Beecher v. Alabama*, 389 U.S. 35 (1967); *Clewis v. Texas*, 386 U.S. 707 (1967).

The net effect of these decisions is that the voluntariness test and the totality of circumstances analysis are very much alive, at least in limited situations including determination of the admissibility of pre-*Miranda* confessions. The endurability of the totality-of-the-circumstances approach is important and crucially relevant in any discussion of the application of *Miranda* safeguards to the juvenile process, because the courts have placed heavy reliance on this approach in evaluating statements given to the police by juveniles.

§ 3.12. Application of Miranda to Juvenile Proceedings.

As mentioned in the preceding section, even prior to the *Miranda* and *Gault* decisions, the Supreme Court in *Haley v. Ohio*, 332 U.S. 596 (1948), and *Gallegos v. Colorado*, 370 U.S. 49 (1962), used the voluntariness test to determine the admissibility of statements made by juveniles to the police. This determination was made by examining the totality-of-the-circumstances surrounding the giving of the statements, specifically for the purpose of deciding whether the procedures employed measured up to the standards of due process and fairness under the fourteenth amendment. *See Gallegos v. Colorado*, 370 U.S. 49, 55 (1962). But the Court went beyond merely applying to juveniles the same standard used in assessing the validity of statements given by adults; it indicated that in the case of juveniles, special care and solicitude have to be exercised. Thus, the age factor was deemed quite significant in evaluating the voluntariness of statements given to the police by juveniles. *See Haley v. Ohio*, 332 U.S. 596, 599-600 (1948).

Haley and *Gallegos*, however, involved juveniles who were prosecuted as adults and dealt with in the confines of the criminal process. Following its decision in the *Gault* case, the Supreme Court has not ruled specifically on the question of the applicability of the *Miranda* safeguards to the juvenile process. Although the Court in *Gault* held the privilege against self-incrimination applicable to juveniles in the same way it is applicable to adults, 387 U.S. at 55, elsewhere in its opinion it qualified the scope of its ruling in general:

"We do not in this opinion consider the impact of these constitutional provisions upon the totality of the relationship of the juvenile and the state. We do not even consider the entire process relating to juvenile 'delinquents.' For example, *we are not here concerned with the procedures or constitutional rights applicable to the pre-judicial stages of the juvenile process....*" 387 U.S. at 13 (emphasis added).

Even though the Court in *Gault* deliberately a-voided the question of police investigatory procedures, does a logical reading of the decision require police officers to give *Miranda* warnings to juveniles? Can a juvenile waive his constitutional rights? What role, if any, do parents play during the investigatory stage of the proceedings? These and other questions were bound to arise and have been answered by a number of legislatures and courts, sometimes reaching differing results.

Following the *Gault* decision the Oklahoma legislature enacted a statute providing that information gained through questioning a child is inadmissible unless the questioning is conducted in the presence of the child's attorney or legal custodian and then only after all parties have been fully advised of their constitutional and legal rights, including the right to a trial by jury, right to counsel, and the right to have counsel appointed by the court and paid out of the court's funds if the party cannot afford retained counsel. Okla. Stat. Ann. tit. 10, § 1109(a) (Supp. 1974). The Oklahoma statute thus requires warnings similar to those required by *Miranda* but oddly does not provide that the child and his parents must be warned of the right to remain silent and that this right may be invoked at any time.

California statutory law now requires that full *Miranda* warnings must be given to juveniles taken into custody by police before any questioning can occur. Cal. Welf. & Inst'ns Code § 625 (1972). Moreover, if the child appears before a probation officer, California law requires the probation officer to give the *Miranda* warnings to the child and his parents. *Id.* § 627.5.

In similar fashion, Colorado has enacted legislation implementing the *Miranda* safeguards in the juvenile process. As an example of such legislation, the statute is set forth in pertinent part:

> "No statements or admissions of a child made as a result of interrogation of the child by a law enforcement official concerning acts which would constitute a crime if committed by an adult shall be admissible in evidence unless a parent, guardian, or legal custodian of the child was present at such interrogation, and the child and his parent, guardian, or legal custodian were advised of the child's right to remain silent, that any statements made may be used against him in a court of law, the right of the presence of an attorney during such interrogation, and the right to have counsel appointed if so requested at the time of the interrogation...."
> Colo. Rev. Stat. Ann. § 22-2-2(3) (c) (Supp. 1971).

Connecticut law makes similar provision. Conn. Gen. Stat. Ann. § 17-66d(a) (Supp. 1973).

Other approaches, while not so direct, are intended to implement the same safeguards. The Uniform Juvenile Court Act, for example, provides as follows:

> "A child charged with a delinquent act need not be a witness against or otherwise incriminate himself. An extra-judicial statement, if obtained in the course of violation of this Act *or which would be constitutionally inadmissible in a criminal proceeding*, shall not be used against him...."

Uniform Juvenile Court Act § 27(b) (1968) (emphasis added).

Jurisdictions that have adopted the Uniform Juvenile Court Act have identical provisions. *See, e.g.,* Ga. Code Ann. § 24A-2002(b) (Supp. 1973); N.D. Cent. Code § 27-20-27(2) (1974); Tenn. Code Ann. § 37-227 (Supp. 1973); *see also* N.M. Stat. Ann. § 13-14-25(C) (1) (Supp. 1973); Pa. Stat. Ann. tit. 11, § 50-325(a)(1), (e) (Supp. 1974); Vt. Stat. Ann. tit. 33, § 652 (Supp. 1973). Since the *Miranda* safeguards are constitutionally required, they are necessarily incorporated into such statutes.

Since the *Gault* decision, virtually all of the courts that have passed on the question of the applicability of the *Miranda* safeguards to the juvenile process have concluded that the safeguards do apply.

The most difficult issue, over which there has been considerable disagreement, is whether a juvenile, by himself, is competent to waive the *Miranda* rights or whether, in addition to the juvenile, a parent or attorney must be present and must waive the rights also. The question of waiver is discussed in § 3.13, *infra*.

New York's statutory law, for example, is silent on whether the *Miranda* safeguards apply to the juvenile process. A statute does provide, however, that if a police officer wishes to question a child, he must

> "[T]ake the child to a facility designated by the appropriate appellate division of the supreme court as a suitable place for the questioning of children and there question him for a reasonable period of time...." N.Y. Fam. Ct. Act § 724(b) (ii) (McKinney Supp. 1972).

The same statute also provides as follows:

> "In determining what is a 'reasonable period of time' for questioning a child, the child's age and

> the presence or absence of his parents or other
> person legally responsible for his care shall be
> included among the relevant considerations."
> *Id.* § 724(d).

Despite an absence of language in the statute reflecting on applicability of the *Miranda* safeguards to juveniles, some lower New York courts held the *Miranda* requirements applicable to juvenile proceedings even prior to the *Gault* decision. *In re Knox*, 53 Misc.2d 889, 280 N.Y.S.2d 65 (Fam. Ct., Monroe Co. 1967); *In re Rust*, 53 Misc.2d 51, 278 N.Y.S.2d 333 (Fam. Ct., Kings Co. 1967). Following the *Gault* decision, two decisions by the Appellate Division held the *Miranda* requirements to be directly applicable to juvenile proceedings. *In re Aaron D.*, 30 App. Div.2d 183, 290 N.Y.S.2d 935 (1968); *In re William L.*, 29 App. Div.2d 182, 287 N.Y.S.2d 218 (1968). In both cases, the juveniles were given the *Miranda* warnings but in the absence of their parents. In still another case, a child's confession was held inadmissible even though he was warned of his *Miranda* rights, because the court found no effective waiver of his rights and further found that the place of questioning—a police station—was not a statutorily approved place for questioning juveniles, and the duration of the questioning—eight hours—exceeded the court's estimate of a "reasonable period of time." *In re Nelson*, 58 Misc.2d 748, 750, 296 N.Y.S.2d 472, 474 (Fam. Ct., Bronx Co. 1969). The court specifically declined, however, to reach the question of whether the literal requirements of *Miranda* should be strictly applied to juvenile proceedings.

Other courts likewise have confronted *Miranda* problems in the context of the juvenile investigatory process and have concluded, for the most part in reliance on *Gault*, that *Miranda* warnings must be given to juveniles during the investigatory stage of a delinquency proceeding; otherwise, incriminating statements elicited from children are inadmissible against them in a court proceeding. *In re Dennis M.*, 70 Cal.2d 444, 450 P.2d 296, 75 Cal. Rptr. 1 (1969); *In re Teters*, 264 Cal. App.2d 816, 70 Cal. Rptr. 749 (1968); *In re Creek*, 243 A.2d 49 (D.C. Ct. App. 1968); *Leach v. State*, 428 S.W.2d 817 (Tex. Civ. App. 1968).

There are indications, moreover, that courts may be going even beyond the requirements of *Miranda* in conducting a scrupulous examination into the circumstances surrounding a juvenile's statement to the police. In *In re Rambeau*, 266 Cal. App.2d 1, 72 Cal. Rptr. 171 (1968), for example, the court conceded that the *Miranda* safeguards were observed but held a juvenile's confession inadmissible because it was taken during a period of unlawful detention following an illegal arrest; furthermore, no attempt had been made to notify the youth's parents or to bring him without unnecessary delay before a juvenile authority, and the questioning of the youth was offensive in nature. *See also Daniels v. State*, 226 Ga. 269, 174 S.E.2d 422 (1970).

This kind of inquiry into the totality-of-the-circumstances extends beyond the usual *Miranda* inquiry, indicating the vitality of Justice Douglas's remarks in *Haley v. Ohio*, 332 U.S. 596, 599 (1948), that special care must be employed in determining the admissibility of confessions and incriminating statements made by juveniles.

§ 3.13. Waiver of Miranda Rights by a Minor.

Perhaps the most perplexing problem that has confronted courts in the post-*Miranda*, post-*Gault* era is that of waiver of the *Miranda* safeguards by a minor. Particularly, the controversy surrounds the competency of a minor, without the guidance of a parent, attorney, or other friendly adult, to make an intelligent, understanding, voluntary waiver of his constitutional rights.

Most courts that have considered this question have concluded that there is no absolute requirement that a parent or attorney be present in order for a child to make an effective waiver, or, put another way, that a child is not presumed, for reasons of age alone, to be incapable of waiving his rights by himself. Rather, the effectiveness of the waiver is determined by examining the totality-of-the circumstances surrounding the giving of the statements, and some courts in using this approach have employed what amounts to a voluntariness test, rather than a literal application of *Miranda*.

Most of the decisions that examine the totality-of-the-circumstances to determine the effectiveness of a minor's waiver rely on *Haley v. Ohio*, 332 U.S. 596 (1948), and *Gallegos v. Colorado*, 370 U.S. 49 (1962) (these cases are discussed in § 3.11(a), *supra*). The leading case so holding is *People v. Lara*, 67 Cal.2d 365, 432 P.2d 202, 62 Cal. Rptr. 586 (1967), *cert. denied*, 392 U.S. 945 (1968). Following *People v. Lara*, or otherwise reaching the same result are *United States v. Miller*, 453 F.2d 634 (4th Cir. 1972); *Lopez v. United States*, 399 F.2d 865 (9th Cir. 1968); *West v. United States*, 399 F.2d 467 (5th Cir. 1968), *cert. denied*, 393 U.S. 1102 (1969); *Mosley v. State*, 438 S.W.2d 311 (Ark. 1969); *In re Dennis M.*, 70 Cal.2d 444, 450 P.2d 296, 75 Cal. Rptr. 1 (1969); *State v. Dillon*, 93 Idaho 698, 471 P.2d 553, *cert. denied*, 401 U.S. 942 (1970); *McClintock v. State*, 253 Ind. 333, 253 N.E.2d 233 (1969); *State v. Hinkle*, 479 P.2d 841 (Kan. 1971); *State v. Melanson*, 259 So.2d 609 (La. 1972); *Walker v. State*, 12 Md. App. 684, 280 A.2d 260 (1971); *Commonwealth v. Cain*, 279 N.E.2d 706 (Mass. 1972); *State v. Sinderson*, 455 S.W.2d 486 (Mo. 1970); *In re Aaron D.*, 30 App. Div.2d 183, 290 N.Y.S.2d 935 (1968); *State v. Dawson*, 278 N.C. 351, 180 S.E.2d 140 (1971); *Commonwealth v.*

Porter, 449 Pa. 153, 295 A.2d 311 (1972); *Vaughn v. State,* 3 Tenn. Crim. App. 54, 456 S.W.2d 879 (1970); *State v. Prater,* 77 Wash.2d 526, 463 P.2d 640 (1970); *State v. Baker,* 4 Wash. App. 121, 480 P.2d 778 (1971).

In *West v. United States,* 399 F.2d 467 (5th Cir. 1968), the court set forth the circumstances to be considered in determining the validity of a minor's waiver of *Miranda* rights:

> "(1) age of the accused; (2) education of the accused; (3) knowledge of the accused as to both the substance of the charge, if any has been filed, and the nature of his rights to consult with an attorney and remain silent; (4) whether the accused is held incommunicado or allowed to consult with relatives, friends or an attorney; (5) whether the accused was interrogated before or after formal charges had been filed; (6) methods used in interrogation; (7) length of interrogations; (8) whether vel non the accused refused to voluntarily give statements on prior occasions; and (9) whether the accused had repudiated an extra judicial statement at a later date." 399 F.2d at 469.

In some of the cases cited above, although the court used a totality-of-the-circumstances approach, it urged in the very strongest terms the importance of a parent's presence in determining the effectiveness of a waiver of constitutional rights. *McClintock v. State,* 253 Ind. 333, 253 N.E.2d 233 (1969); *Commonwealth v. Cain,* 279 N.E.2d 706 (Mass. 1972); *In re Aaron D.,* 30 App. Div.2d 183, 290 N.Y.S.2d 935 (1968). *See also In re William L.,* 29 App. Div.2d 182, 287 N.Y.S.2d 218 (1968); *In re Nelson,* 58 Misc.2d 748, 296 N.Y.S.2d 472 (Fam. Ct., Bronx Co. 1969); *In re Knox,* 53 Misc.2d 889, 280 N.Y.S.2d 65 (Fam. Ct., Monroe Co. 1967); *In re Rust,* 53 Misc.2d 51, 278 N.Y.S.2d

333 (Fam. Ct., Kings Co. 1967). In each of these cases statements by a child made to the police in the absence of parents were held inadmissible.

In other cases employing the totality-of-the-circumstances analysis, statements have been held inadmissible for reasons other than or in addition to the absence of parents. *See, e.g., Walker v. State,* 12 Md. App. 684, 280 A.2d 260 (1971) (parents denied access to minor; intensive questioning; incommunicado interrogation).

Invariably, the cases that hold that age alone is not determinative of the effectiveness of the waiver, have involved minors who are fourteen years of age or older, and most often sixteen or seventeen. Obviously, the younger the child, the more significant the age factor becomes.

In a recent New Jersey case the court concluded that a ten-year old boy was incapable of understanding the *Miranda* warnings and making an intelligent, understanding waiver of his rights, even though the warnings were given and carefully explained. *In re S.H.,* 61 N.J. 108, 115, 293 A.2d 181, 184 (1972). An interesting point about this case is that the court applied a voluntariness test and found that the child's statement was involuntarily given and for that reason inadmissible.

Similarly, the New York cases that have emphasized so strongly the importance of a parent's presence involved children of a very tender age. *In re Knox,* 53 Misc.2d 889, 280 N.Y.S.2d 65 (Fam. Ct., Monroe Co. 1967) (twelve-year old petitioner); *In re Rust,* 53 Misc.2d 51, 278 N.Y.S.2d 333 (Fam. Ct., Kings Co. 1967) (petitioners were nine, ten, twelve, and thirteen years of age); *see also In re Nelson,* 58 Misc.2d 748, 296 N.Y.S.2d 472 (Fam. Ct., Bronx Co. 1969) (fourteen-year old petitioner).

The judgment of the New Jersey court in *In re S.H., supra,* that giving *Miranda* warnings to a ten-year old child is a meaningless gesture, has been empirically reinforced.

A recent California study conducted among a random sampling of mostly fourteen-year old delinquent and nondelinquent children showed that the vast majority failed to understand the *Miranda* warnings although they had voluntarily waived their rights. A. B. Ferguson, and A. Douglas, *A Study of Juvenile Waiver*, 7 San Diego L. Rev. 39, 53-54 (1970). Hence, serious doubt exists whether children, especially young children, are capable of understanding, let alone waiving, their constitutional rights without assistance of a friendly adult.

Perhaps in response to doubts as to a child's capacity to waive his rights, a number of states go beyond emphasizing the importance of a parent's presence and *require* the presence of a parent before an effective waiver can be found. *See, e.g.*, Colo. Rev. Stat. Ann. § 22-2-2(3)(c) (Supp. 1971) (requires that warnings be given to both child and parent or legal custodian and requires presence of parent or legal custodian during any questioning); Conn. Gen. Stat. Ann. § 17-66(a) (Supp. 1973) (identical to Colorado provision); Okla. Stat. Ann. tit. 10, § 1109(a) (Supp. 1973) (requires that warnings be given to both child and parent or legal custodian); *see also* N.M. Stat. Ann. § 13-14-25(A) (Supp. 1973) (child cannot be questioned except in presence of parent or counsel); *Freeman v. Wilcox*, 119 Ga. App. 325, 167 S.E.2d 163 (1969); *Lewis v. State*, Ind. App.   , 288 N.E.2d 138 (1972); *Story v. State*, 452 P.2d 822 (Okla. Crim. App. 1969) (minor incompetent to waive rights without parent or attorney present, unless shown beyond reasonable doubt that minor fully understood nature and consequences of waiver). The Colorado statute cited requires the presence of a parent but waives the requirement if an attorney is in fact present to represent the child.

If a minor asks for an attorney during questioning, some courts have held that any statement he thereafter makes is in violation of *Miranda* and therefore inadmissible. *See, e.g., Arnold v. State*, 265 So.2d 64 (Fla. 1972); *In re Williams*, 49 Misc.2d 154, 267 N.Y.S.2d 91 (Fam. Ct., Ulster Co. 1966) (statement given by child following his request to see an attorney held inadmissible in violation of *Escobedo*).

More importantly, at least one court has held that a minor's request to see a *parent* during questioning invokes the same fifth amendment privilege, and any statement given by him thereafter is inadmissible because it is in violation of *Miranda*. *People v. Burton*, 6 Cal.3d 375, 491 P.2d 793, 99 Cal. Rptr. 1 (1971); *contra People v. Pierre*, 114 Ill. App.2d 283, 252 N.E.2d 706 (1969), *cert. denied*, 400 U.S. 854 (1970) (minor's request to see parent does not invoke sixth amendment right to counsel; sixth amendment right recognized under *Escobedo* limited to requests to see attorney). The California court's rationale for this position is that, while an adult in trouble normally requests an attorney's assistance, a child logically expresses his desire for help and his unwillingness to proceed alone by requesting a parent's presence. Reinforcing this notion is the judgment that in the case of a child the right to assistance of counsel is hollow unless a parent is present, for a parent is normally the child's only avenue through which to evaluate and exercise the right to counsel. *See Commonwealth v. Cain*, 279 N.E.2d 706, 710n.3 (Mass. 1972).

Even more protective of a child's rights is the requirement that an attorney be present before an effective waiver of rights can occur. In *Ezell v. State*, 489 P.2d 781 (Okla. Crim. App. 1971), the court held statements by a minor inadmissible even though his parent and legal guardian were present when the minor was advised of his constitutional rights. The basis of the court's decision was that the parent and guardian were not knowledgeable about the law and were not in a position to counsel the minor or make an effective waiver themselves; therefore, only the presence of an attorney would have effectuated the minor's right to counsel and enabled him to make a knowing, understanding waiver of his right to remain silent if he so chose. 489 P.2d at 783-84. *Cf.* Tex. Fam. Code Ann. § 51.09 (1973).

Other decisions have specifically rejected the necessity of counsel where a parent was present. *State v. Hinkle*, 479 P.2d 841 (Kan. 1971); *State v. Fernald*, 248 A.2d 754 (Me. 1968); *State v. Sinderson*, 455 S.W.2d 486 (Mo. 1970).

V. LINEUPS.

§ 3.14. General Background.

In *United States v. Wade*, 388 U.S. 218 (1967), the Supreme Court held that a pretrial confrontation between an accused and his accuser is a "critical stage" of criminal proceedings at which the accused is entitled to be represented by counsel under the sixth amendment. Since the witnesses in *Wade* did not testify at trial regarding the illegal lineup identification, but simply identified the defendant in court, the Supreme Court remanded the case for a hearing on whether the in-court identifications were tainted by the objectionable pretrial lineups or whether they had a source independent of the pretrial lineups, or whether, in any event, introduction of the identification evidence was harmless error.

In *Gilbert v. California*, 388 U.S. 263 (1967), decided the same day, the witnesses had not only identified the defendant at trial, but testified that they identified him at the pretrial lineups as well. Accordingly, the Court stated that testimony relating to out-of-court identifications at which the accused is not represented by counsel is *per se* inadmissible. Moreover, the Court, as in *Wade*, vacated the defendant's conviction and remanded his case to the trial court for a determination of whether the in-court identifications had an independent source, or whether their admission into evidence was harmless error.

In a companion case to *Wade* and *Gilbert*, the Court held that the rules announced in those decisions would not be retroactive in application. *Stovall v. Denno*, 388 U.S. 293 (1967). However, the Court recognized in *Stovall v. Denno* a means of challenging identification evidence independent of the right to counsel claim recognized in *Wade* and *Gilbert*. Examining the totality-of-the-circumstances, the Court considered whether the pretrial identification procedures employed were "so unnecessarily suggestive and conducive to irreparable mistaken identification that [the petitioner] was denied due process of law." 388 U.S. at 301-02.

In *Stovall* the facts were as follows. The victim, whose husband had been killed in the same vicious assault that left her seriously wounded, was recovering in the hospital from surgery undertaken to save her life. The police arrested a suspect less than twenty-four hours after the attack. No one knew at that point whether the victim would survive. To be sure, her condition would not permit her to come down to the police station to observe a standard lineup. Moreover, if the suspect was in fact innocent, she was the only person who could exonerate him. Such being the case, the police immediately took the suspect to the victim's hospital room where she identified him as her attacker. Under the circumstances here outlined, the Court felt that the defendant was not denied due process of law. 388 U.S. at 302.

Both the *Wade* and *Gilbert* cases involved post-indictment lineups. One of the nagging questions left unanswered by both cases was whether the rules announced in the decisions were restricted to post-indictment identification procedures or whether the right to counsel attaches at an earlier stage of the proceedings, for example, at the arrest stage. Subsequent decisions by state courts and lower federal courts indicated that *Wade* and *Gilbert* were not applicable to on-the-scene identifications, *see, e.g., Russell v. United States,* 408 F.2d 1280 (D.C. Cir. 1969); *Commonwealth v. Bumpus,* 238 N.E.2d 343 (Mass. 1968), but certainly there are many situations that fall between an on-the-scene identification and a post-indictment identification.

The Supreme Court seemed to answer this question in *Kirby v. Illinois,* 406 U.S. 682 (1972). This decision, while not expressly stating that the right to counsel attaches only after indictment, certainly implied as much, since it stated that the right to counsel and all the safeguards announced in *Wade* and *Gilbert* apply only after "adversary judicial criminal proceedings" have commenced. In the language of the Court, such "proceedings" might be "by way of formal charge, preliminary hearing, indictment, information, or arraignment." 406 U.S. at 689-90.

A literal application of *Kirby v. Illinois* would limit *Wade* and *Gilbert* to their facts, *i.e.,* only where a lineup is held following indictment or other formal charge. Indeed, most courts have strictly interpreted *Kirby* as applicable only to post-indictment identification procedures. *See, e.g., Thomas v. State,* 278 So.2d 230 (Ala. Crim. App. 1973); *West v. State,* 229 Ga. 427, 192 S.E.2d 163 (1972); *People v. Reese,* 54 Ill.2d 51, 294 N.E.2d 288 (1973); *Williamson v. State,* 201 N.W.2d 490 (Iowa 1972); *State v. Edgecombe,* 275 So.2d 740 (La. 1973); *Commonwealth v. Lopes,* 287 N.E.2d 118 (Mass. 1972); *State v. Northup,* 303 A.2d 1 (Me. 1973); *Reed v. Warden,* 508 P.2d 2 (Nev. 1973); *State v. Rollins,* 16 N.C. App. 616, 192 S.E.2d 606 (1972); *Stewart v. State,* 509 P.2d 1402 (Okla. Crim. App. 1973); *State v. McLeod,* 196

S.E.2d 645 (S.C. 1973); *Turner v. State*, 486 S.W.2d 797 (Tex. Crim. App. 1972); *State v. Easthope*, 29 Utah 2d 400, 510 P.2d 933 (1973).

A few courts, however, have held that within the terms of *Kirby v. Illinois*, the commencement of adversary criminal proceedings begins with issuance of an arrest warrant and the arrest itself, and any subsequent identification procedures must comport with the requirements of *Wade* and *Gilbert*, notwithstanding that no indictment has issued. *See, e.g., United States ex rel. Robinson v. Zelker*, 468 F.2d 159 (2d Cir. 1972); *Arnold v. State*, 484 S.W.2d 248 (Mo. 1972).

In any event, while there may be disagreement over the extent to which *Kirby v. Illinois* has limited the application of the *Wade-Gilbert* safeguards, it is clear that it limits application of the sixth amendment right to counsel only. It does not limit the due process requirements of *Stovall v. Denno*. *Kirby v. Illinois*, 406 U.S. 682, 690-91 (1972).

§ 3.15. **Applicability of Wade, Gilbert, and Stovall to Juvenile Proceedings.**

Are the constitutional safeguards set forth in the *Wade-Gilbert-Stovall* trilogy applicable to juvenile proceedings? The courts were just beginning to probe the depths of this question when *Kirby v. Illinois* was decided. To the extent any answers were formulated prior to its decision, all conclusions reached will likely have to be reassessed in light of the *Kirby* decision. In any event, a discussion of the impact of lineup identification requirements on juvenile proceedings follows.

In *In re McKelvin*, 258 A.2d 452 (D.C. Mun. Ct. App. 1969), the court declined to reach the question of the applicability of the *Wade, Gilbert*, and *Stovall* requirements to the juvenile process. The court felt that it was not confronted directly with this question, since its conclusion was that the in-court identification had a source independent of the questioned stationhouse identification. Specifically, the witness testified that he had seen the appellant several times in the neighborhood, that he knew where he lived and that he recognized him at the time of the incident. This independent basis for the in-court identification negated the applicability of *Wade* and *Gilbert* in the court's opinion, and the fact that the witness knew appellant negated the fear of suggestiveness and the risk of irreparable mistaken identification outlined in *Stovall*.

The court, however, seems to have overlooked an objection on the basis of *Gilbert*. *Gilbert* did not deal exclusively with establishing an independent basis for an in-court identification; it also established a *per se* exclusionary rule with respect to testimony describing an out-of-court identification at which constitutional protections were not afforded. The witness in *McKelvin* actually testified regarding the stationhouse identification, which would appear to raise directly the question of *Gilbert's* applicability to juvenile proceedings. The court, however, chose not to reach this question. Instead, its decision seems to have been prompted by the notion that children are entitled only to "fundamentally fair identification procedures." 258 A.2d 454.

Two other courts have reached the question, however, and have concluded that the *Wade, Gilbert,* and *Stovall* decisions are applicable to juvenile proceedings. In *In re Carl T.*, 1 Cal. App.3d 344, 81 Cal. Rptr. 655 (1969), the witness identified the appellant in a single suspect confrontation arranged by the police. The witness identified the appellant at the adjudicatory hearing and also testified that she had identified him earlier at the probation office. Thus, questions of the dimensions of *Wade, Gilbert,* and *Stovall* were squarely presented. The court held that the safeguards announced in these decisions were applicable to juvenile proceedings for two reasons. First, under state law, a child may be adjudicated a ward of the state only on the basis of evidence "legally admissible in the trial of criminal cases." Cal. Welf. & Inst'ns Code § 701 (1972). Secondly, aside from statutory law, the court felt its decision was compelled by a reading of *Gault*.

Since the identification occurred before the appellant had been charged, the court specifically reserved decision on the question of whether *Wade* and *Gilbert* were applicable to the identification in the case before it. The question of whether *Wade* and *Gilbert* were limited to post-indictment identifications or applied as well to pre-indictment identifications was then before the California Supreme Court. The court did hold *Stovall* applicable, however, since *Stovall* applies to all prehearing identifications arranged by the police that might be unnecessarily suggestive. Applying the standards of *Stovall*, the court concluded that the identification was constitutionally defective, since it consisted of a one-on-one confrontation with no apparent justification. 1 Cal. App.3d at 353, 81 Cal. Rptr. at 661.

Likewise, the court in *In re Holley*, 268 A.2d 723 (R.I. 1970), relying on the due process requirements of the *Gault* decision, held that *Wade*, *Gilbert*, and *Stovall* were fully applicable to juvenile proceedings. More importantly, the court held that the requirements set forth in *Wade* and *Gilbert* were not restricted to post-indictment identification procedures but extended as well to pre-indictment procedures. An interesting note is that in reaching this decision the court relied very heavily on *People v. Fowler*, 1 Cal.3d 335, 461 P.2d 643, 82 Cal. Rptr. 363 (1969), the case that was still pending at the time of the decision in *In re Carl T.*, and in deference to which the California Court of

Appeals declined to apply *Wade* and *Gilbert* to an identification occurring before filing of formal proceedings.

Of course, the Rhode Island court's decision in *In re Holley* was decided prior to *Kirby v. Illinois,* and is therefore subject to reformulation in light of the *Kirby* decision. The Maryland Court of Appeals, for example, held, in the aftermath of the *Wade* and *Gilbert* decisions, that the requirements announced in those decisions applied also to pre-indictment lineups. *Palmer v. State,* 5 Md. App. 691, 249 A.2d 482 (1969). But following the Supreme Court's decision in *Kirby v. Illinois,* the Maryland court reversed itself, holding that the right to counsel requirements announced in *Wade* and *Gilbert* are applicable only to identification procedures occurring after commencement of adversary criminal proceedings within the meaning of *Kirby. Jackson v. State,* 17 Md. App. 167, 171-72, 300 A.2d 430, 434 (1973).

The Maryland court further intimated that the constitutional requirements of *Wade* and *Gilbert* might not be applicable in juvenile proceedings at all. The court pointed out that juvenile proceedings are not criminal proceedings, and that criminal proceedings under Maryland law cannot be brought against a juvenile until the juvenile court has waived jurisdiction in accordance with statute. 17 Md. App. at 174n.5, 300 A.2d at 435n.5. Since it had already concluded that the sixth amendment right to counsel at a lineup applies only after commencement of adversary *criminal* proceedings, the court seemed to be saying that criminal proceedings do not commence until the case has been transferred to the criminal court for prosecution. The court expressly declined to reach a decision on whether proceedings in the juvenile court might be regarded as adversary criminal proceedings within the meaning of *Kirby.* 17 Md. App. at 174, 300 A.2d at 435.

The prevailing view, therefore, appears to be that the *Wade, Gilbert,* and *Stovall* safeguards are applicable to the juvenile process. The only real question that remains is to what extent their applicability has been altered, if at all, by *Kirby v. Illinois.*

Chapter 4

WAIVER OF JURISDICTION

§ 4.01. General
§ 4.02. Waiver Hearing and Requirements of Due Process
§ 4.03. Waiver Standards
§ 4.04. Vagueness in Waiver Standards

---

§ 4.01. General.

Waiver of jurisdiction by a juvenile court is the process whereby the court relinquishes its jurisdiction over a child and transfers the case to a court of criminal jurisdiction for prosecution as in the case of an adult.

The effect of a decision to waive jurisdiction over a child is to deny to the child the protection and ameliorative treatment afforded by the juvenile process, substituting therefor the punitive treatment found in the criminal process. To be sure, in a criminal prosecution the juvenile will enjoy all the rights guaranteed to adults in the criminal process, but a great deal is given up to secure those rights. The fact that a juvenile often is faced with such a choice is perhaps the strongest argument in favor of securing procedural rights for juveniles in the juvenile process as well as in the criminal process.

Most jurisdictions provide by statute for waiver of jurisdiction or a functional equivalent. A recent perusal of the statutes of the fifty states and the District of Columbia, however, revealed that Arizona, Louisiana, Nebraska, New York, and Vermont do not provide for waiver of jurisdiction. In some of these instances, the absence of waiver provisions is explainable by the fact that the jurisdictional age of the juvenile court is set very low, at sixteen — the youngest jurisdictional age recognized in any state. Presumably, since the jurisdictional age is already set low, waiver is not considered a plausible alternative. *See, e.g.,* N.Y. Fam. Ct. Act § 712(a) (McKinney 1963); Vt. Stat. Ann. tit. 33, § 632(a)(1) (Supp. 1973) (jurisdictional age is sixteen in case of delinquent child).

In other cases, the absence of a waiver provision is perhaps explainable because the more serious offenses are excluded from the juvenile court's jurisdiction and are within the exclusive province of the criminal courts, or else the juvenile and criminal courts have concurrent jurisdiction over the more serious offenses. *See, e.g.,* La. Rev. Stat. Ann. § 13.1570(A)(5) (1968) (excludes capital offenses and crime of attempted aggravated rape when committed by child fifteen years of age or older); *State v. McCoy,* 145 Neb. 750, 18 N.W.2d 101 (1945); *Fugate v. Ronin,* 167 Neb. 70, 91 N.W.2d 240 (1958) (these cases hold that the juvenile court does not have exclusive jurisdiction over children, that other courts have concurrent jurisdiction over children charged with criminal violations).

Among the jurisdictions in which waiver is permitted, waiver provisions are quite varied in setting forth the circumstances under which jurisdiction may be waived. Most jurisdictions require that the child be over a certain age and be charged with a particularly serious offense before jurisdiction may be waived. Colo. Rev. Stat. Ann. § 22-1-4(4)(a), (b) (Supp. 1969) (fourteen or older and charged with a felony); Conn. Gen. Stat. Ann. § 17-60a (Supp. 1973) (charged with murder allegedly committed after reaching fourteen); Hawaii Rev. Stat. § 571-22(a)(1), (2) (Supp. 1972) (sixteen or older and charged with a felony, or eighteen or older and charged with commission of any crime allegedly committed before reaching eighteen); Idaho Code § 16-1806(1)(a)-(b) (2), (Supp. 1973) (sixteen or older and charged with felony, or eighteen or older and charged with any offense allegedly committed prior to becoming eighteen; waiver mandatory where person charged with offense is over eighteen and already under supervision of court); Mich. Comp. Laws Ann. § 712A.4 (Supp. 1974) (fifteen or older and charged with felony); Miss. Code Ann. § 43-21-31 (1972) (thirteen or older and charged with felony); Mo. Ann. Stat. § 211.071 (1962) (fourteen or older and charged with felony, or between seventeen and twenty-one and charged with any delinquent act allegedly occurring before reaching seventeen); Mont. Rev. Codes Ann. § 10-603(c) (Supp. 1973) (sixteen or older and charged with murder, attempted murder, manslaughter, arson in first or second degree, assault in first or second degree, robbery, burglary, carrying a deadly weapon with intent to assault, or forcible rape); Nev. Rev. Stat. § 62.080 (1973) (sixteen or older and charged with felony); N.M. Stat. Ann. § 13-14-27(A)(1) (Supp. 1973) (sixteen or older and charged with felony); N.C. Gen. Stat. § 7A-280 (1969) (fourteen or older and charged with felony; waiver mandatory if act is capital offense); Ohio Rev. Code Ann. § 2151.26(A), (C) (1971) (fifteen or older and charged with felony); R.I. Gen. Laws Ann. § 14-1-7 (Supp. 1972) (sixteen or older and charged with indictable offense); Tex. Fam. Code Ann. § 54.02(a)(1), (2) (1973) (fifteen or older and charged with felony); Utah Code Ann. § 55-10-86 (Supp. 1973) (fourteen or older and charged with felony); Va. Code Ann. § 16.1-176(a) (Supp. 1973) (fifteen or older and charged with felony).

A number of other states permit waiver of jurisdiction over children above a certain age, without regard to the nature of the offense charged. Ala. Code tit. 13, § 364 (1959) (fourteen); Del. Code Ann. tit. 11, § 2711 (Supp. 1970) (fourteen); Ill. Ann. Stat. ch. 37, § 702-7(3), (5) (1972) (thirteen); Ind. Ann. Stat. § 9-3214 (Supp. 1972) (fifteen); Iowa Code Ann. § 232.72 (1969) (fourteen); Mass. Gen. Laws Ann. ch. 119, § 61 (1965) (fourteen); Minn. Stat. Ann. § 260.125(1) (1971) (fourteen); N.J. Stat. Ann. § 2A:4-15 (1952) (sixteen); N.D. Cent. Code § 27-20-34(1)(a) (1974) (sixteen); Ore. Rev. Stat. § 419.533(1)(a) (1971) (sixteen); W. Va. Code Ann. § 49-5-14(3) (1966) (sixteen); Wis. Stat. Ann. § 48.18 (Supp. 1973) (sixteen).

Two states permit waiver on the basis of the seriousness of the conduct alone, without regard to age. N.H. Rev. Stat. Ann. § 169:21 (1964) (waiver permitted if child is charged with felony); Okla. Stat. Ann. tit. 10, § 1112(b) (Supp. 1974) (waiver permitted if child is charged with felony).

Still other jurisdictions place no limitations on waiver, permitting waiver without regard to the age of the child or the nature of the offense. Alaska Stat. § 47.10.060 (1962); Ark. Stat. Ann. § 45-224 (1964); Cal. Welf. & Inst'ns Code §§ 603, 606 (1972) (however, the Attorney General has expressed the opinion that the juvenile court may not transfer a child under eighteen to criminal court for prosecution on a misdemeanor charge and may not transfer in any event a child under fifteen. 40 Ops. Atty. Gen. 83); Me. Rev. Stat. Ann. tit. 15, § 2611(3) (1965); S.C. Code Ann. § 15-1171 (1962); S.D. Compiled Laws Ann. § 26-11-4 (Supp. 1973); Wash. Rev. Code Ann. § 13.04.120 (1962); Wyo. Stat. Ann. § 14-115.38 (Supp. 1973).

Finally, a number of states permit waiver based on a combination of the above factors. D.C. Code Ann. § 16-2307(a) (1973) (fifteen or older and charged with felony, or sixteen or older and already under commitment as a delinquent child, or eighteen or older and charged with commission of any delinquent act alleged to have been committed before reaching eighteen); Fla. Stat. Ann. § 39.02(6)(a), (b) (Supp. 1973) (waiver permitted where child is fourteen or older and charged with felony, except upon demand of child and parents, judge *must* waive jurisdiction without regard to nature of offense); Ga. Code Ann. § 24A-2501(a)(4) (Supp. 1973) (waiver permitted where child is thirteen or older and charged with an act punishable by death or life imprisonment, or fifteen or older and charged with any delinquent act); Kan. Stat. Ann. § 38-808(a), (b) (Supp. 1972) (waiver permitted where child was sixteen or older at time of alleged act, without regard to offense charged; also, in case of any child under eighteen charged with felony, case may be transferred to criminal court for trial and then remanded to juvenile court for disposition); Ky. Rev. Stat. Ann. § 208.170(1) (1972) (waiver permitted where child is sixteen or older and charged with felony, and in case of any child charged with murder or rape, including being accessory before fact to either offense, without regard to age); Md. Ann. Code, Cts. & Jud. Proc. § 3-816(b) (1974) (waiver permitted where child is fourteen or older, without regard to offense, and in case of any child charged with offense punishable by death or life imprisonment, without regard to age); Pa. Stat. Ann. tit. 11, § 50-325(a)(1), (e) (Supp. 1974) (waiver permitted where child is fourteen or older; waiver mandatory where child charged with murder, unless case has been transferred to juvenile court as elsewhere provided); Tenn. Code Ann. § 37-234(a)(1) (Supp. 1973) (waiver permitted where child is sixteen or older, without regard to offense, and where child is fifteen or older and charged with murder, rape, robbery with a deadly weapon, or kidnapping).

§ 4.02. Waiver Hearing and Requirements of Due Process.

The decision to waive jurisdiction is a critical determination because it affects the tenor of the juvenile's subsequent treatment. Even so, prior to 1966 very few states sought to protect the juvenile against procedural arbitrariness in the waiver process.

In a 1962 decision the Alabama Supreme Court held that juvenile court jurisdiction can be waived only after a full and thorough investigation and the submission of findings supported by proof that the child cannot be made to lead a correct life and cannot be properly disciplined by the juvenile court. *Stapler v. State*, 273 Ala. 358, 141 So.2d 181 (1962).

Similarly, the Delaware court in 1965 held that if a child is not given the assistance of counsel during determination of the question of transfer to a court of criminal jurisdiction, such transfer amounts to a denial of due process of law. *State v. Naylor*, 207 A.2d 1 (Del. 1965).

In 1966 the Supreme Court in *Kent v. United States*, 383 U.S. 541 (1966), reviewed a District of Columbia case in which the petitioner challenged the validity of the juvenile court's decision to waive jurisdiction over him, on the ground that the procedure by which the court reached its decision constituted a denial of due process of law. The Court was called upon to construe a provision of the District of Columbia Code that stated in part that the juvenile court could waive jurisdiction after a full investigation. In nullifying the juvenile court's decision to waive jurisdiction, the Supreme Court held that waiver of jurisdiction was a "critically important" stage in the juvenile process and must be attended by minimum requirements of due process and fair treatment required by the fourteenth amendment. 383 U.S. at 560.

Specifically, the Court set forth four basic

safeguards required by due process during the waiver proceedings:

(1) If the juvenile court is considering waiving jurisdiction, the juvenile is entitled to a hearing on the question of waiver.

(2) The juvenile is entitled to representation by counsel at such hearing.

(3) The juvenile's attorney must be given access to the juvenile's social records on request.

(4) If jurisdiction is waived, the juvenile is entitled to a statement of reasons in support of the waiver order. 383 U.S. at 561-63.

The *Kent* decision was initially limited in scope since it was seemingly based on an interpretation of the requirements under the District of Columbia waiver statute, rather than on constitutional principles. However, following references to *Kent* in *In re Gault*, 387 U.S. 1, 12 (1967), the weight of authority now favors the judgment that the principles stated in *Kent* are of constitutional dimensions. *United States ex rel. Turner v. Rundle*, 438 F.2d 839, 842 (3d Cir. 1971), and cases cited therein at 842n.11; *Powell v. Hocker*, 453 F.2d 652 (9th Cir. 1971); *In re Harris*, 67 Cal.2d 876, 434 P.2d 615, 64 Cal. Rptr. 319 (1967); *see People v. Fields*, 30 Mich. App. 390, 186 N.W.2d 15 (1971), *rev'd on other grounds*, 388 Mich. 66, 199 N.W.2d 217 (1972). *Contra Stanley v. Peyton*, 292 F. Supp. 209 (W.D. Va. 1968); *State v. Acuna*, 78 N.M. 119, 428 P.2d 658 (1967); *Cradle v. Peyton*, 208 Va. 243, 156 S.E.2d 874 (1967), *cert. denied*, 392 U.S. 945 (1968).

In any event, at the very minimum, most of the jurisdictions that permit waiver of jurisdiction require by statute a hearing on the waiver decision. Colo. Rev. Stat. Ann. §§ 22-1-4(4)(a), 22-3-8 (Supp. 1969); Conn. Gen. Stat. Ann. § 17-60a (Supp. 1973); D.C. Code Ann. § 16-2307(d) (1973); Fla. Stat. Ann. § 39.02(6)(a) (Supp. 1973); Ga. Code

Ann. § 24A-2501(a)(1) (Supp. 1973); Hawaii Rev. Stat. § 571-22(a) (Supp. 1972); Idaho Code § 16-1806(1) (Supp. 1973); Ill. Ann. Stat. ch. 37, § 702-7(3) (1972); Iowa Code Ann. § 232.72 (1969); Md. Ann. Code, Cts. & Jud. Proc. § 3-816(a) (1974); Mass. Gen. Laws Ann. ch. 119, § 61 (1965); Mich. Compiled Laws Ann. § 712A.4(2) (Supp. 1974); Minn. Stat. Ann. § 260.125(2)(c) (1971); Mont. Rev. Codes Ann. § 10-603(c) (Supp. 1973); N.M. Stat. Ann. § 13-14-27(A)(2) (Supp. 1973); N.C. Gen. Stat. § 7A-280 (1969); N.D. Cent. Code § 27-20-34(1)(b) (1974); Ohio Rev. Code Ann. § 2151.26(A), (B) (1971); Okla. Stat. Ann. tit. 10, § 1112(b) (Supp. 1974); Pa. Stat. Ann. tit. 11, § 50-325(a)(2) (Supp. 1974); S.D. Compiled Laws Ann. § 26-11-4 (Supp. 1973); Tenn. Code Ann. § 37-234(a)(2) (Supp. 1973); Tex. Fam. Code Ann. § 54.02(c) (1973); Utah Code Ann. § 55-10-86 (Supp. 1973); Va. Code Ann. § 16.1-176(a)(2) (Supp. 1973); Wyo. Stat. Ann. § 14-115.38 (Supp. 1973).

Hearings have also been required in a number of instances by judicial decision, in some cases in reliance on *Kent,* and in others not. In addition to the cases cited in *United States ex rel. Turner v. Rundle,* 438 F.2d 839, 842n.11 (3d Cir. 1971), see *Powell v. Hocker,* 453 F.2d 652 (9th Cir. 1971); *Miller v. Quatsoe,* 332 F. Supp. 1269 (E.D. Wis. 1971) (by implication); *Hopkins v. State,* 209 So.2d 841 (Miss. 1968); *State v. Van Buren,* 29 N.J. 548, 150 A.2d 649 (1969); *Dillenburg v. Maxwell,* 68 Wash.2d 481, 413 P.2d 940 (1966).

§ 4.03. Waiver Standards.

In making a waiver determination the juvenile court judge is called upon to decide whether the child is amenable to the treatment and rehabilitation afforded by the juvenile processes. This hardly satisfies the requirement of a standard, however, since it represents little more than the judge's conclusion that the interests of society and the interests of the child suggest that the child is not an appropriate subject for treatment as a juvenile. Prudence, if nothing more, suggests that such a critical decision should depend on objective considerations that evaluate the child's receptiveness to juvenile treatment.

As an appendix to its decision in *Kent*, the Supreme Court suggested the following criteria to be used in determining whether to waive jurisdiction over a child and transfer him to criminal court:

> "1. The seriousness of the alleged offense to the community and whether the protection of the community requires waiver.
>
> "2. Whether the alleged offense was committed in an aggressive, violent, premeditated or willful manner.
>
> "3. Whether the alleged offense was against persons or against property, greater weight being given to offenses against persons especially if personal injury resulted.
>
> "4. The prosecutive merit of the complaint, i.e., whether there is evidence upon which a Grand Jury may be expected to return an indictment....
>
> "5. The desirability of trial and disposition of the entire offense in one court when the juvenile's associates in the alleged offense are adults who will be charged with a crime in the [criminal court].
>
> "6. The sophistication and maturity of the juvenile as determined by consideration of his home, environment situation, emotional attitude and pattern of living.
>
> "7. The record and previous history of the juvenile....
>
> "8. The prospects for adequate protection of the public and the likelihood of reasonable rehabilitation of the juvenile (if he is found to have committed the alleged offense) by the use of procedures, services and facilities currently available to the Juvenile Court." 383 U.S. at 566-67.

A comprehensive survey of some 207 juvenile courts in the country showed that two factors were cited by the courts as weighing most heavily in the decision to waive jurisdiction: the seriousness of the offense and the past history of the juvenile. The President's Commission on Law Enforcement and Administration of Criminal Justice, *Task Force Report: Juvenile Delinquency and Youth Crime*, Appendix B, Table 5, at 78 (1967).

The study further revealed that after the above two considerations, the following factors, in order of reported frequency, were utilized by judges in determining waiver questions:

1. Aggressive, violent, premeditated, or willful manner by which the offense was committed.

2. Sophistication, maturity, emotional attitude of the juvenile.

3. Proximity of juvenile's age to the maximum age of juvenile court jurisdiction.

4. More appropriate procedures, services, and facilities available in the adult court for the likelihood of reasonable rehabilitation.

5. The possible need for a longer period of incarceration.

6. Evidence apparently sufficient for grand jury indictment.

7. The juvenile's associates in the alleged offense will be charged with a crime in adult court.

8. Effect of judgment of waiver on public's respect for law enforcement and law compliance.

9. Community attitude toward the specific offense. *Id.* With the exception of the last two criteria, these factors correspond to those listed by the Supreme Court in *Kent.* 383 U.S. at 566-67.

Following the Supreme Court's decision in *Kent,* the suggested criteria were incorporated as closely as possible into the new District of Columbia Juvenile Court Code. D.C. Code Ann. § 16-2307(e) (1973). In addition, at least four other states have codified waiver criteria identical or very similar to those enumerated in *Kent* and subsequently embodied in the District of Columbia Juvenile Court Code. Ill. Ann. Stat. ch. 37, § 702-7(3)(a) (1972); Okla. Stat. Ann. tit. 10, § 1112(b) (Supp. 1974); Tex. Fam. Code Ann. § 54.02(f) (1973); Wyo. Stat. Ann. § 14-115.38 (Supp. 1973).

The pertinent Alaska statute provides:

> "In determining whether a minor is unamenable to treatment, the court may consider the seriousness of the offense the minor is alleged to have committed, the minor's history of delinquency, the probable cause of the minor's delinquent behavior, and the facilities available to the division of youth and adult authority for treating the minor." Alaska Stat. § 47.10.060(d) (1971). *See also* the criteria set forth in Md. Ann. Code, Cts. & Jud. Proc. § 3-816(c) (1974); Mich. Compiled Laws Ann. § 712A.4(4) (Supp. 1974).

Most states, however, do not attempt to set forth the criteria by which the waiver question is to be determined. If any attempt is made to set forth a standard at all, it is usually in the form of a statement of the last criterion suggested in *Kent*—i.e., that the child is not amenable to the rehabilitative processes of the juvenile court, *see, e.g.,* Ga. Code Ann. § 24A-2501(a)(2) (Supp. 1973), or else a statement that the "interests of the public require" that he be tried as an adult, *see, e.g.,* Mass. Gen. Laws Ann. ch. 119, § 61 (1965).

Again, such provisions merely state the conclusion to be reached without stating the considerations to be weighed in reaching the conclusion. Nevertheless, as a practical matter most states simply leave the waiver determination to the discretion of the juvenile court judge. *See, e.g., State ex rel. Londerholm v. Owens,* 197 Kan. 212, 224-29, 416 P.2d 259, 270-73 (1966); *Lewis v. State,* 86 Nev. 889, 478 P.2d 168 (1970).

On the other hand, an Indiana court held it insufficient to support waiver of jurisdiction for the juvenile court judge to merely recite the language of the statute authorizing waiver, and further held that the court must accompany its waiver order with a statement of reasons or considerations explaining with specificity why jurisdiction was waived. *Summers v. State,* 248 Ind. 551, 559-60, 230 N.E.2d 320, 324-25 (1967). *See also D.M.N. v. State,* 129 Ga. App. 165, 199 S.E.2d 114 (1973) (waiver order invalid where it merely recited, in language of waiver statute, that child was not amenable to rehabilitation or treatment, that probable guilt was shown, and that safety of the community required that child be placed under legal restraint).

Failure to state any waiver standard whatsoever exposes a statute to still another hazard. Such a statute may be found wanting in regard to the essentials of due process a.ʾd equal protection guaranteed under the fourteenth amendment, since it fails to set forth with sufficient particularity the basis on which some children are to be treated differently than others. This problem is discussed in § 4.04, *infra.*

§ 4.04. Vagueness in Waiver Standards.

As noted in the preceding section, a few jurisdictions have codified fairly detailed criteria by which waiver determinations are to be made. (*See* statutes cited in § 4.03, *supra.*)

Most jurisdictions, however, do not attempt to set forth ascertainable standards but rather simply state the basis on which waiver is allowed—*i.e.,* where the child "is not amenable to treatment or rehabilitation," Ga. Code Ann. § 24A-2501(a)(3) (Supp. 1973), or where "the needs of the child or best interest of the State" require that the child's case be transferred to adult court for prosecution, N.C. Gen. Stat. § 7A-280 (1969).

If standards by which such a conclusion is to be reached are not set forth, how is the conclusion to be fairly drawn at all? Some courts may assume that if the statute fails to state a waiver standard, or if the standard expressed is a single, conclusory standard, then standards similar to those stated by the Supreme Court in the *Kent* decision can be read into or inferred from the statute.

For example, in *State v. Gibbs*, 94 Idaho 908, 500 P.2d 209 (1972), after noting that the Idaho waiver statute contained "no known or ascertainable criteria" on which to base a waiver decision, the court proceeded to formulate standards to guide the juvenile court judges in exercising their discretion:

> "[T]he state courts, when the discretionary waiver statutes of their respective jurisdictions are subjected to constitutional challenge, must fashion the controlling criteria.
>
> "Jurisdiction ordinarily is waived when (1) the defendant has acquired such a degree of emotional or mental maturity that he is not receptive to rehabilitative programs designed for children; (2) although the defendant is immature, his disturbance has eluded exhaustive prior efforts at correction through existing juvenile programs; or (3) the defendant is immature and might be treated, but the nature of his difficulty is likely to render him dangerous to the public, if released at age twenty-one, or to disrupt the rehabilitation of other children in the program prior to his release." 94 Idaho at 916, 500 P.2d at 217.

Since the Indiana waiver statute likewise does not express a waiver standard, the Indiana Supreme Court also judicially adopted waiver criteria to be applied by juvenile court judges:

> "[A]n offense committed by a juvenile may be waived to a criminal court if the offense has specific prosecutive merit in the opinion of the prosecuting attorney; or if it is heinous or of an aggravated character, greater weight being given to offenses against the person than to offenses against property; or, even though less serious, if the offense is part of a repetitive pattern of juvenile offenses which would lead to a determination that said juvenile may be beyond rehabilitation...; or where it is found to be in the best interest of the public welfare and for the protection of the public security generally that said juvenile be required to stand trial as an adult offender." *Summers v. State*, 248 Ind. 551, 561, 230 N.E.2d 320, 325-26 (1967).

Similarly, the Michigan Court of Appeals was content that its waiver statute, which at that time contained no ascertainable standards, could be read consistently with the due process requirements of *Kent. People v. Fields*, 30 Mich. App. 390, 392-93, 186 N.W.2d 15, 16 (1971). The statute in question specifically provided for a waiver hearing, notice and right to counsel and otherwise passed muster under the standards articulated in *Kent.* However, on appeal the Michigan Supreme Court stated:

> "It is important to understand the precise issue in this case. It is not whether the constitutional requirements of due process stated in *Kent v. United States* ... were met. Rather, it is whether the lack of standards in the statute preclude a

waiver proceeding." *People v. Fields*, 388 Mich.
66, 75, 199 N.W.2d 217, 221 (1972).

The court was very disturbed at the absence of standards in this statute and disapproved of the lower court's attempt to read standards into the statute. Its opinion further stated:

> "If the Legislature is to treat some persons under the age of 17 differently from the entire class of such persons, excluding them from the beneficient [sic] processes and purposes of our juvenile courts, the Legislature must establish suitable and ascertainable standards whereby such persons are to be deemed adults and treated as such subject to the processes and penalties of our criminal law. The statute is unconstitutional because it lacks standards." 388 Mich. at 77, 199 N.W.2d at 222.

As a result of the ruling in *People v. Fields*, the Michigan statute was amended to embody the following waiver considerations:

> "(a) The prior record and character of the child, his physical and mental maturity and his pattern of living.
> "(b) The seriousness of the offense.
> "(c) Whether the offense, even if less serious, is part of a repetitive pattern of offenses which would lead to a determination that the child may be beyond rehabilitation under existing juvenile programs and statutory procedures.
> "(d) The relative suitability of programs and facilities available to the juvenile and criminal courts for the child.
> "(e) Whether it is in the best interests of the public welfare and the protection of the public security that the child stand trial as an adult

offender." Mich. Compiled Laws Ann. §
712.4(4) (Supp. 1974).

It should be noted that these criteria are virtually identical to those set forth by the Indiana Supreme Court in *Summers v. State*, 248 Ind. 551, 561, 230 N.E.2d 320, 325-26 (1967).

Of course, the Michigan statute, and consequently the *People v. Fields* decision, might be distinguished from others by virtue of the fact that previously the statute *totally* lacked standards. Although a statute that employs nonamenability of the child to rehabilitation as its principal or only standard may be imprecise or even vague, at least it can be said to furnish a semblance of a standard, even if it represents a conclusion rather than considerations by which the conclusion is reached.

Perhaps the whole problem can be remitted to the integrity of the judicial process. If the juvenile court judge is required to include a statement of reasons supporting a waiver order, appellate courts can carefully scrutinize the record to ascertain whether the evidence supports the findings of fact and whether the facts as established indeed warrant waiver of jurisdiction under the articulated standard.

As was stated in *Summers v. State*, 248 Ind. 551, 230 N.E.2d 320 (1967), a statement by the judge, worded in the language of a statute devoid of an ascertainable waiver standard, is insuffcient to support waiver of jurisdiction. Likewise, a statement by the judge, worded in the bare language of a statute that *does* include an ascertainable waiver standard, is insufficient to support waiver of jurisdiction. *D.M.N. v. State*, 129 Ga. App. 165, 199 S.E.2d 114 (1973). What is needed is a statement demonstrating in specific terms *why* the child is not amenable to rehabilitation or treatment and *why* the needs of the child and the safety of the community require that the child be tried as an adult. *See Summers v. State,* 248 Ind. 551, 559-60, 230 N.E.2d 320, 324-25 (1967).

Nevertheless, there are remaining doubts about the constitutional validity of a statute that contains only a single, conclusory standard. While *People v. Fields* might tentatively be distinguished on the basis that the Michigan statute there reviewed contained no standard, the following language in the court's opinion should be noted:

> "Absent *carefully defined standards* in the statute itself which would justify such disparity of treatment, there is no way by which it can be determined what standard a probate judge should apply in a waiver proceeding....He might use the standard contended for by the prosecutor — 'the child's welfare and the best interest of the state.' [*Cf.* N.C. Gen. Stat. § 7A-280 (1969)] *This standard is so vague and subject to so many possible interpretations as to be no standard at all.*" 388 Mich. at 75-76, 199 N.W.2d at 221-22 (emphasis added).

The court thus called for legislative creation of "carefully defined standards" (note the use of the plural), not creation of a single standard that only sets forth the basis for waiver of jurisdiction. A standard employing terms such as "the child's welfare and the best interest of the state" would, in the court's estimation, be impermissibly vague.

State legislatures would do well, for the sake of clarification of a question that is sure to arise again and again, to create statutory waiver criteria to guide judges in making the critically important waiver decision.

Chapter 5

THE ADJUDICATORY PROCESS

§ 5.01. The Adjudicatory Hearing.

The adjudicatory hearing is a fact-finding hearing at which the court determines the existence or nonexistence of the allegations contained in the petition. *See, e.g.,* Ill. Ann. Stat. ch. 37, § 701-4 (1972); N.Y. Fam. Ct. Act § 742 (McKinney Supp. 1973); N.C. Gen. Stat. § 7A-285 (Supp. 1973).

The court's function at the adjudicatory hearing is to determine, for example, in a delinquency or need-of-supervision case, whether the child committed the delinquent act alleged or committed the acts that cause him to be in need of supervision, or in a neglect or abandonment proceeding, whether the child is in fact neglected or aban-

123

doned. In this sense, the adjudicatory hearing is the functional equivalent of the trial in the regular criminal or civil process. In a case in which the act charged is an act that would be a crime if committed by an adult, the juvenile is entitled to certain procedural safeguards, as discussed subsequently in this chapter.

The action against a child, whether it arises from conditions of neglect or abandonment, or conduct indicating delinquency, or a need for supervision, is commenced by filing a petition. *See, e.g.,* Alaska Stat. § 47.10.020 (1973); Hawaii Rev. Stat. § 571-21 (1968); Ind. Ann. Stat. § 9-3208 (Supp. 1972); Iowa Code Ann. § 232.3 (1969); Ky. Rev. Stat. Ann. § 208.070 (1971); La. Rev. Stat. Ann. § 13:1574 (Supp. 1974); Mass. Gen. Laws Ann. ch. 119, § 54 (1965); Mich. Compiled Laws Ann. § 712A.11 (1968); Minn. Stat. Ann. § 260.131 (1971); Miss. Code Ann. § 43-21-11 (1972); Mont. Rev. Codes Ann. § 10-605.1 (Supp. 1973); N.M. Stat. Ann. §§ 13-14-14 to 13-14-17 (Supp. 1973); Ore. Rev. Stat. § 419.482 (1971).

Once the petition is filed commencing action against the child or on his behalf, a date for the adjudicatory hearing is set. At this point, *In re Gault*, 387 U.S. 1 (1967), requires that the child be given adequate notice of the proceedings and of the nature of the conduct alleged in the petition. The Court in *Gault* set forth the notice requirement as follows:

> "Notice, to comply with due process requirements, must be given sufficiently in advance of scheduled court proceedings so that reasonable opportunity to prepare will be afforded, and it must 'set forth the alleged misconduct with particularity.' . . . Due process of law requires notice of the sort we have described-- that is, notice which would be deemed constitutionally adequate in a civil or criminal proceeding." 387 U.S. at 33 & n.53.

Most states have statutes requiring notice to be given to the child and, particularly in the case of a young child, to the parents of the child as well. *See, e.g.,* Cal. Welf. & Inst'ns Code §§ 658, 659 (1972); Ga. Code Ann. §§ 24A-1701,24A-1702 (Supp. 1973); Minn. Stat. Ann. §§ 260.135, 260.141 (1971); N.D. Cent. Code §§ 27-20-22, 27-20-23 (1974); Ore. Rev. Code § 419.486 (1971); Tenn. Code Ann. §§ 37-221, 37-223 (Supp. 1973); Tex. Fam. Code Ann. §§ 53.06, 53.07 (1973).

§ 5.02. Right to Counsel.

In *Kent v. United States,* the Supreme Court held that fundamental fairness required that juveniles have assistance of counsel at a waiver hearing. 383 U.S. at 561-62.

In *In re Gault,* the Court underscored the importance of what it considered to be a fundamental right, this time in conjunction with an adjudicatory hearing:

> "A proceeding where the issue is whether the child will be found to be 'delinquent' and subjected to the loss of his liberty for years is comparable in seriousness to a felony prosecution. The juvenile needs the assistance of counsel to cope with problems of law, to make skilled inquiry into the facts, to insist upon regularity of the proceedings, and to ascertain whether he has a defense and to prepare and submit it." 387 U.S. at 36.

The Court concluded, therefore, that in delinquency proceedings in which the child faces a risk of commitment to an institution, the child and his parents must be notified of the right to counsel and that if they cannot afford retained counsel, counsel will be appointed by the court to represent the child. 387 U.S. at 41.

Prior to the *Gault* decision, there was no prohibition

against permitting lawyers inside the juvenile courtroom. Their role was certainly limited, however, and was not at all the same role customarily played in a full adversary proceeding. Generally, those who could afford it were allowed to have the "family lawyer" come in to stand by the child's side. Indeed, this "right" was sometimes provided by statute. *See* Miss. Code Ann. § 43-21-17 (1972) (any party in juvenile proceeding may be represented by counsel of his own choosing, paid at his own expense).

A number of states already provided a right to counsel, including court-appointed counsel, even prior to *Gault.* Now most states provide by statute for representation of juveniles by counsel, in one form or another. The provisions are varied.

Some jurisdictions express the right to counsel by declaring that a juvenile is entitled to be represented by counsel, including court-appointed counsel if he is unable to afford retained counsel, at all stages of the proceedings. *See, e.g.,* Colo. Rev. Stat. Ann. § 22-1-6(1) (Supp. 1967); D.C. Code Ann. § 16-2304(a) (1973); Ga. Code Ann. § 24A-2001(a) (Supp. 1973); Md. Ann. Code, Cts. & Jud. Proc. § 3-830(d) (1974); N.M. Stat. Ann. § 13-14-25(E) (Supp. 1973); N.D. Cent. Code § 27-20-26 (1974); Ohio Rev. Code Ann. § 2151.352 (1971); Pa. Stat. Ann. tit. 11, § 50-317 (Supp. 1974); S.D. Compiled Laws Ann. §§ 26-8-22.1, 26-8-22.2 (Supp. 1973); Tenn. Code Ann. § 37-226(a) (Supp. 1973); Tex. Fam. Code Ann. § 51.10(a), (b) (1973); Utah Code Ann. § 55-10-96 (Supp. 1973); Va. Code Ann. § 16.1-173(a), (c) (Supp. 1973); Wyo. Stat. Ann. § 14-115.23 (Supp. 1973). This represents an extension of both *Kent* and *Gault,* since they required counsel only at the waiver and adjudicatory stages, respectively.

Other jurisdictions simply provide that a juvenile is entitled to be represented by counsel, without specifying whether this right extends to all stages of the proceedings or whether it applies to all forms of conduct for which the juvenile might be before the court. *See, e.g.*, Ill. Ann. Stat. ch. 37, § 701-20(1) (1972); Iowa Code Ann. § 232.28 (1969); La. Rev. Stat. Ann. § 13: 1579 (Supp. 1974); Minn. Stat. Ann. § 260.155(2) (1971); Neb. Rev. Stat. § 43-205.06 (1968); N.Y. Fam. Ct. Act § 741(a) (McKinney 1963); W. Va. Code Ann. § 49-5-13 (Supp. 1973).

Still other jurisdictions provide for a more limited right to counsel. Some states require the court to appoint counsel only where the juvenile requests counsel and is financially unable to retain counsel of his own choice, *see, e.g.*, Ariz. Rev. Stat. Ann. § 8-225(A) (Supp. 1973); Ore. Rev. Stat. § 419.498(2) (1971); Vt. Stat. Ann. tit. 33, § 653 (Supp. 1973), while others permit the judge to appoint counsel in his discretion, *see, e.g.*, Mich. Compiled Laws Ann. § 712A.17 (1968); Nev. Rev. Stat. § 62.085 (1973); Wis. Stat. Ann. § 48.25(6) (1957).

One remaining question is to what extent the right to counsel is accorded as a matter of right to children who are before the juvenile court for conduct other than a violation of law. The Supreme Court in *Gault*, after all, indicated that a juvenile is entitled to representation by counsel in "proceedings to determine delinquency which may result in commitment to an institution." 387 U.S. at 41. The classification "delinquency" increasingly is restricted to violations of law, although some jurisdictions include within the "delinquency" category other forms of conduct, such as truancy, incorrigibility, and running away from home.

In jurisdictions that limit the definition of delinquency to violations of law, these latter forms of conduct are grouped under the heading of "incorrigibility" or "children in need of supervision" or a similar category. (See various classifications of conduct described in § 2.06, *supra*.)

As mentioned earlier, some states accord to juveniles a general right to counsel without describing the kinds of cases to which the right is applicable. Consequently, it is difficult to determine whether the right extends to cases other than those in which a violation of law is the basis for the petition.

Some jurisdictions, however, specifically indicate that the right to counsel is applicable both to delinquency cases (*i.e.*, cases in which a violation of law is involved) and cases involving a child in need of supervision (*i.e.* where the petition is based on truancy, incorrigibility, running away from home, etc.). *See, e.g.*, Cal. Welf. & Inst'ns Code § 679 (1972) (right extends to children alleged to be wards of state under § 601, which describes children in need of supervision, and § 602, which is concerned with children who are accused of violating a law); Colo. Rev. Stat. Ann. § 22-1-6 (1) (Supp. 1967) (by reference to other statutes, right extends to children charged with violations of law and children in need of supervision); Conn. Gen. Stat. Ann. § 17-66b (a) (Supp. 1973) (right extends to children alleged to be delinquent, which under § 17-53, includes law violations as well as truancy, running away from home, etc.); D.C. Code Ann. § 16-2304 (a) (1973); Ga. Code Ann. § 24A-2001 (a) (Supp. 1973); N.M. Stat. Ann. § 13-14-25 (E) (Supp. 1973).

Some jurisdictions also provide that a child has a right to be represented by counsel in neglect or dependency proceedings, which clearly goes beyond any requirement of *Gault*, since the proceeding does not allege an act of delinquency nor does it ordinarily entail a loss of liberty by the child, unless delinquent conduct is also alleged in the petition. *See, e.g.*, Colo. Rev. Stat. Ann. § 22-1-6(1) (Supp. 1967) (by reference to other sections, right extends to children alleged to be neglected or dependent, where termination of parental rights is a possibility); Ga. Code Ann. § 24A-2001(a) (Supp. 1973).

In addition, some jurisdictions provide that in a neglect or dependency proceeding, the *parent* is entitled to representation by counsel, which includes court-appointed counsel if the parent cannot afford retained counsel. Conn. Gen. Stat. Ann. § 17-66b (b) (Supp. 1973); D.C. Code Ann. § 16-2304 (b) (1973); N.M. Stat. Ann. § 13-14-25 (F) (Supp. 1973).

In any event, in whatever form counsel might be provided, or whether provision is made by statute for representation by counsel at all, a juvenile is entitled to the assistance of counsel as a matter of constitutional due process. Notice to that effect and notice that counsel will be appointed to represent him if he cannot afford counsel are also required by due process.

§ 5.03. Right to Jury.

In terms of a delineation of the rights of juveniles, without a doubt the major setback of the post-*Gault* period is the Supreme Court's decision in *McKeiver v. Pennsylvania*, 403 U.S. 528 (1971), in which the Court held that due process of law under the fourteenth amendment does not require the states to provide a jury trial in juvenile proceedings. The Court listed a number of reasons in support of its decision, but these reasons have a common thread running throughout that seems to spell out the Court's underlying concern, *i.e.*, that imposing a jury trial in the conduct of juvenile hearings would be disruptive to its informal fact-finding setting and its basically nonadversary process. 403 U.S. at 545-51.

Nevertheless, a number of states provide for jury trial in adjudicatory hearings, either by statute or judicial decision. Colo. Rev. Stat. Ann. § 22-1-6 (4) (a) (Supp. 1967); Mich. Compiled Laws Ann. § 712A.17 (1968); Mont. Rev. Codes Ann. § 10-604.1 (Supp. 1973); Okla. Stat. Ann. tit. 10, § 1110 (Supp. 1974);S.D. Compiled Laws Ann. §

26-8-31 (1967); Tex. Fam. Code Ann. § 54.03 (c) (1973); W. Va. Code Ann. § 49-5-6 (1966); Wis. Stat. Ann. § 48.25 (2) (1957); Wyo. Stat. Ann. § 14-115.24 (c) (Supp. 1973); *RLR v. State*, 487 P.2d 27 (Alaska 1971); *Commonwealth v. Thomas*, 269 N.E.2d 277 (Mass. 1971); *Peyton v. Nord*, 78 N.M. 717, 437 P.2d 716 (1968). At least one federal court has agreed. *Nieves v. United States*, 280 F. Supp. 994 (S.D.N.Y. 1968).

Of the four cases mentioned above, none deals directly with the sixth amendment right to trial by jury. The Massachusetts and New Mexico decisions are based on state statutory law. The Alaska decision, which was decided subsequent to *McKeiver v. Pennsylvania*, declined to rule on the federal constitutional right, but held that a child is entitled to a jury trial in a juvenile proceeding under the state constitution. *Nieves* involved the constitutionality of *waiver* of the right to trial by jury. Under then existing federal law a juvenile had a right to trial by jury, but in order to exercise that right, he had to elect to be tried as an adult. Election to be tried as a juvenile under the provisions of the Federal Juvenile Delinquency Act of June 25, 1948, ch.645, § 5033, 62 Stat. 857, operated as a waiver of the sixth amendment right. The three-judge panel held that this imposed a constitutionally impermissible choice on the juvenile and declared § 5033 unconstitutional insofar as it compelled him to make such a choice. Furthermore, the court held that if the plaintiff thereafter elected to be tried as a juvenile, he would have to be accorded the right to a jury trial. 280 F. Supp. at 1000-01, 1006.

Nothing in *McKeiver v. Pennsylvania* changes existing statutory or decisional law providing for jury trials. The Court in *McKeiver* simply stated that the right to jury trial in juvenile proceedings is not one of those rights made obligatory upon the states by the fourteenth amendment due process test announced in *Gault*. This does not prevent the states from affording such a right if they feel compelled, for constitutional or other reasons, to do so.

The majority of jurisdictions, however, have declared by statute that hearings shall be conducted without a jury or have concluded by judicial decision, for the most part prior to *McKeiver*, that jury trials are not constitutionally required in juvenile proceedings. *See, e.g.,* Ark. Stat. Ann. § 45-206 (1964); Del. Code Ann. tit. 10, § 1175 (1953); D.C. Code Ann. § 16-2316 (a) (1973); Fla. Stat. Ann. § 39.02 (2) (1961); Ga. Code Ann. § 24A-1801(a) (Supp. 1973); Hawaii Rev. Stat. § 571-41 (1968); Idaho Code § 16-1813 (Supp. 1973); Ind. Ann. Stat. § 9-3215 (Supp. 1972); Iowa Code Ann. § 232.27 (1969); Ky. Rev. Stat. Ann. § 208.060 (1971); La. Rev. Stat. Ann. § 13.1579 (Supp. 1974); Minn. Stat. Ann. § 260.155(1) (1971); Miss. Code Ann. § 43-21-17 (1972); Neb. Rev. Stat. § 43-206.03(2) (1968); Nev. Rev. Stat. § 62.190(3) (1973);N.J. Stat. Ann. § 2A:4-35 (1952); N.D. Cent. Code § 27-20-24(1) (1974); Ohio Rev. Code Ann. § 2151.35 (1971); Ore. Rev. Stat. § 419.498(1) (1971); Pa. Stat. Ann. tit. 11, § 50-316 (a) (Supp. 1974); S.C. Code Ann. § 15-1095.19 (Supp. 1973); Tenn. Code Ann. § 37-224(a) (Supp. 1973); Utah Code Ann. § 55-10-94 (Supp. 1973); Vt. Stat. Ann. tit. 33, § 651 (a) (Supp. 1973); Wash. Rev. Code Ann. § 13.04.030 (1962); *Robinson v. State*, 227 Ga. 140, 179 S.E.2d 248 (1971); *In re Fucini*, 44 Ill.2d 305, 255 N.E. 2d 380 (1970), *appeal dismissed*, 403 U.S. 925 (1971); *Bible v. State*, 254 N.E.2d 319 (Ind. 1970); *Dryden v. Commonwealth*, 435 S.W.2d 457 (Ky. 1968); *In re Johnson*, 254 Md. 517, 255 A.2d 419 (1969); *In re Fisher*, 468 S.W.2d 198 (Mo. 1971); *In re Hans*, 174 Neb. 612, 119 N.W.2d 72 (1963); *In re J.W.*, 57 N.J. 144, 270 A.2d 273 (1970); *In re Burrus*, 275 N.C. 517, 169 S.E.2d 879 (1969), *aff'd*, 403 U.S. 528 (1971); *In re Daniel D.*, 27 N.Y.2d 90, 261 N.E.2d 627, 313 N.Y.S.2d 704 (1970); *In re Agler*, 19 Ohio St. 2d 70, 249 N.E.2d 808 (1969); *State v. Turner*, 253 Ore. 235, 453 P.2d 910 (1969); *In re Terry*, 438 Pa. 339, 265 A.2d 350 (1970), *aff'd sub nom. McKeiver v.*

Pennsylvania, 403 U.S. 528 (1971); *In re McCloud*, 110 R.I. 431, 293 A.2d 512 (1972); *Estes v. Hopp*, 73 Wash.2d 263, 438 P.2d 205 (1968).

§ 5.04. Burden of Proof.

In *In re Winship*, 397 U.S. 358 (1970), the Supreme Court was called upon to pass on the validity of a New York statute, N.Y. Fam Ct. Act § 744 (b) (McKinney Supp. 1973), that prescribed a preponderance of the evidence as the standard of proof in all adjudicatory hearings. The Court first held that proof beyond a reasonable doubt is the constitutionally required standard in a criminal prosecution, and then held that the same degree of proof is required in the adjudicatory stage of a delinquency proceeding. At least two state courts had already reached this result. *Thomas v. State*, 121 Ga. App. 91, 172 S.E.2d 860 (1970); *In re Urbasek*, 38 Ill.2d 535, 232 N.E.2d 716 (1967). Subsequent to its decision in *Winship*, the Court ruled that the *Winship* mandate was to receive fully retroactive effect. *Ivan V. v. City of New York*, 407 U.S. 203 (1972).

It is important to note that the *Winship* decision was limited to an inquiry into the applicable standard of proof in a *delinquency* proceeding. The Court itself framed the question in the case: "This case presents the single, narrow question whether proof beyond a reasonable doubt is among the 'essentials of due process and fair treatment' required during the adjudicatory stage when a juvenile is charged with an act which would constitute a crime if committed by an adult." 397 U.S. at 358-59. In answering this question, the Court reiterated its view in *Gault* that " '[a] proceeding where the issue is whether the child will be found to be 'delinquent' and subjected to the loss of his liberty for years is comparable in seriousness to a felony prosecution'." 397 U.S. at 366, quoting from *In re Gault*, 387 U.S. 1, 66 (1967).

Moreover, the Court's specific holding, quoting Chief Justice Fuld's dissent in the decision below, was

> " '[T]hat, where a 12-year-old child is charged with an act of stealing which renders him liable to confinement for as long as six years, then, as a matter of due process . . . the case against him must be proved beyond a reasonable doubt'." 397 U.S. at 368, quoting from *In re Samuel W.*, 24 N.Y.2d 196, 207, 247 N.E.2d 253, 260, 299 N.Y.S.2d 414, 423-24 (1969) (Fuld, C.J., dissenting).

A close reading of the *Winship* decision yields the conclusion that the reasonable doubt standard is constitutionally required only in an adjudicatory hearing to determine *delinquency,* and "delinquency" is particularly limited to conduct that would be criminal if committed by an adult. In light of this conclusion, it is interesting to note the various statutory standards of proof observed by the states, in some cases no doubt in compliance with the *Winship* decision, and in other cases despite it.

Many states, for example, observe a literal application of the *Winship* mandate, and require proof beyond a reasonable doubt only in delinquency cases. *See, e.g.*, Cal. Welf. & Inst'ns Code § 701 (1972) (proof beyond reasonable doubt required in cases under § 602, which deals only with conduct in violation of law); Ill. Ann. Stat. ch. 37, § 704-6 (1972) (proof beyond reasonable doubt required in cases under § 702-2, which deals only with conduct in violation of law); La. Rev. Stat. Ann. § 13:1579.1 (Supp. 1974); Md. Ann. Code, Cts. & Jud. Proc. § 3-830(a) (1974); Tenn. Code Ann. § 37-229(b) (Supp. 1973). Generally, these states also provide that in other cases, *i.e.*, need of supervision and neglect or dependency cases, the standard of proof is either clear and convincing evidence, *see* Tenn. Code

Ann. § 37-229(c) (Supp. 1973), or a preponderance of the evidence, see Cal. Welf. & Inst'ns Code § 701 (1972) (refers to § 600 and § 601 cases, which deal with deprivation and incorrigibility); Ill. Ann. Stat. ch. 37, § 704-6 (1972) (refers to §§ 702-3, 702-4, and 702-5, which describe persons in need of supervision, neglected children, and dependent children, respectively); Md. Ann. Code, Cts. & Jud. Proc. § 3-830(c) (1974).

Several states, however, provide that proof beyond a reasonable doubt is the standard of proof in both delinquency cases *and* need of supervision (or incorrigibility) cases. *See, e.g.*, Ga. Code Ann. § 24A-2201(b) (Supp. 1973); N.M. Stat. Ann. § 13-14-28 (E) (Supp. 1973); N.D. Cent. Code § 27-20-29(2) (1974); Pa. Stat. Ann. tit. 11, § 50-320 (b)(Supp. 1974),("delinquent act" under § 50-102(2) includes both violations of law and incorrigible behavior); S.D. Compiled Laws Ann. § 26-8-22.9 (Supp. 1973); Tex. Fam. Code Ann. § 54.03(f) (1973); Wyo. Stat. Ann. § 14-115.26 (Supp. 1973). These states normally provide that neglect or deprivation cases are established on the basis of clear and convincing evidence, see Ga. Code Ann. § 24A-2201(c) (Supp. 1973);N.M. Stat. Ann. § 13-14-28(F) (Supp. 1973); N.D. Cent. Code § 27-20-29 (3) (1974); Pa. Stat. Ann. tit 11, § 50-320(c) (Supp. 1974); or a preponderance of the evidence, see S.D. Compiled Laws Ann. § 26-8-22.10 (Supp. 1973); Wyo. Stat. Ann. § 14-115.26 (Supp. 1973).

The states that apply the reasonable doubt standard to ungovernability and in need of supervision cases, as well as delinquency cases, no doubt do so because in many instances the possibility of commitment is available to both delinquent children and children in need of supervision. Not all states take this view, however. In Iowa, for example, "delinquency" includes both children who are alleged to have violated a law and incorrigible children,

Iowa Code Ann. § 232.2(13) (1969), and both kinds of conduct may result in commitment to an institution. Iowa Code Ann. § 232.34 (1969). The Iowa Supreme Court held that in cases in which the allegation of delinquency rests on conduct other than commission of a public offense, the reasonable doubt standard is not required. *In re Henderson*, 199 N.W.2d 111, 121 (Iowa 1972).

In contrast, the New York Court of Appeals, taking a less restricted view of the *Winship* decision, held that the reasonable doubt standard is also applicable in a proceeding to determine whether a child is a person in need of supervision. *Richard S. v. City of New York*, 27 N.Y.2d 802, 264 N.E.2d 353, 315 N.Y.S.2d 861 (1970) (Mem.).

Despite the constitutional requirements contained in the *Winship* decision, a few states retain the old standards of proof, requiring either clear and convincing evidence, *see* Iowa Code Ann. § 232.31 (1969); Ohio Rev. Code Ann. § 2151.35 (1971), or a preponderance of the evidence, *see* N.Y. Fam. Ct. Act § 744(b) (McKinney Supp. 1973); Wis. Stat. Ann. § 48.25(3) (1957), in *all* cases, regardless of the kind of conduct alleged. These provisions are clearly in violation of the due process requirements announced in *Winship*, at least insofar as they allow a lesser standard of proof in delinquency proceedings. The New York court, of course, recognized the constitutional frailty of its own statute in *Richard S. v. City of New York, supra*.

§ 5.05. Rules of Evidence.

Most states make no particular provision regarding which rules of evidence are applicable in juvenile proceedings. Some of the older cases (*i.e.*, pre-*Gault*) took the view that because of the *parens patriae* philosophy of the juvenile court and because of its nonadversary setting, the formal rules of evidence were inapplicable. *See, e.g., In re*

Holmes, 379 Pa. 599, 109 A.2d 523 (1954) (hearsay evidence admissible in juvenile proceeding). Some of the older statutory provisions were to the same effect. A former Louisiana statute provided that all evidence, including hearsay and opinion evidence, was admissible in juvenile hearings. La. Acts 1956, No. 106, § 1. This statute has been replaced by one that provides that the rules of evidence contained in the Code of Civil Procedure are applicable in juvenile hearings. La. Rev. Stat. Ann. § 13:1579.1 (Supp. 1974).

Similarly, a former Mississippi statute provided that juvenile hearings were to be conducted "without regard to the technicalities of other statutory procedures and rules of evidence." Act of February 20, 1946, ch. 207, § 8 [1946] Gen. Laws Miss. 177. This statute also has been replaced by a statute that requires adjudicatory hearings to be conducted "under such rules of evidence as may comply with applicable constitutional standards." Miss. Code Ann. § 43-21-17 (Supp. 1973). Both the Louisiana and Mississippi statutes were changed following the *Gault* decision, which is perhaps indicative of a trend toward acceptance of formal rules of evidence as governing questions of admissibility in juvenile hearings.

Some jurisdictions, however, continue to follow the view that the nature of juvenile hearings does not require strict compliance with the technical rules of evidence. A current Alaska statute, for example, provides that the rules of evidence do not apply in juvenile hearings. Alaska Stat. § 47.10.070 (1971).

Several states express by statute a standard by which questions of evidence are determined in juvenile hearings. The standard varies from jurisdiction to jurisdiction. At least one state provides that evidence, in order to be admissible in a juvenile proceeding, must be such that it would be "legally admissible" in a criminal case. Cal.

Welf. & Inst'ns Code § 701 (1972). Similarly, another state provides that the rules of evidence applicable in criminal cases apply in delinquency proceedings, and the rules of evidence applicable in civil cases apply in neglect, dependency, and need of supervision cases. Ill. Ann. Stat. ch. 37, § 704-6 (1972).

Other states provide that the rules of evidence applicable in the trial of civil or equity cases are applicable in all juvenile proceedings, regardless of the kind of conduct alleged. *See* Fla. Stat. Ann. § 39.09(2) (1961); Hawaii Rev. Stat. § 571-41 (1968); Iowa Code Ann. § 232.31 (1969); La. Rev.Stat. Ann. § 13:1579.1 (Supp. 1974); Mo. Ann. Stat. § 211.171 (6) (1964); Neb. Rev. Stat. § 43-206.03(2) (1968); Tex. Fam. Code Ann. § 54.03(d) (1973); Wis. Stat. Ann. § 48.25(3) (1957).

Still other jurisdictions don't specify whether the rules of evidence applicable in civil or criminal cases will apply in juvenile hearings, but simply require that evidence, in order to be admissible, must be competent, relevant, and material. *See* D.C. Code Ann. § 16-2316(b) (1973); N.M. Stat. Ann. § 13-14-28(E)-(F) (Supp. 1973); N.Y. Fam. Ct. Act § 744(a) (McKinney Supp. 1973); Wyo. Stat. Ann. § 14-115.27 (Supp. 1973).

To be sure, when the courts have been called upon to decide questions of the admissibility of evidence, they occasionally have held that because of the nature of a juvenile proceeding, the usual rules of evidence do not apply. *See, e.g., In re Holmes, supra.* Most courts, however, have determined that the rules of evidence, particularly those relating to admissibility of hearsay, are applicable in juvenile proceedings. *See, e.g., In re Contreras,* 109 Cal. App.2d 787, 241 P.2d 631 (1952); *In re Ross,* 45 Wash.2d 654, 277 P.2d 335 (1954); *see also Garner v. Wood,* 188 Ga. 463, 4 S.E.2d 137 (1939).

§ 5.06. Confrontation and Cross Examination.

In *In re Gault*, the Supreme Court held that "absent a valid confession, a determination of delinquency and an order of commitment to a state institution cannot be sustained in the absence of sworn testimony subjected to the opportunity for cross examination in accordance with our law and constitutional requirements." 387 U.S. at 57. The particular problem in *Gault* to which the Court was addressing itself was the fact that the complaining witness did not appear at the adjudicatory hearing; her version of what had happened was related in the form of hearsay testimony by a police officer.

A number of courts have permitted use of hearsay testimony in juvenile proceedings where the evidence was received under a recognized exception to the hearsay rule, *see, e.g., C.A.J. v. State*, 127 Ga. App. 813, 195 S.E.2d 225 (1973), or where, for one reason or another, admission of the hearsay was harmless error or otherwise not prejudicial to the child. *See, e.g., P.H. v. State*, 504 P.2d 837 (Alaska 1972); *Campbell v. Siegler*, 10 N.J. Misc. 987, 162 A. 154 (1932); *In re Mont*, 175 Pa. Super. 150, 103 A.2d 460 (1954); *Williams v. State*, 219 S.W.2d 509 (Tex. Civ. App. 1949); *In re Bentley*, 246 Wis. 69, 16 N.W.2d 390 (1944).

Moreover, the Supreme Court has pointed out that although the hearsay rule and the rights to confrontation and cross examination spring from the same source, they are not to be equated. *Dutton v. Evans*, 400 U.S. 74, 86 (1970); *see also California v. Green*, 399 U.S. 149, 155-56 (1970). Therefore, simply because an accused does not have an opportunity to cross examine the out-of-court witness does not mean that the testimony is *per se*, for that reason, inadmissible. If the hearsay exception under which the testimony was admitted is buttressed by "salient and cogent reasons," and the accused's rights were not otherwise prejudiced, admission of the evidence is not violative of the right of confrontation and cross examination. *Dutton v. Evans*, 400 U.S. 74, 80, 87-89 (1970).

In numerous other cases, however, in which hearsay evidence was admitted, usually *not* under the authority of any recognized exception, courts have declared that admission of the hearsay into evidence constituted a denial of the rights to confrontation and cross examination. *See, e.g., In re Dennis H.*, 19 Cal. App.3d 350, 96 Cal. Rptr. 791 (1971); *In re Hill*, 78 Cal. App. 23, 247 P. 591 (1926); *In re Sippy*, 97 A.2d 455 (D.C. Mun. Ct. App. 1953); *State ex rel. Palagi v. Freeman*, 81 Mont. 132, 262 P. 168 (1927); *Ballard v. State*, 192 S.W.2d 329 (Tex. Civ. App. 1946); *In re Baum*, 8 Wash. App. 337, 506 P.2d 323 (1973).

Some states by statute have expressly conferred on juveniles the rights to confrontation and cross examination, apparently intending that juveniles are entitled to those rights to the same extent they are enjoyed by adults. *See, e.g.*, Conn. Gen. Stat. Ann. § 17-66b(a) (Supp. 1973); Ill. Ann. Stat. ch. 37, § 701-20(1) (1972); N.M. Stat. Ann. § 13-14-25(J) (Supp. 1973); Tenn. Code Ann. § 37-227(a) (Supp. 1973) (stated in terms of right to cross examination only); Wyo. Stat. Ann. § 14-115.24(b) (Supp. 1973).

In addition to the affront to a child's rights when a witness is not present, an additional problem is presented when the child himself is not present at the hearing at a time when a witness is testifying against him. Some states provide by statute that the child has a right to be present during the conduct of the hearing. *See, e.g.*, Cal. Welf. & Inst'ns Code § 679 (1972). Additionally, some states provide that the presence of the child may be waived, *except* in delinquency proceedings, apparently out of regard for the significance of the rights to confrontation and cross examination in a case in which the child is alleged to have violated a law. *See, e.g.*, Iowa Code Ann. § 232.30 (1969); Minn. Stat. Ann. § 260.155(5) (1971).

In *RLR v. State*, 487 P.2d 27 (Alaska 1971), an initial hearing was held prior to the adjudicatory hearing, for the sole purpose of perpetuating the testimony of an expert witness who apparently was unable to appear at the adjudicatory hearing, and who in fact did not testify there. The juvenile was not present at the initial hearing, and his attorney declined to waive his statutory right to be present. The juvenile court proceeded to hear the testimony in the juvenile's absence. The Alaska Supreme Court, in reversing the adjudication of delinquency, held that a child's right to be present at an adjudicatory hearing is coequal with an adult's right to be present during a criminal trial. Moreover, the court concluded that the juvenile's absence was not harmless error, since the testimony given in his absence was offered to prove an essential element of the state's case, *i.e.*, that the pill allegedly sold by the juvenile contained LSD. 487 P.2d at 42-43.

§ 5.07. Corroboration of Confessions.

Several states provide by statute that a child's out-of-court confession, even if validly made, is insufficient to support the allegations against him, unless the confession is corroborated by other evidence. *See, e.g.*, Ga. Code Ann. § 24A-2002(b) (Supp. 1973); Md. Ann. Code, Cts. & Jud. Proc. § 3-830(a) (1974); N.M. Stat. Ann. § 13-14-25(C)(3) (Supp. 1973); N.Y. Fam. Ct. Act § 744(b) (McKinney Supp. 1973); N.D. Cent. Code § 27-20-27(2) (1974); Pa. Stat. Ann. tit. 11, § 50-318(b) (Supp. 1974);·Tenn. Code Ann. § 37-227 (b) (Supp. 1973); Tex. Fam. Code Ann. § 54.03(e) (1973); Vt. Stat. Ann. tit. 33, § 652 (Supp. 1973).

Of course, if the child acknowledges in court that he committed the acts in question, this constitutes a judicial admission, which may furnish the basis for an adjudication of delinquency. This assumes, however, that he has been advised in the hearing of his right not to incriminate himself, as required by *Gault.* 387 U.S. at 55-57.

A number of states specifically provide that a child enjoys the privilege against self-incrimination in a juvenile hearing. *See, e.g.,* Ga. Code Ann. § 24A-2002(b) (Supp. 1973); La. Rev. Stat. Ann. § 13:1579 (Supp. 1974); N.D. Cent. Code § 27-20-27(2) (1974); Pa. Stat. Ann. tit. 11, § 50-318(b) (Supp. 1974); Tenn. Code Ann. § 37-227(b) (Supp. 1973); Tex. Fam. Code Ann. § 54.03(e) (1973); Vt. Stat. Ann. tit. 33, § 652 (Supp. 1973); Wyo. Stat. Ann. § 14-115.24(a) (Supp. 1973).

Some older, pre-*Gault* cases upheld adjudications of delinquency or incorrigibility based solely on the child's uncorroborated confession. *See, e.g., In re Tillotson,* 225 La. 573, 73 So.2d 466 (1954); *People v. Lewis,* 260 N.Y. 171, 183 N.E. 353 (1932). However, following the serious doubt cast upon the reliability and trustworthiness of children's confessions by the *Gault* decision, *see* 387 U.S. at 52-55, most courts have been reluctant to endorse an adjudication of delinquency resting solely on a child's confession.

In *In re W.J.,* 116 N.J. Super. 462, 282 A.2d 770 (1971), for example, the court held that an adjudication of delinquency based only on a juvenile's extrajudicial confession was invalid. Where a juvenile's confession is used as evidence, the court said, the state's task is to "show that the confession is trustworthy by proof of facts and circumstances *independent of the confession* and that the loss or injury confessed to did in fact occur." 116 N.J. Super. at 470, 282 A.2d at 774 (emphasis added). By "facts and circumstances" the court apparently was referring to proof of the child's identity or connection with the offense. In emphasizing the element of trustworthiness, the court suggested that in light of the ease with which children confess, a greater quantum of corroboration may be required than is ordinarily demanded in the trial of an adult. *See also In re Carlo,* 48 N.J. 224, 245, 225 A.2d 110, 122 (1966), to which the court refers.

Other states, while requiring corroboration of a child's confession, don't require quite the substantial showing demanded in *In re W.J..* In *People v. Cunningham,* 122 Ill. App.2d 222, 258 N.E.2d 145 (1970), for example, the court held that the independent evidence required for corroboration need not *by itself* establish the fact of commission of the crime by the accused; rather, the corroborating evidence may consist only of proof that a crime has been committed and that someone is criminally responsible therefor, which, *when considered with the accused's confession* of guilt, is sufficient to support the adjudication of delinquency.

A related problem is a situation in which the child's delinquency is established solely on the basis of an accomplice's uncorroborated testimony. Treatment of this question has been varied. In *In re Collins,* 20 Ohio App.2d 319, 253 N.E.2d 824 (1969), the court applied to juvenile proceedings the same rule applicable in the trial of criminal cases in the state, *i.e.,* that a conviction may be upheld on the uncorroborated testimony of an accomplice. The court did indicate, however, that such evidence should be scrutinized with care.

Other courts have reached the opposite result. In *In re Arthur M.,* 34 App. Div.2d 761, 310 N.Y.S.2d 399 (1970) (Mem.), for example, the court observed that under the rules of criminal procedure, a conviction cannot be supported on the basis of the uncorroborated testimony of an accomplice; instead, the accomplice testimony must be supported by independent proof connecting the accused to the offense. Therefore, the court reasoned, failure to hold the same rule applicable in juvenile proceedings would be a denial of fair treatment and equal protection.

Accord: In re Lang, 60 Misc.2d 155, 301 N.Y.S.2d 136 (Fam. Ct., Ulster Co. 1969) (required by due process and equal protection). *See also People v. Davis,* 66 Misc.2d 820, 322 N.Y.S.2d 116 (Co. Ct., Dutchess Co. 1971); *State v. Smith,* 1 Ore. App. 583, 465 P.2d 247 (1970).

For the most part, the change in attitude by the courts has resulted from the Supreme Court's decision in *In re Winship,* 397 U.S. 358 (1970). Prior to the *Winship* decision, courts did not feel compelled to require corroboration of a child's confession or an accomplice's confession simply because the standard of proof in a delinquency proceeding was less than that required in a criminal proceeding. *See, e.g., In re Collins,* 20 Ohio App.2d 319, 253 N.E.2d 824 (1969). But, in some cases even prior to *Winship,* courts concluded that corroboration was required. *See, e.g., In re Lang, supra.* Without question, the decision in *Winship* requiring proof beyond a reasonable doubt — at least in delinquency proceedings — has had and will continue to have an impact on courts considering this question. *See, e.g., In re Arthur M., supra.*

§ 5.08. Double Jeopardy.

The fifth amendment states in part that no person shall "be subject for the same offense to be twice put in jeopardy of life or limb . . . ." U.S. Const. Amend. V. This constitutional guarantee against double jeopardy was held applicable to the states in *Benton v. Maryland,* 395 U.S. 784 (1969).

The double jeopardy provision goes beyond protecting the accused from being punished twice; what it prohibits is being placed in jeopardy twice, *i.e.,* being *tried* twice for the same offense. *See, e.g., Price v. Georgia,* 398 U.S. 323 (1970).

In the context of juvenile proceedings, at least two

possibilities can arise wherein the application of the double jeopardy prohibition is called into question. First, a juvenile may be adjudicated a delinquent (or for that matter, acquitted of a charge of delinquency) and subsequently prosecuted in criminal court for the same act. Secondly, a juvenile may be subjected to two successive delinquency petitions in juvenile court, based on the same act.

Traditionally, at least prior to *Gault*, and perhaps more importantly, prior to *Benton v. Maryland*, 395 U.S. 784 (1969), challenges by juveniles of such procedures as violative of the constitutional protection against double jeopardy had met with failure.Courts held that double jeopardy did not prohibit a juvenile's being adjudged a delinquent and subsequently being tried criminally for the same offense, *see, e.g., Moquin v. State*, 216 Md. 524, 140 A.2d 914 (1958); *Dearing v. State*, 204 S.W.2d 983 (Tex. Crim. App. 1947), *overruled by Garza v. State*, 369 S.W.2d 36 (Tex. Crim. App. 1963), and likewise did not prohibit the filing of successive delinquency petitions in the juvenile court, *see, e.g., In re McDonald*, 153 A.2d 651 (D.C. Ct. App. 1959); *State v. Smith*, 75 N.D. 29, 25 N.W.2d 270 (1946).

Aside from the reason that the fifth amendment protection against double jeopardy had not yet been made applicable to the states, the reason traditionally given for denying its application to juvenile proceedings was that a juvenile proceeding was civil in nature, and because of the protective, rehabilitative philosphy of the juvenile court, a juvenile was not deemed to be in jeopardy in such proceedings. *See, e.g., Moquin v. State*, 216 Md. 524, 527-30, 140 A.2d 914, 916-17 (1958).

However, in *Gault* the Supreme Court emphasized that for some purposes a proceeding in which a child faces the risk of incarceration must be regarded as criminal in nature. 387 U.S. at 36, 49. Consequently, since the *Gault* decision, courts have uniformly held that fundamental fairness bars successive hearings in juvenile court based on the same act of delinquency. *See, e.g., Richard M. v. Superior Court,* 4 Cal.3d 370, 482 P.2d 664, 93 Cal. Rptr. 752 (1971); *Fonseca v. Judges of Family Court,* 59 Misc.2d 492, 299 N.Y.S.2d 493 (Sup. Ct., Kings Co. 1969); *Tolliver v. Judges of Family Court,* 59 Misc.2d 104, 298 N.Y.S.2d 237 (Sup. Ct., Bronx Co. 1969); *Collins v. State,* 429 S.W.2d 650 (Tex. Civ. App. 1968).

In like manner a number of courts have held that an adjudication of delinquency in juvenile court bars subsequent criminal prosecution for the same offense. *Faine v. Duff,* 488 F.2d 218 (5th Cir. 1973); *Hultin v. Beto,* 396 F.2d 216 (5th Cir. 1968); *Commonwealth ex rel. Freeman v. Superintendent,* 212 Pa. Super. 422, 242 A.2d 903 (1968). One court had reached this result even prior to *Gault. Sawyer v. Hauck,* 245 F. Supp. 55 (W.D. Tex. 1965).

Nevertheless, in two decisions subsequent to *Gault,* courts have held, in reliance on *McKeiver v. Pennsylvania,* 403 U.S. 528 (1971), that the double jeopardy provision is not applicable to juveniles and a juvenile may be prosecuted criminally for an act that has already been the basis for an adjudication of delinquency. *State v. R.E.F.,* 251 So.2d 672 (Fla. Dist. Ct. App. 1971), *aff'd,* 265 So. 2d 701 (Fla. 1972); *Lewis v. Commonwealth,* 214 Va. 150, 198 S.E.2d 629 (1973). It should be noted, however, that the juvenile in the Florida case subsequently challenged in federal court his indictment following an adjudication of delinquency in juvenile court. The court held that the double jeopardy provision of the fifth amendment, as well as standards of fundamental fairness under the fourteenth amendment, barred his being subjected to criminal prosecution on the basis of an act for which he had already been adjudicated delinquent in juvenile court. *Fain v. Duff,* 488 F.2d 218, 225-27 (5th Cir. 1973).

Currently, a number of states have statutory provisions that are designed to prevent a child from being prosecuted in criminal court for conduct that has already been the subject of juvenile court action. Some provisions state in specific terms that a subsequent criminal prosecution is barred if a petition based on the same facts has been filed in juvenile court, see Utah Code Ann. § 55-10-105(4) (Supp. 1973), or if the juvenile court has started taking evidence in the case, see Ill. Ann. Stat. ch. 37, § 702-7(3)(b) (1972); N.M. Stat. Ann. § 13-14-25(I) (Supp. 1973), or if the juvenile court has already made disposition in a case involving the same matter, see Wis. Stat. Ann. § 48.39 (1957).

Other states indicate in a more general fashion that a child cannot be the subject of a criminal prosectuion, except as provided by law. This would seem to bar altogether a criminal action against the child unless jurisdiction has been waived by the juvenile court, or the juvenile court has no jurisdiction over the particular offense, or the juvenile court and criminal court have concurrent jurisdiction over the offense. See Cal. Welf. & Inst'ns Code § 606 (1972); Ga. Code Ann. § 24A-2501(c) (Supp.1973); Hawaii Rev. Stat. § 571-49 (1968); Ind. Ann. Stat. § 9-3215 (Supp. 1972); Md. Ann. Code, Cts. & Jud. Proc. § 3-809 (1974); Mo. Ann. Stat. § 211.171(2) (Supp. 1974); Mont. Rev. Codes Ann. § 10-611 (Supp. 1973); N.D. Cent. Code § 27-20-34(3) (1974); Ohio Rev. Code Ann. § 2151.26(D) (1971); Okla. Stat. Ann. tit. 10, § 1112(a) (Supp. 1974); R.I. Gen. Laws Ann. § 14-1-40 (1969); Tenn. Code Ann. § 37-234(c) (Supp. 1973); Tex. Fam. Code Ann. § 54.02(g) (1973).

Still other states simply provide, without more, that the adjudication, disposition or evidence in a juvenile proceeding may not thereafter be used as evidence against the child in a criminal proceeding. See Alaska Stat. § 47.10.080(g) (1971); Ark. Stat. Ann. § 45-205 (1964); Colo.

Rev. Stat. Ann. § 22-1-9(2) (Supp. 1967); Del. Code Ann. tit. 10, § 982(c) (1953); Ky. Rev. Stat. Ann. § 208.350 (1972); Mass. Gen. Laws Ann. ch. 119, § 60 (1969); Mich. Compiled Laws Ann. § 712A.23 (1968); Minn. Stat. Ann. § 260-211(1) (1971); Miss. Code Ann. § 43-21-19 (1972); N.J. Stat. Ann. § 2A:4-39 (1952); S.D. Compiled Laws Ann. § 26-8-57 (Supp.1973); Vt. Stat. Ann. tit. 33, § 662 (e) (Supp. 1973). While the latter statutes do not explicity forbid institution of criminal proceedings against a child who has already been subjected to juvenile court action for the same conduct, the argument has been made that the prohibition against use of evidence in a subsequent criminal proceeding achieves the same result. *See* D. Rudstein, *Double Jeopardy in Juvenile Proceedings,* 14 Wm. & Mary L. Rev. 266, 293-94 (1972).

Chapter 6

THE DISPOSITIONAL PROCESS

§ 6.01. The Disposition Hearing.

The most immediate question regarding the dispositional hearing is whether there has to be a hearing at all, or at least a hearing separate from the adjudicatory hearing. The trend seems to be toward a bifurcated hearing process, whereby the adjudicative and dispositional hearings are separate and distinct. *See, e.g.,* Cal. Welf. & Inst'ns Code §§ 701, 702 (1972); D.C. Code Ann. § 16-2317(c) (1973); Ga. Code Ann. § 24A-2201(b)-(c) (Supp. 1973); Ill. Ann. Stat. ch. 37, § 705-1 (1972); Md. Ann. Code,

149

Cts. & Jud. Proc. § 3-829 (1974); N.Y. Fam. Ct. Act § 743 (McKinney 1963), § 746 (McKinney Supp. 1972); N.D. Cent. Code § 27-20-29(2)-(3) (1974).

The principal concern for separating the adjudicatory and dispositional processes arises out of the fact that different evidentiary rules are applicable in the two phases of the court's consideration. As demonstrated in § 6.02, *infra*, virtually any evidence that is material and relevant on the issue of disposition is admissible, because for purposes of making an appropriate disposition, the court needs to know as much about the child as possible. The same is not at all true of the adjudicatory phase, however, since it is comparable to the trial phase of a criminal prosecution. In the adjudicatory hearing, rules of evidence generally prevail. (*See* § 5.05, *supra*.)

Where a bifurcated hearing process is authorized, it is important that the court observe a strict separation of the two hearings. In *In re Gladys R.*, 1 Cal.3d 855, 464 P.2d 127, 83 Cal. Rptr. 671 (1970), the juvenile court judge acknowledged that he had thoroughly studied the child's social report during the adjudicatory stage of the proceedings. The California Supreme Court held that this constituted reversible error. The court found that the clear legislative intent in creating a bifurcated hearing process was to provide a safeguard against inadmissible evidence being considered on the issue of whether the child committed the alleged offense. This basic purpose was thwarted when the juvenile court judge reviewed the child's social report, since his action went squarely to the fairness of the hearing.

In jurisdictions in which a dispositional hearing is required, whether heard separately from or contiguously with the adjudicatory hearing, courts have held that the child has a right to a dispositional hearing. In *In re J.L.P.*, 25 Cal. App.3d 86, 100 Cal. Rptr. 601 (1972), the court held that it was error for the juvenile court judge to refuse to hear evidence on disposition and to commit the minor to the California Youth Authority without conducting a dispositional hearing. The court held that following adjudication, the dispositional phase must be conducted and all relevant evidence heard. Under California law, commitment may not be based on the gravity of the offense alone, but rather, if ordered at all, must be based on a finding that (1) the parents are unable to control the child, (2) prior probation has failed, or (3) the welfare of the child requires his removal from parental custody.

Similarly, in a series of Maryland cases the court held that where commitment to a training school was ordered without conducting a dispositional hearing, reversible error was committed. The mere finding of delinquency does not require commitment or separation from parents; instead, commitment should be ordered only where necessary for the safety of the public or where the child is beyond the control of his parents. To make the latter determination, the judge must conduct a separate hearing, following adjudication, for the purpose of hearing evidence relevant to appropriate disposition in each case. In re Roberts, 13 Md. App. 644, 284 A.2d 621 (1971); In re Wooten, 13 Md. App. 521, 284 A.2d 32 (1971); see also In re Arnold, 12 Md. App. 384, 278 A.2d 658 (1971); In re Hamill, 10 Md. App. 586, 271 A.2d 762 (1970).

On the other hand, if the statutes fail to provide for a separate dispositional hearing or are unclear on the point, courts are usually disinclined to require a separate dispositional phase. In AS v. Murphy, 487 S.W.2d 589 (Mo. 1972), the court held that if the child is found to be within the jurisdiction of the juvenile court and is adjudicated delinquent or in need of supervision, the court may proceed immediately to make a disposition in the case as warranted by statute. To the same effect is Johnson v.

People, 170 Colo. 137, 459 P.2d 579 (1969). Although statutes provided for a dispositional hearing and authorized the juvenile court to make a "proper disposition best serving the interests of the child and the public," the court held that under Colorado's statutory scheme, the juvenile court may hold a separate hearing on disposition or may conduct the dispositional phase coextensively with the adjudicatory phase. In this particular case, involving issues of child neglect, ample evidence was presented at the adjudicatory hearing to support the court's order of disposition. This approach, however, would appear to thwart the purpose of having a bifurcated hearing process in the first instance.

§ 6.02. Procedures in the Disposition Hearing.

The Supreme Court in *Gault* specifically refrained from commenting on the applicability of due process requirements to the dispositional phase of juvenile proceedings. 387 U.S. at 13, 31n.48. Likewise, the Court in *Winship* declined to address itself to the requirements to be observed during the dispositional stage of the proceedings. To determine the procedures to be followed, one has to turn to the statutes and the decisions of lower courts.

First of all, to the extent a separate dispositional hearing is conducted, the procedures attending the hearing are quite different from those required during the adjudicatory phase. The adjudicatory hearing is essentially a fact-finding hearing at which the court determines whether the child did or did not commit the alleged delinquent act, is or is not in need of supervision, is or is not a dependent child, etc. Such a hearing, comparable to the fact-finding phase of an ordinary trial must be conducted in accordance with certain recognized safeguards and procedures. (*See* Chapter 5, *supra.*) The dispositional hearing, however, is concerned only with correctional considerations of what is best for the child, or what disposition in the case seems most suited to the child's individual needs.

To render a weighted judgment on this question, the court must have at its disposal all possible information on the child's background, family, environment, education, health, etc. Any evidence that is relevant to the issue of the child's welfare and need of treatment is generally admissible for this purpose, without regard to whether it would be competent evidence at the adjudicatory stage of the proceedings. Many states specifically provide by statute that the usual rules of evidence do not apply at the dispositional stage of the proceedings. *See, e.g.,* D.C. Code Ann. § 16-2316(b) (1973); Ga. Code Ann. § 24A-2201(d) (Supp. 1973); Ill. Ann. Stat. ch. 37, § 705-1(1) (1972); N.M. Stat. Ann. § 13-14-28(G) (Supp. 1973); N.Y. Fam. Ct. Act § 745(a) (McKinney 1963); N.D. Cent. Code § 27-20-29(4) (1974); Pa. Stat. Ann. tit. 11, § 50-320(d) (Supp. 1974); Tenn. Code Ann. § 37-229(d) (Supp. 1973).

In addition, juveniles are not entitled to a jury trial at the dispositional stage of the proceedings. *See, e.g., Alford v. Carter,* 504 P.2d 436 (Okla. Crim. App. 1972). As pointed out earlier (*see* § 5.03, *supra*), *McKeiver v. Pennsylvania,* 403 U.S. 528 (1971), held that states are not compelled by constitutional due process to provide a jury trial at the *adjudicatory* hearing. Nevertheless, some states, including Oklahoma, have provided for a right to trial by jury at the adjudicatory hearing. Okla. Stat. Ann. tit. 10, § 1110 (Supp. 1974). The Oklahoma Court of Criminal Appeals, however, concluded that the statute giving juveniles a right to trial by jury at the adjudicatory stage did not by its terms include a right to trial by jury during the dispositional hearing.

Although the enumeration of rights in *Gault* was specifically limited to the adjudicatory stage, 387 U.S. at

13, a juvenile may very well have a right to be represented by counsel at the dispositional hearing, if a separate hearing is held on the question of disposition. The child certainly has a right to counsel at a dispositional hearing, if one is held, in those states that by statute accord a right to representation by counsel at "all stages of the proceedings." (*See* statutes cited in § 5.02, *supra*.)

Regardless of how the statutory right to counsel is worded, or whether the right is granted by statute at all, the child may be entitled to representation by counsel as a matter of due process. In *In re Robert F.*, 30 App. Div.2d 933, 293 N.Y.S.2d 873 (1968) (Mem.), the court said: "The need for legal representation is just as fundamental and essential at a dispositional hearing as at a fact-finding hearing." The case concerned a child who was alleged to be a person in need of supervision, based on his truancy from school. Some two months elapsed between the fact-finding hearing and the dispositional hearing, and the child's court-appointed attorney was not notified of the dispositional hearing, nor was he present at the hearing. On these facts, the court held that the child was entitled to representation by counsel at the dispositional hearing and could not by himself waive the right to have counsel present.

§ 6.03. Available Dispositions: Delinquent Children.

Delinquent conduct always includes, and more often than not is limited to, violations of law, *i.e.*, conduct that if committed by an adult would be criminal. For this reason, the disposition that may be ordered in a delinquency case normally includes commitment to an institution for juveniles. There are other available dispositions, albeit less severe ones. With some variation, most states follow the dispositional scheme outlined by the Uniform Juvenile Court Act:

> "If the child is found to be a delinquent child the court may make any of the following orders of disposition best suited to his treatment, rehabilitation, and welfare:
>
> "(1) any order authorized by section 30 for the disposition of a deprived child;
>
> "(2) placing the child on probation under the supervision of the probation officer of the court or the court of another state as provided in section 41, or [the Child Welfare Department operating within the county,] under conditions and limitations the court prescribes;
>
> "(3) placing the child in an institution, camp, or other facility for delinquent children operated under the direction of the court [or other local public authority;] or
>
> "(4) committing the child to [designate the state department to which commitments of delinquent children are made or, if there is no department, the appropriate state institution for delinquent children]." Uniform Juvenile Court Act § 31 (1968).

The reference to other dispositions available under § 30, which deals with disposition of deprived children, includes permitting the child to remain with his parents subject to the court's supervision, and temporarily transferring custody of the child to another person or agency. Section 30 is set out in full in Appendix A, *infra*.

Occasionally, states will permit an additional alternative, namely, commitment to the state's department of corrections, or the equivalent agency responsible for treatment of adult offenders. *See, e.g.*, Ga. Code Ann. § 24A-2304 (Supp. 1973); Ill. Ann. Stat. § 705-10 (1972). The Georgia provision is particularly puzzling, since Georgia has adopted, with some modification, the Uniform Juvenile Court Act, which provides in pertinent part: "A child shall not be committed or transferred to a penal institution or other facility used primarily for the execution of sentences of persons convicted of crime." Uniform Juvenile Court Act § 33(a) (1968). The Georgia Code contains an identical provision. Ga. Code Ann. § 24A-2401(a) (Supp. 1973). The provision permitting commitment of a child to the department of corrections seems to be directly in conflict with the provision prohibiting incarceration of a child in an institution primarily designed for treatment of adult criminals.

The Georgia courts, however, have held that the two statutes can be read consistently with one another. In *A.B.W. v. State*, 129 Ga. App. 346, 199 S.E.2d 636 (1973), the Georgia Court of Appeals summarily held that the two sections were not in conflict, but omitted explanation of the basis for the decision. This decision was subsequently affirmed by the Georgia Supreme Court, which ruled that the two statutes are consistent provided that the department of corrections has an available program *not* primarily designed for treatment of adults, into which the child can be placed. *A.B.W. v. State*, 231 Ga. 699, 203 S.E.2d 512 (1974).

While at one extreme, commitment to an adult correctional agency may indicate a complete abandonment of the rehabilitative ideal, still there are some imaginative efforts being made to explore alternative measures for treatment of delinquent children, particularly alternatives to institutionalization of any kind. One such effort is concerned with community-based programs in which the juveniles spend half their time working at the center or elsewhere and the other half of their time participating in group therapy sessions designed to focus on each child's problem and to direct the resources of the group toward dealing with those problems. The juveniles spend nights and weekends at home. These programs have met with a great deal of success, particularly in terms of reduced recidivism. For a full discussion and evaluation of these community-based programs, see H. Weeks, *Youthful Offenders at Highfields: An Evaluation of the Effects of the Short-Term Treatment of Delinquent Boys* (1958); L. Empey, and J. Rabow, *The Provo Experiment In Delinquency Rehabilitation,* 26 Am. Soc. Rev. 679 (1961); S. Pilnick, A. Elias, and N. Clapp, *The Essexfields Concept: A New Approach to the Social Treatment of Juvenile Delinquents,* 2 J. Applied Behav. Sci. 109 (1966); F. Scarpitti, and R. Stephenson, *The Use of the Small Group in the Rehabilitation of Delinquents,* 30 Fed. Prob., Sept. 1966, at 45.

In addition to the community-based group therapy programs, one of the most imaginative treatment programs is California's Community Treatment Project. This project is designed to provide differential treatment based on each particular child's needs. A child's needs are determined according to his classification based on his maturity, his self-perception, his perception of others, and his means of satisfying his needs. Thus, for one child, a severe reprimand might suffice as the only necessary form of rehabilitation. For another, a traditional form of institutionalization might be required. Another child might be responsive to a group therapy program. In any event, the program points out that responses to juvenile problems must be flexible and varied, rather than uniform. Children are different, and each child, because of his particular make-up, will be more responsive to a particular kind of treatment than any other. The program is designed to identify just that particular kind of treatment to which an individual child will respond. For an explanation and evaluation of the program, see M. Warren, *The Community Treatment Project: History and Prospects,* in *Law*

Enforcement Science and Technology 191 (S. Yefsky ed. 1967).

Other programs have explored the use of "halfway houses" in the treatment of juvenile delinquents. *See, e.g.,* the program described in P. Keve, *Imaginative Programming in Probation and Parole* (1967). Still others have attempted to treat the family as a whole rather than focusing only on the juvenile, since many juvenile problems are family-related. *See, e.g.,* the programs described in The President's Commission on Law Enforcement and the Administration of Justice, *Task Force Report: Corrections* 30-31 (1967).

§ 6.04 Available Dispositions: Children in Need of Supervision.

Following the statutory scheme of dispositions contained in the Uniform Juvenile Court Act, the Act provides as follows with respect to disposition of "unruly" children:

> "If the child is found to be unruly the court may make any disposition authorized for a delinquent child except commitment to [the state department or state institution to which commitment of delinquent children may be made]. [If after making the disposition the court finds upon a further hearing that the child is not amenable to treatment or rehabilitation under the disposition made it may make a disposition otherwise authorized by section 31.]" Uniform Juvenile Court Act § 32 (1968).

The Act thus prohibits committing an unruly child to a juvenile institution, although such commitment is authorized under § 32 if the court finds, pursuant to a new hearing, that the child has not responded to rehabilitative treatment under a disposition earlier ordered.

Some states permit commitment of an unruly child to a juvenile institution, just as in the case of a delinquent child, although in some instances courts have held that children in need of supervision must be kept separate from delinquent children. *See, e.g., Martarella v. Kelley,* 349 F. Supp. 575 (S.D.N.Y. 1972).

The provisions vary. Some statutes provide that "delinquent" children may be committed to an institution. Since they provide elsewhere that "delinquency" includes conduct in violation of law as well as conduct that ordinarily would be termed "incorrigible" or "unruly", these statutes authorize commitment of a child in need of supervision. *See, e.g.,* Iowa Code Ann. § 232.2(13) (1969), § 232.34 (Supp. 1973); Miss. Code Ann. §§ 43-21-5(g), 43-21-19 (1972). Other jurisdictions permit commitment of children in need of supervision in a more direct way, with little or no qualification. *See, e.g.,* Ga. Code Ann. § 24A-2303 (Supp. 1973) (requires only a finding that the child is not amenable to treatment or rehabilitation); Ill. Ann. Stat. ch. 37, § 705-2(b)(1) (1972).

In contrast, some statutes specifically prohibit commitment of children in need of supervision to a juvenile institution. *See, e.g.,* Md. Ann. Code, Cts. & Jud. Proc. § 3-832(a),(c) (1974). Moreover, courts occasionally have limited the commitment powers of juvenile courts. In *In re E.M.D.,* 490 P.2d 658 (Alaska 1971), for example, the court held that even though the statute authorized commitment of a child in need of supervision to the department of health and welfare, the statute contemplated that only delinquent children, *i.e.,* children accused of violations of law, would be committed to institutions; therefore, under the particular Alaska statutory scheme, commitment of a child in need of supervision is not authorized.

Other jurisdictions authorize commitment of a child in need of supervision only as a last resort, after other attempts at rehabilitation have been attempted and have failed. In New York, the courts have held that a child in need of supervision cannot be committed to an institution for treatment of juveniles until all other avenues for placement have been exhausted or earlier attempts at rehabilitation have resulted in failure. *See In re Jeanette M.*, 40 App. Div.2d 977, 338 N.Y.S.2d 177 (1972); *In re Stanley M.*, 39 App. Div.2d 746, 332 N.Y.S.2d 125 (1972); *In re Ellery C.*, 40 App. Div.2d 862, 337 N.Y.S.2d 936 (1972).

Georgia authorizes commitment of an unruly child to the state department of corrections (adult corrections) in certain instances. Ga. Code Ann. § 24A-2304 (Supp. 1973). This statute was discussed in § 6.03, *supra*. This statute is rather unusual, since it represents an aberration from the usual dispositions available in such a case. In contrast, Maryland law expressly provides what most states implicitly follow in practice, *i.e.*, that no child may be committed to a penal institution. Md. Ann. Code, Cts. & Jud. Proc. § 3-832(b) (1974).

§ 6.05. Available Dispositions: Abandoned and Neglected Children.

The Uniform Juvenile Court Act provides as follows for disposition in the case of a deprived child:

"(a) If the child is found to be a deprived child the court may make any of the following orders of disposition best suited to the protection and physical, mental, and moral welfare of the child:
"(1) permit the child to remain with his parents, guardian, or other custodian, subject to

conditions and limitations as the court prescribes, including supervision as directed by
the court for the protection of the child;
"(2) subject to conditions and limitations as
the court prescribes transfer temporary legal
custody to any of the following:
"(i) any individual who, after study by the
probation officer or other person or agency
designated by the court to be qualified to
receive and care for the child;
"(ii) an agency or other private organization licensed or otherwise authorized by
law to receive and provide care for the
child; or
"(iii) the Child Welfare Department of the
[county] [state,] [or other public agency authorized by law to receive and provide care
for the child;]
"(iv) an individual in another state with or
without supervision by an appropriate officer under section 40; or
"(3) without making any of the foregoing orders transfer custody of the child to the
juvenile court of another state if authorized
by and in accordance with section 39 if the
child is or is about to become a resident of that
state.
"(b) Unless a child found to be a deprived child
is found also to be delinquent he shall not be
committed to or confined in an institution or
other facility designed or operated for the benefit of delinquent children." Uniform Juvenile
Court Act § 30 (1968).

Moreover, the Act also provides for termination of
parental rights in a case where removal of custody of the
child seems warranted:

"(a) The court by order may terminate the parental rights of a parent with respect to his child if:

> "(1) the parent has abandoned the child;
>
> "(2) the child is a deprived child and the court finds that the conditions and causes of the deprivation are likely to continue or will not be remedied and that by reason thereof the child is suffering or will probably suffer serious physical, mental, moral, or emotional harm; or
>
> "(3) the written consent of the parent acknowledged before the court has been given.
>
> "(b) If the court does not make an order of termination of parental rights it may grant an order under section 30 if the court finds from clear and convincing evidence that the child is a deprived child." *Id.* § 47.

Most jurisdictions follow a similar scheme providing for the same kinds of dispositions, *i.e.*, permitting the child to remain with the parents under the supervision of the court, temporary withdrawal of custody from the parents and placement in a foster home or with a public or private agency, or, where necessary, termination of parental rights and placement of the child in a foster home or with an adoption agency. Occasionally, some states may elaborate on the conditions under which a child is allowed to remain in the custody of his parents under the court's supervision. For example, California requires the parents to undergo therapy if the child is left in their custody. Cal. Welf. & Inst'ns Code § 727 (1972). Commitment of a neglected or abandoned child to a juvenile institution is generally not authorized unless, as the Uniform Act points out, the petition also alleges delinquent conduct. *See, e.g.,* Md. Ann. Code, Cts. & Jud. Proc. § 3-832(c) (1974); Pa. Stat. Ann. tit. 11, § 50-321(b) (Supp. 1974).

One of the major questions arising over disposition of a neglected or deprived child is the standard to be applied in reaching a determination that the child is a neglected child. Judge Thomas Gill offered the following standard in 1960, quoting in part from *People ex rel. Wallace v. Labrenz*, 411 Ill. 618, 624, 104 N.E.2d 769, 773 (1952):

> " 'Neglect, however, is the failure to exercise the care that the circumstances justly demand. It embraces willful as well as unintentional disregard of duty. It is not a term of fixed and measured meaning. It takes its context always from specific circumstances and its meaning varies as the context of surrounding circumstances changes.'
>
> "It is evident that this decision is indebted to the law of negligence for its governing principle, and appropriately and happily so." T. Gill, *The Legal Nature of Neglect*, 6 N.P.P.A.J. 1, 6 (1960).

However, Dean Monrad Paulsen sharply disagrees with this formulation and offers a different standard:

> "The meaning of the standard is given by community minimums in regard to family conduct. In the writer's view, Judge Gill of Connecticut is quite wrong when he draws a parallel between negligence and neglect. Nothing could be further from the truth than to assert that 'neglect' is measured by the 'reasonably prudent parent.' A reasonably prudent parent would hardly refuse to correct a cleft palate if resources were available. Such a prudent parent would not frequent taverns or train his child in a strange and obscure religious belief. The 'reasonably prudent parent' is defined by a kind of community average. In contrast, the parent who 'neglects' falls below the very minimum of acceptable parental behavior. Furthermore, 'negligence' im-

> plies inadvertence. It refers to harm done
> though *not foreseen* — obviously an idea not
> approximate to the problem of deficiency in car-
> ing for children. In practice, the meaning of the
> neglect standard varies according to the prob-
> lem, the relationship of the custodian to the
> child, and the disposition that is sought in the
> case. The last factor is important to note. In neg-
> lect cases, the petitioners almost always have a
> specific objective in relation to disposition.
> Temporary custody and termination of parental
> rights are the most common aims. Not surpris-
> ingly the meaning of 'neglect' turns on the goal
> of the proceeding." M. Paulsen, *The Delin-
> quency, Neglect, & Dependency Jurisdiction of the
> Juvenile Court,* in *Justice for the Child* 44, 74 (M.
> Rosenheim ed. 1962).

By his comments, Dean Paulsen indicates that the applicable "neglect" standard falls considerably below the standard of conduct required of ordinary persons in the "negligence" formulation. Simply because the conduct of parents might not measure up to the conduct of reasonably prudent parents would *not*, in Dean Paulsen's estimation, warrant a juvenile court in terminating the parents' rights of custody of the child. Something evidencing a more severe failing on the part of parents is required in order to justify intervention of the state into the parent-child relationship. This, after all, is the very essence of the concept of *parens patriae.*

Although delinquent conduct, and all its attendant constitutional problems, draws the most concern and comment, the area of dependency and neglect is one of the areas of greatest difficulty and frustration in the spectrum of children's problems. Particularly where a child has been removed from parental custody or is otherwise without parents (caused by intentional abandonment or death of parents), and has thus become the responsibility of the court, the juvenile court often encounters severe problems in determining what to do with the child. Often the court simply lacks the available resources to make an adequate disposition of the child, or where a potential disposition exists, the child often becomes a victim of an immense bureaucratic system, shuffled from one agency to another, never quite within reach of a final disposition.

The latter problem typically results from the fact that, especially in the urban areas, the number of children needing placement is far greater than the number of willing recipients. For an expression of the kind of anguish and exasperation that an inability to act can produce, *see In re Bonez*, 48 Misc.2d 900, 266 N.Y.S.2d 756 (Fam. Ct., New York Co. 1966), and its follow-up case, *In re Bess P.*, 52 Misc.2d 528, 276 N.Y.S.2d 257 (Fam. Ct., New York Co. 1966).

§ **6.06. Duration of Commitment.**

When the decision is finally made to commit a child to an institution, what is the permissible duration of the commitment? The Uniform Juvenile Court Act places a maximum limit of two years on the duration of a commitment order and allows an extension of the order if a new hearing is held to determine whether further commitment of the child is required. Uniform Juvenile Court Act § 36(b).

Jurisdictions that have adopted the Uniform Juvenile Court Act have identical provisions. Ga. Code Ann. § 24A-2701(b) (Supp. 1973); N.D. Cent. Code § 27-20-36(2) (1974); *see also* Conn. Gen. Stat. Ann. § 17-69(a)-(b) (Supp. 1973) (this permits indeterminate sentencing, but at least the maximum initial period of commitment is two years).

In some jurisdictions a child may be committed to an institution for the remainder of his majority, which usually means until he becomes twenty-one years of age. *See, e.g.*, La. Rev. Stat. Ann. §§ 13:1572, 13:1580 (1968); Mass. Gen. Laws Ann. ch. 119, § 58 (Supp. 1973); Miss. Code Ann. § 43-21-19 (1972); Tenn. Code Ann. §§ 37-203(c), 37-237 (Supp. 1973); Va. Code Ann. § 16.1-180 (1960). This indeterminate sentencing often means that a child may be committed for a longer period than possible in the case of his adult counterpart charged with committing the same offense. This raises a potential question of equal protection.

In *Abernathy v. United States*, 418 F.2d 288 (5th Cir. 1969), the minor was sentenced to a six-year term under the provisions of the Federal Youth Corrections Act, but complained that under the provisions of the Dyer Act (under which he was convicted of interstate transportation of a stolen vehicle) he would have received a maximum of five years had he been an adult. The court dismissed his argument on the basis that the Youth Corrections Act is rehabilitative in nature and scope; thus, the longer period of confinement was warranted as being consonant with the needs of the minor for rehabilitative treatment.

Similarly, a number of state courts have concluded that committing juveniles to institutions for longer periods than would be permissible in the case of adults charged with the same offense violates neither due process nor equal protection of the law for three basic reasons: the juvenile court system is protective and not punitive in nature; under juvenile court philosophy and practice, a juvenile is not committed to an institution for purposes of punishment but rather for rehabilitative purposes; a longer commitment might be required to achieve the latter purpose. *See, e.g., In re Blakes*, 4 Ill. App.3d 567, 281 N.E.2d 454 (1972); *In re Tyler*, 262 So.2d 815 (La. App.

1972); *In re K.V.N.*, 112 N.J. Super. 544, 271 A.2d 921 (1970); *Smith v. State*, 444 S.W.2d 941 (Tex. Civ. App. 1969).

It was reliance on the rehabilitative purposes of the juvenile court, however, that prompted most courts, prior to the *Gault* decision, to deny application of constitutional safeguards to the juvenile process. As a basis for depriving constitutional rights, this justification was thoroughly discredited in *Kent*, 383 U.S. at 555-56, and in *Gault*, 387 U.S. at 15-21. Even in *McKeiver v. Pennsylvania*, the Court acknowledged that the rehabilitative processes of the juvenile court had largely failed. 403 U.S. at 543-44 and accompanying notes.

Moreover, in light of the number of successful claims being brought in favor of a right to treatment for juveniles (see discussion in § 6.07, *infra*), the evidence continues to mount that reliance on the juvenile process as rehabilitative rather than punitive in nature has paid more heed to rhetoric than to reality.

Not all courts have swept aside differential treatment on the basis of the tenuous distinction between punishment and treatment, however. In *In re Wilson*, 438 Pa. 425, 264 A.2d 614 (1970), the court was not persuaded that there was a rational basis sufficient to warrant differential sentencing according to age. The court acknowledged that longer commitment *might* be authorized in some cases if (1) the juvenile has notice at the outset of all factors upon which the court might base an adjudication of delinquency; (2) the conclusions on which a delinquency adjudication is based, plus all facts supporting the conclusions, are set forth in the court's order; and (3) it appears that the longer commitment will insure rehabilitative treatment and not just deprivation of liberty. If any one of these factors is absent, the court held, there is no constitutionally valid distinction between juvenile and adult offenders to warrant subjecting one class to a longer maximum commitment for the same offense. 438 Pa. at 431-32, 264 A.2d at 617-18.

§ 6.07. Post Disposition: Right to Treatment.

If indeterminate commitment and a relaxation of constitutional safeguards are justified in the case of juveniles on the notion that the juvenile court system affords regenerative treatment rather than punishment, how is this argument affected by knowledge that in fact the child may not be receiving the rehabilitative treatment to which he is entitled? Judge Orman Ketcham has asserted the existence of a right to treatment based on what he described as a "mutual compact theory of *parens patriae*." Under Judge Ketcham's theory the state is bound by compact to rehabilitate the delinquent child, based on the premise that the child has bargained away some of his constitutional rights in consideration of the state's promise of rehabilitative treatment. Unless the state satisfactorily performs its obligation under the compact, the juvenile and his parents should have the right to consider the agreement broken and insist upon restoration of the child's full constitutional rights. *See* O. Ketcham, *The Unfulfilled Promise of the American Juvenile Court* in *Justice for the Child* 22, 25-26 (M. Rosenheim ed. 1962).

Along these same lines, in *Creek v. Stone*, 379 F.2d 106, 109 (D.C. Cir. 1967), the court said:

> ". . . Juvenile Court legislation rests, in various aspects, on the premise that the state is acting as parens patriae, that it is undertaking in effect to provide for the child the kind of environment he should have been receiving at

home, and that it is because of this that the
appropriate officials . . . are permitted to take
and retain custody of the child without affording
him all the various procedural rights available to
adults suspected of crime."

From this, it might be argued that by failing to
provide treatment for a delinquent child, the state forfeits
its right to exercise custody over that child.

This has given rise, in the juvenile context, to
claims of a "right to treatment" for children committed to
juvenile institutions. Antecedents for the existence of a
right to treatment may be traced back to *Rouse v. Cameron*,
373 F.2d 451 (D.C. Cir. 1966), which accorded a "right to
treatment" to patients involuntarily committed to mental
institutions. Even earlier arguments for a right to treatment for mentally ill persons can be found in M.
Birnbaum, *The Right to Treatment*, 46 A.B.A.J. 499 (1960).
In any event, while the right to treatment for mentally ill
persons was arguably based on statutory interpretation in
Rouse v. Cameron, the right to treatment accorded persons
involuntarily committed to mental institutions was placed
on a constitutional footing in *Wyatt v. Stickney*, 325 F.
Supp. 781 (M.D. Ala. 1971).

Judge Frank Johnson's thesis in *Wyatt v. Stickney* is
that since the justification for the involuntary commitment
of mentally ill persons without due process of law (*i.e.*,
without having been convicted of a crime) is that they will
receive treatment, then treatment must be provided in fact
or the involuntary incarceration must be held to be violative of due process of law:

"To deprive any citizen of his or her liberty upon
the altruistic theory that the confinement is for
humane therapeutic reasons and then fail to

provide adequate treatment violates the very
fundamentals of due process." 325 F. Supp. at
785.

Under this analysis, then, the right to treatment is
not a *substantive* right but an alternative that must be
available in the absence of due process safeguards. If
treatment is not afforded, then release must be effected.

In light of these antecedents, it is not surprising that
juveniles have made similar claims of a right to treatment.
In *Martarella v. Kelley*, 349 F. Supp. 575 (S.D.N.Y. 1972),
for example, suit was brought against New York state
officials for injunctive and declaratory relief on behalf of
minors classified as persons in need of supervision. The
minors claimed violations of due process and equal protection under the fourteenth amendment and a violation of
the eighth amendment's prohibition against cruel and
unusual treatment, in that they were detained, without
treatment, in the same facilities with children classified as
juvenile delinquents. The court began by observing that
the concept of treatment in a constitutional sense goes
beyond kindness, requiring instead delivery of therapeutic services, which in turn are evaluated in terms
of sufficiency of numbers of staff, staff training, relations
between staff and children, and staff knowledge of children's problems. Finding grave deficiencies in these
areas, the court found the existence of a general right to
treatment on due process grounds, citing *Wyatt v. Stickney*
for the proposition that to deny liberty for therapeutic
reasons and then to deny the promised treatment constitutes a denial of due process of law. 349 F. Supp at 586-590,
600.

Similarly, other courts have held that children confined in juvenile institutions are entitled to programs designed to afford the rehabilitative treatment promised by

the *parens patriae* ideal. The cases typically share certain salient features: inadequate physical facilities, lack of educational and rehabilitative programs, occasional incarceration with adults, and unregulated use of certain punitive measures, such as corporal punishment, solitary confinement, and punitive use of tranquilizing drugs. *See, e.g., Morales v. Turman*, 364 F. Supp. 166 (E.D. Tex. 1973); *Nelson v. Heyne*, 355 F. Supp. 451 (N.D. Ind. 1972) (supplemental opinion filed February 8, 1973); *Inmates v. Affleck*, 346 F. Supp. 1354 (D.R.I. 1972).

Most of the cases recognizing a right to treatment for juveniles emphasize the state statutes creating a system of juvenile courts, which uniformly point out that the juvenile court exists to provide rehabilitative treatment for youths in trouble and to afford them the same kind of treatment they would receive in the family setting. *See, e.g.*, R.I. Gen. Laws Ann. § 14-1-2 (1970). As the court pointed out in *Inmates v. Affleck*, however, conditions in one of the confinement units were so poor that if parents of the youths had provided the same kind of treatment, the state would have been authorized by law to remove the children from parental custody.

To return to Judge Ketcham's mutual compact theory, where the child is not receiving the treatment to which he is entitled, and his constitutional rights were forgone *solely* on the basis that they were not necessary in light of the ameliorative treatment postulated for children, the child is entitled to have his constitutional rights restored. In the context of constitutional requirements, the courts have recognized a constitutional right to treatment and have required implementation of minimum standards of treatment in some cases, or in the absence of a minimally acceptable program of treatment, have declared that the child is entitled to be released. *See, e.g., Inmates v. Affleck*, 346 F. Supp. 1354 (D.R.I. 1972).

On the right to treatment generally, *see* A. Gough, *The Beyond Control Child and the Right to Treatment: An Exercise in the Synthesis of Paradox,* 16 St. Louis U.L.J. 182 (1971); N. Kittrie, *Can the Right to Treatment Remedy the Ills of the Juvenile Process?,* 57 Geo. L.J. 848 (1969); Note, *A Right to Treatment for Juveniles?,* 1973 Wash. U.L.Q. 157.

§ 6.08. Post Disposition: Transfer to Penal Institution.

Judge Orman Ketcham's "mutual compact theory of *parens patriae*" whereby a juvenile forgoes constitutional rights in exchange for a promise of rehabilitative treatment (*see* § 6.07, *supra*), was put to the test in *In re Rich*, 125 Vt. 373, 216 A.2d 266 (1966). This case involved the constitutionality of the transfer of an adjudged juvenile delinquent to an adult state facility because of disciplinary problems encountered with the juvenile at a state juvenile institution. Holding the transfer to be constitutionally impermissible, the court accepted the thesis that the prior surrender of a constitutional right in a juvenile court proceeding could come only in exchange for a right to "rehabilitative caretaking." The court thus based its analysis on the following principle: "The validity of the whole juvenile system is dependent upon its adherence to its protective, rather than its penal aspects." 125 Vt. at 377, 216 A.2d at 269.

Some courts, however, have not taken this view, but instead have taken the position that transferring a juvenile from a juvenile institution to an adult institution may sometimes be necessary for the good of the child and for the good of the other children in the juvenile institution. If done with one of these purposes or a similar purpose in mind, the transfer is not regarded as constitutionally impermissible.

In *Long v. Langlois*, 93 R.I. 23, 170 A.2d 618 (1961), for example, the court upheld the transfer of a juvenile from a training school to a penal institution, noting that once committed to a training school, "[the juvenile] is on his own and his conduct must to a degree determine where he shall remain. If removal of a boy by reason of his conduct is determined upon as a means of saving him or the rest of the school or both, such determination would appear to be in harmony with the purpose of the juvenile court." 93 R.I. at 28, 170 A.2d at 620. *Accord: Suarez v. Wilkinson*, 133 F. Supp. 38 (M.D. Pa. 1955); *Wilson v. Coughlin*, 259 Iowa 1163, 147 N.W.2d 175 (1966); *Sheehan v. Superintendent*, 254 Mass. 342, 150 N.E. 231 (1926); *In re Darnell*, 173 Ohio St. 335, 182 N.E.2d 321 (1962).

Most of the decisions sustaining transfers from juvenile facilities to adult institutions were decided before the Supreme Court's decision in *In re Gault*, 387 U.S. 1 (1967). One of the factors leading to the Court's decision to accord juveniles certain constitutional rights was its recognition that "in over half the States, there is not even assurance that the juvenile will be kept in separate institutions, apart from adult 'criminals.' In those States juveniles may be placed in or transferred to adult penal institutions after having been found 'delinquent' by a juvenile court." 387 U.S. at 50.

Certainly since the *Gault* decision, and to a great degree prior to that decision, most courts that have examined the question have agreed with the result in *In re Rich, supra*, that transfer of a juvenile to a penal institution is inconsistent with the ameliorative goals of the juvenile process, and such a transfer is not constitutionally valid unless the child has been afforded a trial or hearing at which he was given all the constitutional rights of a criminally accused. *See, e.g., Kautter v. Reid*, 183 F. Supp. 352 (D.D.C. 1960); *United States ex rel. Stinnet v. Hegstrom*, 178

F. Supp. 17 (D. Conn. 1959); *White v. Reid*, 125 F. Supp. 647 (D.D.C. 1954); *State ex rel. Londerholm v. Owens*, 197 Kan. 212, 416 P.2d 259 (1966); *OH v. French*, 504 S.W.2d 269 (Mo. App. 1973); *State v. Fisher*, 17 Ohio App.2d 183, 245 N.E.2d 358 (1969); *State ex rel. McGilton v. Adams*, 143 W. Va. 325, 102 S.E.2d 145 (1958).

Of course, it might have been argued, prior to *Mc-Keiver v. Pennsylvania*, 403 U.S. 528 (1971), that because of the *Gault* decision and the results flowing from it, a child received a hearing at which he was entitled to the whole panoply of constitutional rights available to adults. However, because *McKeiver* denied one of those rights — the right to a jury trial — to juveniles, this argument must fail. It was the absence of the right to a jury trial that persuaded the Vermont Supreme Court in *In re Rich, supra,* of the constitutional invalidity of the transfer of a juvenile to an adult institution.

In parallel situations in which an individual was transferred from one institution to another "functionally distinct" institution, the Supreme Court has held transfer procedures which ignore the fundamental constitutional rights of the transferee are violative of due process and equal protection of the laws. *Baxstrom v. Herold*, 383 U.S. 107 (1966); *see also Specht v. Patterson*, 386 U.S. 605 (1967). In *Baxstrom v. Herold*, after the petitioner had served two years of his two and a half year sentence, he was certified insane and transferred to a mental institution for prisoners. Shortly thereafter, the petitioner was involuntarily ordered to be held in custody at the hospital where he was then being confined, upon expiration of his prison sentence. In finding each phase of this procedure a denial of equal protection of the laws because the petitioner had not been afforded the standard hearing that any other person would have received to determine his mental fitness, the Court emphasized that the petitioner was administratively transferred to a "functionally distinct" institution without the same procedural safeguards that would have been required had he not already been a prisoner.

This same rationale has an obvious application to the juvenile transfer question. For one thing, it furnishes an answer to some justifications given by courts for upholding transfers of juveniles to adult institutions — for example, that the transfer was purely an administrative action, necessary to the management of the institution and the discipline of its inmates, *see, e.g., Shone v. State*, 237 A.2d 412 (Me. 1968), or that the possibility of transfer is implied within the juvenile court's original sentence, by virtue of the statute authorizing transfer, *see, e.g., Sheehan v. Superintendent*, 254 Mass. 342, 150 N.E. 231 (1926); *Long v. Langlois*, 93 R.I. 23, 170 A.2d 618 (1961).

A number of cases, in fact, have involved direct attacks on the *procedures* whereby the transfer decision is made, and in each case great reliance has been placed on *Baxstrom v. Herold* and *Specht v. Patterson*.

In *Shone v. Maine*, 406 F.2d 844, 848 (1st Cir. 1969), for example, the court stated:

> "*Baxstrom* and *Specht* require that substantially the same procedural protection be extended to a juvenile committed to [a juvenile institution] before he can be lawfully transferred to a functionally distinct institution on the basis of a critically new finding of fact."

Other courts have agreed with the court in *Shone v. Maine* that before a juvenile may be transferred to a penal institution, he must be accorded a hearing with all the requisite procedural safeguards to which other persons would be entitled before commitment to the penal institution. *See, e.g., Boone v. Danforth*, 463 S.W.2d 825 (Mo. 1971); *People ex rel. Goldfinger v. Johnson*, 53 Misc.2d 949, 280 N.Y.S.2d 304 (Sup. Ct., Dutchess Co. 1967).

Chapter 7

FUTURE DIRECTION OF THE JUVENILE COURT

The future course of decisions affecting the constitutional rights of juveniles is difficult to chart, to say the least. Perhaps the simplest and most logical approach is briefly to trace the development of the constitutionalization of the juvenile process as it has been revealed in the decisions of the United States Supreme Court. Only in understanding its beginnings can one hope to understand, if not its ending, its future direction.

Courts initially applied traditional — as opposed to constitutional — standards of fundamental fairness and due process in determining the applicability of certain procedural rights to the juvenile process. When the *Gault* case was decided by the Arizona Supreme Court, for example, the court applied these traditional standards of fairness in reaching its determination that juveniles were not entitled to the right to counsel, the privilege against self-incrimination, etc. *Application of Gault*, 99 Ariz. 181, 407 P.2d 760 (1965).

Even in *Kent v. United States*, 383 U.S. 541 (1966), the Supreme Court stated that although it did not hold that a juvenile hearing "must conform with all of the requirements of a criminal trial . . . the hearing must measure up to the essentials of due process and fair treatment." 383

U.S. at 562. The required standards apparently were to be "determined from the requirements of due process and fair treatment, and not by the direct application of the clauses of the Constitution which . . . apply to criminal cases." 383 U.S. at 562, *citing Pee v. United States*, 274 F.2d 556, 559 (D.C. Cir. 1959). This language suggests something less than a new constitutional standard, although subsequent to its decision, *Kent* has been read as stating constitutional requirements. *See United States ex rel. Turner v. Rundle*, 438 F.2d 839, 842 (3d Cir. 1971), and cases cited therein at 842n.11.

Lest *Kent* left any doubt as to the emerging constitutionalism, the Supreme Court in *In re Gault*, 387 U.S. 1 (1967), placed the requisite fairness and due process squarely on the fourteenth amendment, using the specific provisions of the Bill of Rights as a reference point for determining the requirements of due process. In *Gault* the Court reiterated the view it had taken in *Kent* but went on to add that the "essentials of due process and fair treatment" standard was "a requirement which is part of the Due Process Clause of the Fourteenth Amendment." 387 U.S. at 30-31.

It is extremely significant to notice, beginning with the *Gault* decision, the various rationales offered for the reshaping of the juvenile process. Justice Harlan, for example, would have fashioned the fourteenth amendment test along a more fundamental design: "Among the first premises of our constitutional system is the obligation to conduct any proceeding in which an individual may be deprived of liberty or property in a fashion consistent with the 'traditions and conscience of our people'." 387 at 67 (concurring opinion). With this in mind, he said the Court's task was to "measure the requirements of due process by reference both to the problems which confront the State and to the actual character of the procedural system which the State has created." 387 U.S. at 68. The sources for making such a determination are three-fold: "first, the 'settled usages and modes of proceeding' . . .; second, the 'fundamental principles of liberty and justice which lie at the base of all our civil and political institutions' . . .; and third, the character and requirements of the circumstances presented in each situation." 387 U.S. at 68. Based on "fair distillations of relevant judicial history," his test did not use the Bill of Rights provisions as a reference point for determining the essentials of due process, a method of analysis that Justice Black found extremely upsetting. 387 U.S. at 61-64 (Black, J., concurring).

Justice Black felt that the particular rights granted in *Gault* were required by the specific provisions of the Bill of Rights, and he further believed that the only relevance of the fourteenth amendment was that it made the particular provisions of the Bill of Rights mandatory upon the states. To Justice Black, it followed naturally that if a particular right was not a requirement of the Bill of Rights, the Court could not make it so by relying solely on the due process clause of the fourteenth amendment. To do so, he felt, would be to attach some independent significance to the due process clause that was never intended. 387 U.S. at 61, 64.

This fundamental constitutional debate continued in the next case decided by the Court, *In re Winship*, 397 U.S. 358 (1970). Paradoxically, *Winship* represents in a sense a return to Justice Harlan's broader concept of due process, because, as Justice Black correctly pointed out, the requirement of proof beyond a reasonable doubt is not to be found in the Bill of Rights. For that reason Justice Black felt that it was not a right to be made applicable to the states. Therefore, he dissented in *Winship*. 397 U.S. at 377. Justice Black's dissent in *Winship* is a logical, if problematical consequence of his belief expressed in *Gault* that due process means the "law of the land," which in the *Gault* context he translated literally as the Bill of Rights. Thus, he felt that *all* of the provisions of the Bill of Rights should be applicable to the states. According to his view, judges were not free to withhold any of them; by the same token they were not free to add to them, either. *See In re Gault*, 387 U.S. 1, 61, 64 (1967) (Black, J., concurring). However — and herein lies the paradox — had Justice Black's view prevailed it would have produced the anomaly that in parallel proceedings involving violations of the same criminal statute, adults would be entitled to proof beyond a reasonable doubt while juveniles could be adjudicated delinquent on the basis of some lesser standard.

The Court in *Gault* reiterated the position taken earlier in *Kent* that its decision did not require that *all* of the familiar requirements of the criminal process be extended to the juvenile process. 387 U.S. at 30; *see also Kent v. United States*, 383 U.S. 541, 562 (1966). Yet, the decision in *Gault* had a profound effect on the state courts, which systematically extended the requirements of *Gault* far beyond its mandate, particularly in the area of procedural rights during the police investigatory stage of the proceedings. (*See* Chapter 3, *supra*.) Likewise, the tendency was to extend *Winship* beyond its ostensible scope. (*See* § 5.04, *supra*.) While the Court in *Gault* specifically stated that *all* rights of adults in criminal proceedings are not *necessarily* applicable to juvenile proceedings, courts in effect moved rapidly in that direction.

The states overwhelmingly balked, however, when the question of the right to jury trial arose. (*See* § 5.02, *supra*.) They uniformly relied on the limiting language in *Gault* in determining, with few exceptions, that constitutional due process did not require a jury trial in juvenile hearings. The stage was set for a momentous decision by the Supreme Court. The decision came in *McKeiver v. Pennsylvania*, 403 U.S. 528 (1971).

The Court had been confronted earlier with the jury trial issue in *DeBacker v. Brainard,* 396 U.S. 28 (1969), but because the hearing had been held prior to the Court's decision in *Duncan v. Louisiana,* 391 U.S. 145 (1968), which applied the sixth amendment right to jury trial to the states through the fourteenth amendment, the Court did not decide the question. The Court already had declared in *DeStefano v. Woods,* 392 U.S. 631 (1968), that *Duncan* would not receive retroactive application.

The decision in *McKeiver* came as no surprise. Prior to its announcement, the only two members of the Court who could be counted as solidly supporting the right to trial by jury for juveniles were Justices Black and Douglas. Both would have reached the merits in *DeBacker v. Brainard* and would have held that the sixth and fourteenth amendments compel a jury trial in juvenile proceedings in which the delinquent act charged is one that would be criminal if committed by an adult. 396 U.S. at 33-38 (Black and Douglas, J.J., dissenting). Referring to the rights granted juveniles earlier in *Gault,* Justice Black in *Debacker v. Brainard* said: "I can see no basis whatsoever in the language of the Constitution for allowing persons like appellant the benefit of those rights and yet denying them a jury trial, a right which is surely one of the fundamental aspects of criminal justice in the English-speaking world." 396 U.S. at 34.

While the Court had lost Chief Justice Warren and Justices Fortas and Black, critics of expanding constitutionalism in the juvenile court had remained and had been strengthened by the addition of Chief Justice Burger and Justice Blackmun. Chief Justice Burger revealed his feelings in *In re Winship,* 397 U.S. 358, 375-76 (1970) (dissenting opinion), and Justice Blackmun evidenced his leanings by writing the plurality opinion in the *McKeiver* case itself.

Justice Stewart's credentials as an opponent of the expanding role of the Constitution in the juvenile process go back even further. *See* his dissenting opinion in *In re Gault,* 387 U.S. 1, 78-81 (1967). Justice Harlan had given previous indications that he could not be relied upon to support the right to jury trial for juveniles. In *Gault* he voiced strong opposition to any requirement that might "radically alter the character of the juvenile court proceedings." Such requirements, he said, "would contribute materially to the creation in these proceedings of the atmosphere of an ordinary criminal trial, and would, even if they do no more, thereby largely frustrate a central purpose of these specialized courts." 387 U.S. at 75. Elaborating on this in *Winship,* he intimated disfavor with any action that would, *inter alia,* "burden the juvenile courts with a procedural requirement that will make juvenile adjudications significantly more time consuming or rigid." 397 U.S. at 375 (concurring opinion).

By the time the Court decided the jury question, the forces were already deployed and a few skirmishes had taken place. The campaign oratory was over. All that remained was the inevitable counting of the votes.

McKeiver, however, does not represent a departure from but rather an adherence to the same method of analysis the Supreme Court has used in the past. All of the Court's decisions in the juvenile area have been highly informative in terms of giving an observant bystander insights into the Court's emerging doctrine. One need only read the *Gault* and *Winship* decisions, and particularly the concurring opinions of Justices Black and Harlan in *Gault,* and their respective dissenting and concurring opinions in *Winship* (referred to earlier), to get a flavor for the kinds of considerations that go into determination of whether a particular right should be accorded to juveniles. The *McKeiver* decision is no exception to this analytical development, but instead represents a continuation of this trend.

The Court in *McKeiver*, for example, was very concerned about the impact of a jury trial requirement on the informal juvenile proceedings. This concern is identical to that expressed by Justice Harlan in his concurring opinions in *Gault*, 387 U.S. at 75, and in *Winship*, 397 U.S. at 375. In *McKeiver* the Court expressed fear "that the jury trial, if required as a matter of constitutional precept, will remake the juvenile proceeding into a fully adversary process and will put an effective end to what has been the idealistic prospect of an intimate, informal protective proceeding." 403 U.S. at 545.

Also, the Court was concerned that imposing a requirement of jury trials in juvenile proceedings "would bring with it into that system the traditional delay, the formality and the clamor of the adversary system and, possibly, the public trial." 403 U.S. at 550. An integral part of the Court's decision in *Gault* was the Court's belief that according juveniles the rights granted in that decision was *consistent with* the beneficent purposes of juvenile court treatment. 387 U.S. at 21-27. The Court in *McKeiver*, however, felt that granting a right to jury trial would be destructive of those same purposes.

The *McKeiver* case should not be viewed with particular alarm, therefore. It is simply one in a series of cases that have examined the rights of juveniles in light of the requirements imposed by the "essentials of due process and fair treatment." If there is anything at all alarming about the *McKeiver* decision, it is perhaps Justice Blackmun's enigmatic remarks at the close of his opinion:

> "[T]he arguments advanced by the juveniles here are, of course, the identical arguments that underlie the demand for the jury trial for crimi-

nal proceedings. The arguments necessarily equate the juvenile proceedings — or at least the adjudicative phase of it — with the criminal trial. Whether they should be so equated is our issue....

"*If the formalities of the criminal adjudicative process are to be superimposed upon the juvenile court system, there is little need for its separate existence.* Perhaps that ultimate disillusionment will come one day, but for the moment we are disinclined to give impetus to it." 403 U.S. at 550-51 (emphasis added).

This language may be read to have a very ominous portent. However, the *McKeiver* case by itself has not marked the beginning of a return to the pre-*Gault* days. While there are some indications that courts have relied on the rationale in *McKeiver* to deny juveniles protective rights, *see, e.g., State v. R.E.F.*, 251 So.2d 672 (Fla. Dist. Ct. App. 1971); *Lewis v. Commonwealth*, 214 Va. 150, 198 S.E.2d 629 (1973) (denying application of double jeopardy to prohibit juvenile being prosecuted as criminal, subsequent to adjudication of delinquency for same act), there are also indications that courts have ignored the thrust of *McKeiver* and have held that juveniles are entitled to certain rights to which adults would be entitled in the criminal process. *See, e.g., Fain v. Duff*, 488 F.2d 218 (5th Cir. 1973) (prohibits subsequent criminal prosecution of juvenile on basis of same act for which he had already been adjudicated delinquent); *RLR v. State*, 487 P.2d 27 (Alaska 1971) (juveniles have right to jury trial under state constitution).

Perhaps the true import of *McKeiver* is its shock value. The Court in *Gault* had warned: "We do not mean by this to indicate that the hearing to be held must conform with all of the requirements of a criminal trial."

387 U.S. at 30. *McKeiver* was a tangible indication that the Court meant precisely what it said in *Gault*. Its language in *Gault* was not simply an abstention from deciding questions that were not presented; the Court meant to establish a framework whereby each claimed right in turn would have to be subjected to the constitutional standards of due process and fair treatment, and an independent determination made in each case whether those standards demanded application of the right to the juvenile process. In *McKeiver* the Court simply felt that due process of law could be afforded juveniles without requiring a trial by jury.

The foregoing discussion was intended as more than a recitation of recent judicial history. Its purpose was to furnish insights into the approach used by the Supreme Court in the past, as a basis for predicting what the Court might do in the future. While the path of future decisions affecting the juvenile process, particularly those of constitutional dimensions, is not clear, at least some guidelines have emerged.

First, the Supreme Court is now prepared to effectuate the limitation expressed in *Gault, i.e.,* that not all of the procedural requirements of the criminal process are required perforce in the juvenile process. This conclusion is manifested in the *McKeiver* decision.

Secondly, one may refer to Justice Harlan's concurring opinions in *Gault* and *Winship*, plus Justice Blackmun's opinion in *McKeiver*, to establish the framework of a test for determining the applicability of particular rights to the juvenile process.

With regard to the hearing itself, for example, the Court does not appear to favor applicability of any procedure that will be disruptive of the basically informal juvenile process, that will cause unnecessary delay, that will tend to transform it into a fully adversary process, or that will largely frustrate the ameliorative purposes of the juvenile court. On the basis of these considerations, one might predict, with a fair degree of accuracy, the direction in which the Court might move.

The more difficult question, of course, is the Court's uncertain direction in the area of pre and posthearing rights, such as right to bail, right to counsel at a lineup, applicability of the prohibition against double jeopardy, and right to rehabilitative treatment. The Court's recent tendency has been to dilute or diminish some of the rights earlier promulgated in the criminal process as applicable to adults. *See, e.g., Gustafson v. Florida*, 414 U.S. 260 (1973) (expands scope of permissible search incident to traffic arrest); *Kirby v. Illinois*, 406 U.S. 682 (1972) (limits applicability of right to counsel during lineups to those lineups occurring after commencement of adversary criminal process, which likely means postindictment lineups); *Harris v. New York*, 401 U.S. 222 (1971) (statements otherwise inadmissible in violation of *Miranda* are admissible to show prior inconsistency for purpose of impeachment). This tendency, coupled with the Court's recent decision in *McKeiver*, may foretell a predisposition of the Court to retreat from the position it took in *Gault*.

Yet, two factors appear to mitigate the latter conclusion. First, following the Court's decision in *Gault*, there was a tremendous outpouring of decisions by state courts implementing its constitutional mandate, expanding its scope to embrace other rights not included in its mandate, and extending its applicability to other stages of the process. The impact of the *Gault* decision has been profound, and states have relied on it extensively in forming an entirely new and different perspective of the juvenile court and the juvenile process. This new perspective is not going to be altered, nor the force of *Gault* turned around, by the *McKeiver* decision or any other single decision by the Court, short of an outright overruling of *Gault*, which is not likely.

Secondly, the *McKeiver* decision itself has not enjoyed the same kind of impact *Gault* manifested. Had it done so, one might have expected a reversal of the trend prompted by *Gault*. As mentioned earlier in this section, the experience following *McKeiver* has indicated that in some cases courts have relied on it to deny certain rights to juveniles, but other courts have ignored it and have placed continued reliance on *Gault* in guaranteeing to juveniles many of the rights guaranteed to adults in the criminal process.

This leads to the conclusion that *McKeiver* is simply one in a series of cases and represents only one particular right that the Court has found not to be required in the juvenile process. It has no overall significance comparable to *Gault's*; it did not, for example, change the relationship between the child and the state or give rise to a new manner of perceiving the juvenile process or the setting of the juvenile court, as did *Gault*. The process of decision following *McKeiver* is the same as that existing prior to *McKeiver*. The Court will decide each case and the applicability of each right independently and individually; and importantly, it will do so on the basis of the standards enunciated in *Gault*, *i.e.*, whether the particular right is required as a matter of due process of law under the fourteenth amendment to the Constitution.

APPENDIX A

UNIFORM JUVENILE COURT ACT

Drafted by the

NATIONAL CONFERENCE OF COMMISSIONERS ON
UNIFORM STATE LAWS

and by it

APPROVED AND RECOMMENDED FOR ENACTMENT
IN ALL THE STATES

at its

ANNUAL CONFERENCE
MEETING IN ITS SEVENTY-SEVENTH YEAR
PHILADELPHIA, PENNSYLVANIA
JULY 22—AUGUST 1, 1968

WITH
PREFATORY NOTE AND COMMENTS

℞

APPROVED BY THE AMERICAN BAR ASSOCIATION AT ITS
MEETING AT PHILADELPHIA, PENNSYLVANIA, AUGUST 7, 1968

The Committee which acted for the National Conference of Commissioners on Uniform State Laws in preparing the Uniform Juvenile Court Act was as follows:

MAYNARD E. PIRSIG, Law School, University of Minnesota, Minneapolis, Minn. 55455. *Chairman.*

EUGENE A. BURDICK, P.O. Box 757, Williston, N. Dak. 58801.

M. KING HILL, JR., 1700 One Charles Center, Baltimore, Md. 21201.

THOMAS H. NEEDHAM, The Dolphin House, 403 So. Main St., Providence, R. I. 02903.

RICHARD J. RABBITT, 7 No. 7th St., St. Louis, Mo. 63101.

ROBINSON O. EVERETT, P.O. Box 586, Durham, N. C. 27701, *Chairman, Section G.*

Copies of all Uniform and Model Acts and other printed matter issued by the Conference may be obtained from

NATIONAL CONFERENCE OF COMMISSIONERS ON
UNIFORM STATE LAWS
1155 East Sixtieth Street
Chicago, Illinois 60637

UNIFORM JUVENILE COURT ACT
PREFATORY NOTE

The decisions in *Kent v. United States*, 383 U.S. 541, 86 S. Ct. 1045, 16 L. Ed. 84, (1966), and *Application of Gault*, 387 U.S. 1,87 S. Ct. 1428, 18 L. Ed. 2d 527 (1967), have led to a nationwide re-examination by the several states of their respective juvenile court codes.

The *Kent* case held that before a case can be transferred by a juvenile court to another court for criminal prosecution,. a hearing must be held, and counsel for the child must be given a right to examine and an opportunity to refute any information given the judge. It also held that the judge must render a statement of the reasons for the transfer so that his decision might be subject to review. These requirements were held necessary in view of the "critically important" decision that transfer entails. The court stated, ". . . There is no place in our system of law for reaching a result of such tremendous consequences without ceremony—without hearing, without effective assistance of counsel, without a statement of reasons."

The *Gault* case had under review an adjudication of delinquency and commitment to an institution. The court held that the child and his parents are entitled to notice of the specific charges made, and a reasonable opportunity to refute them, to be advised of the right to be represented by counsel, and by appointed counsel if unable to employ one, to have the charges substantiated by witnesses appearing in court and subject to cross-examination, and to be advised that the child need not give evidence against himself. The court expressly excluded consideration of procedures prior and subsequent to the hearing on the petition.

The decision in *Gault* is clearly based on the requirements of the due process clause as applied to juvenile court proceedings. While *Kent* involved the construction of the District of Columbia Juvenile Court Code, the discussion in the opinion is in the context of constitutional requirements.

In both cases the language of the opinions and the implications contained in them go beyond the specific holdings. They indicate that if the departures in juvenile court from criminal procedure are to be justified when delinquent conduct is alleged involving what for an adult would be a criminal act, the juvenile court proceedings and dispositions must be governed in fact by the objectives of treatment and rehabilitation. If the approach is a punitive one, these cases indicate that the procedure must adhere to the constitutional requirements which characterize a criminal proceeding.

The Uniform Juvenile Court Act has been drawn with a view to fully meeting the mandates of these decisions. At the same time, the aim has been to preserve the basic objectives of the juvenile court system and to promote their achievement. In short, the Act provides for judicial intervention when necessary for the care of deprived children and for the treatment and rehabilitation of delinquent and unruly children, but under defined rules of law and through fair and constitutional procedure.

General adoption of this Act will also assure much needed uniformity in the law among the several states. The common underlying pattern of existing juvenile court codes demonstrates the need for such uniformity. The trend in all areas of court procedure is in the direction of uniformity and the major part of a juvenile court code deals with matters of procedure. Moreover, one of the results of *Kent* and *Gault* will be an increase in judicial review of questions of law arising in juvenile court cases. If the codes of the several states are the same, the resulting development of a common body of judicial precedent will greatly benefit the states generally.

With the greatly increased mobility of families among the states, there is need for a simple means of interstate cooperation between the several states in handling of delinquent, unruly, and deprived children. The Council of State Governments prepared, in 1958, an Interstate Compact on Juveniles which has been adopted by substantially all of the states. (*Suggested State Legislation, Program for* 1958, Council of State Governments.) This interstate agreement was designed to cover multi-state problems of delinquents. The reciprocal provisions contained in this Act will further interstate cooperation in the handling of unruly and deprived children as well as delinquents. This objective requires a uniform act containing not only reciprocal provisions but providing the same law in each of the states.

In the preparation of this Act, the Conference has had the advice and assistance of Mr. William H. Sheridan, Assistant Director, Division of Juvenile Delinquency Service, U.S. Children's Bureau; Mr. Jacob Isaacs, Chairman of the American Bar Association Committee on Family and Juvenile Court Law; a committee of the National Council of Juvenile Court Judges specially appointed to consider the draft of this Act and headed by Honorable Lindsay G. Arthur; and Honorable Thomas Tollakson, representing the National Council on Crime and Delinquency.

UNIFORM JUVENILE COURT ACT

1 SECTION 1. [*Interpretation.*] This Act shall be construed to
2 effectuate the following public purposes:
3   (1) to provide for the care, protection, and wholesome moral,
4 mental, and physical development of children coming within its
5 provisions;
6   (2) consistent with the protection of the public interest, to re-
7 move from children committing delinquent acts the taint of crimi-
8 nality and the consequences of criminal behavior and to substi-
9 tute therefor a program of treatment, training, and rehabilitation.
10   (3) to achieve the foregoing purposes in a family environment
11 whenever possible, separating the child from his parents only
12 when necessary for his welfare or in the interest of public safety;
13   (4) to provide a simple judicial procedure through which
14 this Act is executed and enforced and in which the parties are
15 assured a fair hearing and their constitutional and other legal
16 rights recognized and enforced; and
17   (5) to provide simple interstate procedures which permit
18 resort to cooperative measures among the juvenile courts of the
19 several states when required to effectuate the purposes of this
20 Act.

1 SECTION 2. [*Definitions.*] As used in this Act:
2   (1) "child" means an individual who is:
3   (i) under the age of 18 years; or
4   (ii) under the age of 21 years who committed an act of
5   delinquency before reaching the age of 18 years; [or]
6   [(iii) under 21 years of age who committed an act of de-
7   linquency after becoming 18 years of age and is transferred
8   to the juvenile court by another court having jurisdiction
9   over him;]

COMMENT

Clause (ii) is intended to overcome the tendency to delay bringing children into court when the act committed was near age 18 in order to bring criminal prosecution after reaching that age.

Clause (iii) is bracketed to leave its inclusion optional with the state. Some states now have provisions of this character.

10   (2) "delinquent act" means an act designated a crime under
11 the law, including local [ordinances] [or resolutions] of this
12 state, or of another state if the act occurred in that state, or
13 under federal law, and the crime does not fall under paragraph
14 (iii) of subsection (4) [and is not a juvenile traffic offense as

15   defined in section 44] [and the crime is not a traffic offense as de-
16   fined in [Traffic Code of the State] other than [designate the more
17   serious offenses which should be included in the jurisdiction of the
18   juvenile court such as drunken driving, negligent homicide, etc.];

COMMENT

If sections 44, 45, and 46 are retained, the first pair of brackets should be removed. If these sections are not retained, the second pair of brackets should be removed.

19   (3) "delinquent child" means a child who has committed a
20   delinquent act and is in need of treatment or rehabilitation;

COMMENT

The conjunctive "and" should be noted. Before the child can be characterized as a "delinquent child" he must be found (1) to have committed a "delinquent act" *and* (2) to be in need of treatment or rehabilitation. The first finding is made in the adjudicative hearing on the merits of the allegations of delinquent acts ascribed to the child and involves all of the due process of law safeguards prescribed by *Gault*. The second finding is made in the dispositional hearing and involves the "good will and compassion" of the "kindly juvenile judge," taking into account the "emotional and psychological attitude" of the child and having greater latitude in the information he may consider in making a disposition of the case. *Gault* and *Williams v. People*, 337 U.S. 241, 69 S. Ct. 1079, 93 L. Ed. 1337.

21   (4) "unruly child" means a child who:
22   (i) while subject to compulsory school attendance is ha-
23   bitually and without justification truant from school;
24   (ii) is habitually disobedient of the reasonable and lawful
25   commands of his parent, guardian, or other custodian and is
26   ungovernable; or
27   (iii) has committed an offense applicable only to a child;
28   and
29   (iv) in any of the foregoing is in need of treatment or
30   rehabilitation;

COMMENT

The "unruly child" category is needed to limit the disposition that can be made of a child who is in need of treatment or rehabilitation, but who has committed no offense applicable to adults. The "unruly child" is usually unmanageable and in need of supervision but not to the extent that he should be institutionalized with delinquent children. See section 32.

31   (5) "deprived child" means a child who:
32   (i) is without proper parental care or control, subsistence,
33   education as required by law, or other care or control neces-
34   sary for his physical, mental, or emotional health, or morals,
35   and the deprivation is not due primarily to the lack of finan-

36   cial means of his parents, guardian, or other custodian;
37   (ii) has been placed for care or adoption in violation of
38   law; [or]
39   (iii) has been abandoned by his parents, guardian, or
40   other custodian; [or]
41   [(iv) is without a parent, guardian, or legal custodian;]

COMMENT

This definition of "deprived child" avoids stigmatization of parents in "neglect" cases and focuses upon the needs of the child regardless of parental fault. It also eliminates poverty of the parents as a basis for juvenile court jurisdiction. See Task Force Report: Juvenile Delinquency and Youth Crime, pages 27 and 28. Clause (iv) is intended for states that do not have other adequate resources with which to provide care for dependent children or other judicial machinery for the appointment of a guardian of the person of a dependent child.

42   (6) "shelter care" means temporary care of a child in physi-
43   cally unrestricted facilities;

COMMENT

Shelter is thus distinguished from detention which relates to the temporary care of delinquent children.

44   (7) "protective supervision" means supervision ordered by
45   the court of children found to be deprived or unruly;

COMMENT

Protective supervision is used in this Act to distinguish from probation. Probation is used to refer to the supervision ordered by the court in delinquency cases.

46   (8) "custodian" means a person, other than a parent or
47   legal guardian, who stands in *loco parentis* to the child or a
48   person to whom legal custody of the child has been given by
49   order of a court;
50   (9) "juvenile court" means the [here designate] court of this
51   state.

COMMENT

The court which a state designates to administer this Act should be qualified for this special type of function. This calls not only for a knowledge of the law, but also a knowledge of the behavioral sciences and a sympathetic understanding of the problems and needs of children. When possible, juvenile court jurisdiction should be vested in the trial court of general jurisdiction as a branch or division of that court.

In states which have, or adopt, a Family Court system, this Act should be integrated with the laws relating thereto.

1 SECTION 3. [*Jurisdiction.*]
2 (a) The juvenile court has exclusive original jurisdiction of
3 the following proceedings, which are governed by this Act:
4   (1) proceedings in which a child is alleged to be delinquent,
5 unruly, or deprived [or to have committed a juvenile traffic
6 offense as defined in section 44;]
7   (2) proceedings for the termination of parental rights except
8 when a part of an adoption proceeding; and
9   (3) proceedings arising under section 39 through 42.
10 (b) The juvenile court also has exclusive original jurisdiction
11 of the following proceedings, which are governed by the laws
12 relating thereto without regard to the other provisions of this Act:
13   [(1) proceedings for the adoption of an individual of any
14 age;]
15   (2) proceedings to obtain judicial consent to the marriage,
16 employment, or enlistment in the armed services of a child, if
17 consent is required by law;
18   (3) proceedings under the Interstate Compact of Juveniles;
19 [and]
20   (4) proceedings under the Interstate Compact on the Place-
21 ment of Children; [and]
22   [(5) proceedings to determine the custody or appoint a guar-
23 dian of the person of a child.]

COMMENT

The retention of the bracketed portion of subsection (a)(1) depends on whether sections 44, 45, and 46, dealing with juvenile traffic offenses, are retained.

Subsection (b)(1) is bracketed since some states may have some juvenile court judges who are not admitted to the Bar and may not wish to confer this jurisdiction upon them.

Subsection (5) is bracketed for those states where guardianship jurisdiction is constitutionally conferred on another court. The provisions of this Act do not apply to proceedings falling under this subsection.

1 [SECTION 4. [*Concurrent Jurisdiction.*] The juvenile court has
2 concurrent jurisdiction with [_____] court of proceedings
3 to treat or commit a mentally retarded or mentally ill child.]

COMMENT

While it is desirable that this jurisdiction should be given to the juvenile court, constitutional provisions may confer this jurisdiction on another court. Hence, the section is bracketed.

1 SECTION 5. [*Probation Services.*]
2   [(a) [In [counties] of over _____ population] the

3   [_____] court may appoint one or more probation officers
4   who shall serve [at the pleasure of the court] [and are subject to
5   - removal under the civil service laws governing the county]. They
6   have the powers and duties stated in section 6. Their salaries shall
7   be fixed by the court with the approval of the [governing board
8   of the county]. If more than one probation officer is appointed,
9   one may be designated by the court as the chief probation officer
10 or director of court services, who shall be responsible for the
11 administration of the probation services under the direction of
12 the court.]
13   [(b) In all other cases the [Department of Corrections] [state
14 [county] child welfare department] [or other appropriate state
15 agency] shall provide suitable probation services to the juvenile
16 court of each [county.] The cost thereof shall be paid out of the
17 general revenue funds of the [state] [county]. The probation
18 officer or other qualified person assigned to the court by the
19 [Department of Corrections] [state [county] child welfare depart-
20 ment] [or other appropriate state agency] has the powers and
21 duties stated in section 6.]

COMMENT

A competent probation staff is essential to achieving the objectives of the juvenile court system. The staff must be adequately trained, working loads must be
limited, and conditions must be provided that permit the giving of the required
time and attention called for by each individual case.

A probation service may be established on either a local or a statewide basis.
Competent authorities disagree on the relative merits of the two alternatives. The
National Council of Juvenile Court Judges favors a local system stressing the
importance of having these services provided by court personnel responsible to
and under the direction of the juvenile court judge since he is responsible for the
successful conduct of the juvenile program. Proponents of the statewide system
stress the frequent inadequacy of local resources to provide the needed minimum
service required and contend that better probation service is provided by a state
system, and that the prospect of the judge successfully achieving the objectives
of the court's program is therefore enhanced.

The above bracketed sections leave the choice to each state on how best to
provide the needed services, whether by the local court or by a statewide system
or by some combination of the two.

No attempt is made to deal with clerical staff, reporters, and other supporting
personnel. In most states, the juvenile court is and will continue to be assigned
to a court structure already providing for these facilities.

1   Section 6. [*Powers and Duties of Probation Officers.*]
2   (a) For the purpose of carrying out the objectives and pur-
3   poses of this Act and subject to the limitations of this Act or
4   imposed by the Court, a probation officer shall
5   (1) make investigations, reports, and recommendations to

6   the juvenile court;

7   (2) receive and examine complaints and charges of de-
8   linquency, unruly conduct or deprivation of a child for the
9   purpose of considering the commencement of proceedings
10   under this Act;

11   (3) supervise and assist a child placed on probation or in his
12   protective supervision or care by order of the court or other
13   authority of law;

14   (4) make appropriate referrals to other private or public
15   agencies of the community if their assistance appears to be
16   needed or desirable;

17   (5) take into custody and detain a child who is under his
18   supervision or care as a delinquent, unruly or deprived child
19   if the probation officer has reasonable cause to believe that
20   the child's health or safety is in imminent danger, or that he
21   may abscond or be removed from the jurisdiction of the court,
22   or when ordered by the court pursuant to this Act. Except as
23   provided by this Act a probation officer does not have the
24   powers of a law enforcement officer. He may not conduct ac-
25   cusatory proceedings under this Act against a child who is or
26   may be under his care or supervision; and

27   (6) perform all other functions designated by this Act or by
28   order of the court pursuant thereto.

29   (b) Any of the foregoing functions may be performed in
30   another state if authorized by the court of this state and per-
31   mitted by the laws of the other state.

COMMENT

This section brings together the various functions of the probation officer under this Act. Specific powers also appear in other sections in the Act.

The primary role of the probation officer is the care and protection of the child, and in delinquency cases, his treatment and rehabilitation as well. Incompatible roles such as the power of arrest, conducting the accusatory proceeding in juvenile court, representing the child in court, have been excluded.

The several powers stated are subject to limitations imposed by the court.

The second sentence of paragraph (6) complements the provisions of section 43.

1   [SECTION 7. [*Referees.*]

2   (a) The judge may appoint one or more persons to serve at
3   the pleasure of the judge as referees on a full or part-time basis.
4   A referee shall be a member of the bar [and shall qualify under
5   the civil service regulations of the County]. His compensation
6   shall be fixed by the judge [with the approval of the [governing
7   board of the County] and paid out of [_____]].

8   (b) The judge may direct that hearings in any case or class

9 of cases be conducted in the first instance by the referee in the
10 manner provided by this Act. Before commencing the hearing
11 the referee shall inform the parties who have appeared that they
12 are entitled to have the matter heard by the judge. If a party
13 objects the hearing shall be conducted by the judge.
14   (c) Upon the conclusion of a hearing before a referee he shall
15 transmit written findings and recommendations for disposition to
16 the judge. Prompt written notice and copies of the findings and
17 recommendations shall be given to the parties to the proceeding.
18 The written notice also shall inform them of the right to a re-
19 hearing before the judge.
20   (d) A rehearing may be ordered by the judge at any time and
21 shall be ordered if a party files written request therefor within 3
22 days after receiving the notice required in subsection (c).
23   (e) Unless a rehearing is ordered the findings and recommen-
24 dations become the findings and order of the court when con-
25 firmed in writing by the judge.]

COMMENT

Provisions for referees are fairly common. They serve a purpose where a case
load is greater than the judge can effectively handle, but not sufficiently great
to warrant the appointment of an additional judge. In such situations, the use of
referees is warranted to relieve the judge of these routine and simple matters
which do not call for the qualifications of a judge.

But referees should not be resorted to as a substitute for additional judges
when these are needed. The need for referees will vary among the states. Hence,
the section is bracketed.

In view of *Kent* and *Gault*, with their emphasis on the legal and constitutional
rights of the parties, it is believed important that training in the law should be
required of referees in addition to the other qualifications that participation in
the juvenile court function requires.

1   SECTION 8. [*Commencement of Proceedings.*] A proceeding
2 under this Act may be commenced:
3   (1) by transfer of a case from another court as provided in
4 section 9;
5   [(2) as provided in section 44 in a proceeding charging the
6 violation of a traffic offense;] or
7   (3) by the court accepting jurisdiction as provided in sec-
8 tion 40 or accepting supervision of a child as provided in
9 section 42; or
10   (4) in other cases by the filing of a petition as provided in
11 this Act. The petition and all other documents in the proceed-
12 ing shall be entitled "In the interest of _____, a
13 [child] [minor] under [18] [21] years of age."

COMMENT

This is principally a clarifying section to indicate the methods by which cases may come before the court and the particular sections which control.
Paragraph (2) should be deleted if section 44 is not retained.

1 SECTION 9. [*Transfer from Other Courts.*] If it appears to the
2 court in a criminal proceeding that the defendant [is a child]
3 [was under the age of 18 years at the time the offense charged
4 was alleged to have been committed], the court shall forthwith
5 transfer the case to the juvenile court together with a copy of
6 the accusatory pleading and other papers, documents, and tran-
7 scripts of testimony relating to the case. It shall order that the
8 defendant be taken forthwith to the juvenile court or to a place
9 of detention designated by the juvenile court, or release him to
10 the custody of his parent, guardian, custodian, or other person
11 legally responsible for him, to be brought before the juvenile
12 court at a time designated by that court. The accusatory pleading
13 may serve in lieu of a petition in the juvenile court unless that
14 court directs the filing of a petition.

COMMENT

The appropriate brackets are to be removed depending on the retention of section 2(1) (iii).
A few states permit criminal proceedings to be brought in the discretion of the prosecuting attorney or, sometimes, of the criminal court. The intent of this Act is to make this exclusively the decision of the juvenile court. See section 34, infra. This avoids any constitutional objection which might otherwise be raised under *Kent*.

1 SECTION 10. [*Informal Adjustment.*]
2 (a) Before a petition is filed, the probation officer or other
3 officer of the court designated by it, subject to its direction, may
4 give counsel and advice to the parties with a view to an informal
5 adjustment if it appears:
6 (1) the admitted facts bring the case within the jurisdiction
7 of the court;
8 (2) counsel and advice without an adjudication would be
9 in the best interest of the public and the child; and
10 (3) the child and his parents, guardian or other custodian
11 consent thereto with knowledge that consent is not obligatory.
12 (b) The giving of counsel and advice cannot extend beyond
13 3 months from the day commenced unless extended by the court
14 for an additional period not to exceed 3 months and does not
15 authorize the detention of the child if not otherwise permitted
16 by this Act.

17   (c) An incriminating statement made by a participant to the
18   person giving counsel or advice and in the discussions or con-
19   ferences incident thereto shall not be used against the declarant
20   over objection in any hearing except in a hearing on disposition
21   in a juvenile court proceeding or in a criminal proceeding against
22   him after conviction for the purpose of a presentence investi-
23   gation.

COMMENT

Informal conferences leading to the adjustment of the case are widespread
even without explicit provision. There is, however, danger that, unless controlled,
the prospect that court proceedings will be commenced and the fear of their
consequences may make the participation of parties an involuntary one, and
their agreeing to prescribed terms a product of compulsion. The provisions of
this section are intended to avoid possible abuse of these otherwise desirable
efforts.

1   SECTION 11. [Venue.] A proceeding under this Act may be
2   commenced in the [county] in which the child resides. If de-
3   linquent or unruly conduct is alleged, the proceeding may be
4   commenced in the [county] in which the acts constituting the
5   alleged delinquent or unruly conduct occurred. If deprivation is
6   alleged, the proceeding may be brought in the [county] in which
7   the child is present when it is commenced.

COMMENT

Ordinarily the proceedings will be brought in the county where the child
resides since this is the community primarily concerned with its welfare. Section
12 authorizes the transfer if brought in another county.

1   SECTION 12. [Transfer to Another Juvenile Court Within the
2   State.]
3   (a) If the child resides in a [county] of the state and the pro-
4   ceeding is commenced in a court of another [county], the court,
5   on motion of a party or on its own motion made prior to final dis-
6   position, may transfer the proceeding to the county of the child's
7   residence for further action. Like transfer may be made if the resi-
8   dence of the child changes pending the proceeding. The proceed-
9   ing shall be transferred if the child has been adjudicated delin-
10   quent or unruly and other proceedings involving the child are
11   pending in the juvenile court of the [county] of his residence.
12   (b) Certified copies of all legal and social documents and rec-
13   ords pertaining to the case on file with the clerk of the court shall
14   accompany the transfer.

This section places primary responsibility for care and supervision of a child with the court of the county of the child's residence. This court is usually in a better position to deal effectively with the child's welfare.

1   SECTION 13. [*Taking into Custody.*]
2   (a) A child may be taken into custody:
3   (1) pursuant to an order of the court under this Act;
4   (2) pursuant to the laws of arrest;
5   (3) by a law enforcement officer [or duly authorized officer
6   of the court] if there are reasonable grounds to believe that the
7   child is suffering from illness or injury or is in immediate danger
8   from his surroundings, and that his removal is necessary; or
9   (4) by a law enforcement officer [or duly authorized officer
10   of the court] if there are reasonable grounds to believe that the
11   child has run away from his parents, guardian, or other cus-
12   todian.
13   (b) The taking of a child into custody is not an arrest, except
14   for the purpose of determining its validity under the constitution
15   of this State or of the United States.

This is typical of the statutes on the subject, except that the final clause of the last sentence is new. It is believed to state the law on the subject.

1   SECTION 14. [*Detention of Child.*] A child taken into custody
2   shall not be detained or placed in shelter care prior to the hearing
3   on the petition unless his detention or care is required to protect
4   the person or property of others or of the child or because the
5   child may abscond or be removed from the jurisdiction of the
6   court or because he has no parent, guardian, or custodian or other
7   person able to provide supervision and care for him and return
8   him to the court when required, or an order for his detention or
9   shelter care has been made by the court pursuant to this Act.

This section should be read in conjunction with the next two sections. Its provisions are consistent with not only current juvenile court acts but the modern trend not to hold persons in confinement unless necessary to assure their appearance in court.

1   SECTION 15. [*Release or Delivery to Court.*]
2   (a) A person taking a child into custody, with all reasonable
3   speed and without first taking the child elsewhere, shall:
4   (1) release the child to his parents, guardian, or other cus-.

5   todian upon their promise to bring the child before the court
6   when requested by the court, unless his detention or shelter
7   care is warranted or required under section 14; or
8   (2) bring the child before the court or deliver him to a de-
9   tention or shelter care facility designated by the court or to a
10   medical facility if the child is believed to suffer from a serious
11   physical condition or illness which requires prompt treatment.
12   He shall promptly give written notice thereof, together with a
13   statement of the reason for taking the child into custody, to a
14   parent, guardian, or other custodian and to the court. Any tem-
15   porary detention or questioning of the child necessary to comply
16   with this subsection shall conform to the procedures and condi-
17   tions prescribed by this Act and rules of court.
18   (b) If a parent, guardian, or other custodian, when requested,
19 fails to bring the child before the court as provided in subsection
20 (a) the court may issue its warrant directing that the child be
21 taken into custody and brought before the court.

COMMENT

This draft does not authorize police detention for questioning except for the purpose stated in subsection (a).

1   SECTION 16. [*Place of Detention.*]
2   (a) A child alleged to be delinquent may be detained only in:
3   (1) a licensed foster home or a home approved by the court;
4   (2) a facility operated by a licensed child welfare agency;
5   (3) a detention home or center for delinquent children which
6   is under the direction or supervision of the court or other public
7   authority or of a private agency approved by the court; or
8   (4) any other suitable place or facility, designated or oper-
9   ated by the court. The child may be detained in a jail or other
10   facility for the detention of adults only if the facility in para-
11   graph (3) is not available, the detention is in a room separate
12   and removed from those for adults, it appears to the satisfaction
13   of the court that public safety and protection reasonably re-
14   quire detention, and it so orders.
15   (b) The official in charge of a jail or other facility for the de-
16 tention of adult offenders or persons charged with crime shall
17 inform the court immediately if a person who is or oppears to be
18 under the age of 18 years is received at the facility and shall bring
19 him before the court upon request or deliver him to a detention
20 or shelter care facility designated by the court.
21 (c) If a case is transferred to another court for criminal prose-
22 cution the child may be transferred to the appropriate officer or

23 detention facility in accordance with the law governing the deten-
24 tion of persons charged with crime.
25 (d) A child alleged to be deprived or unruly may be detained
26 or placed in shelter care only in the facilities stated in paragraphs
27 (1), (2), and (4) of subsection (a) and shall not be detained in
28 a jail or other facility intended or used for the detention of adults
29 charged with criminal offenses or of children alleged to be de-
30 linquent.

COMMENT

These provisions are designed to avoid the harm resulting from exposing
children to adult criminals and the degrading effect of jails, lockups, and the like.

1 SECTION 17. [*Release from Detention or Shelter Care—Hearing*
2 *—Conditions of Release.*]
3 (a) If a child is brought before the court or delivered to a de-
4 tention or shelter care facility designated by the court the intake
5 or other authorized officer of the court shall immediately make an
6 investigation and release the child unless it appears that his deten-
7 tion or shelter care is warranted or required under section 14.
8 (b) If he is not so released, a petition under section 21 shall be
9 promptly made and presented to the court.
10 An informal detention hearing shall be held promptly and not
11 later than 72 hours after he is placed in detention to determine
12 whether his detention or shelter care is required under section 14.
13 Reasonable notice thereof, either oral or written, stating the time,
14 place, and purpose of the detention hearing shall be given to the
15 child and if they can be found, to his parents, guardian, or other
16 custodian. Prior to the commencement of the hearing, the court
17 shall inform the parties of their right to counsel and to appointed
18 counsel if they are needy persons, and of the child's right to re-
19 main silent with respect to any allegations of delinquency or
20 unruly conduct.
21 (c) If the child is not so released and a parent, guardian or cus-
22 todian has not been notified of the hearing, did not appear or
23 waive appearance at the hearing, and files his affidavit showing
24 these facts, the court shall rehear the matter without unnecessary
25 delay and order his release, unless it appears from the hearing that
26 the child's detention or shelter care is required under section 14.

1 [SECTION 18. [*Subpoena.*] Upon application of a party the court
2 or the clerk of the court shall issue, or the court on its own motion
3 may issue, subpoenas requiring attendance and testimony of wit-
4 nesses and production of papers at any hearing under this Act.]

COMMENT

If a state's general subpoena statutes or court rules apply to juvenile court proceedings, this section is unnecessary and hence is bracketed.

1   SECTION 19. [*Petition—Preliminary Determination.*] A petition
2   under this Act shall not be filed unless the [probation officer,] the
3   court, or other person authorized by the court has determined and
4   endorsed upon the petition that the filing of the petition is in the
5   best interest of the public and the child.

COMMENT

This section provides for a preliminary screening before a petition may be filed in order to avoid groundless and ill-advised petitions.

1   SECTION 20. [*Petition—Who May Make.*] Subject to section 19
2   the petition may be made by any person, including a law enforce-
3   ment officer, who has knowledge of the facts alleged or is informed
4   and believes that they are true.

1   SECTION 21. [*Contents of Petition.*] The petition shall be verified
2   and may be on information and belief. It shall set forth plainly:
3   (1) the facts which bring the child within the jurisdiction of
4   the court, with a statement that it is in the best interest of the
5   child and the public that the proceeding be brought and, if de-
6   linquency or unruly conduct is alleged, that the child is in need
7   of treatment or rehabilitation;
8   (2) the name, age, and residence address, if any, of the child
9   on whose behalf the petition is brought;
10   (3) the names and residence addresses, if known to petitioner,
11   of the parents, guardian, or custodian of the child and of the
12   child's spouse, if any. If none of his parents, guardian, or cus-
13   todian resides or can be found within the state, or if their re-
14   spective places of residence address are unknown, the name of
15   any known adult relative residing within the [county,] or, if
16   there be none, the known adult relative residing nearest to the
17   location of the court; and
18   (4) if the child is in custody and, if so, the place of his deten-
19   tion and the time he was taken into custody.

COMMENT

The allegation that the child is in need of treatment or rehabilitation is a necessary one and, in the light of the *Gault* case, must be established if the proceedings are to retain their non-criminal character. See also section 2 (3) and (4).

Juvenile court acts rarely have provisions for a formal answer to the petition. The parties simply appear at the hearing and state whether they admit or deny allegations. If admitted, the hearing proceeds to the disposition stage. If denied, the hearing continues to determine the facts. There is likewise no provision for default for non-appearance. If the child is before the court, the appropriate disposition is made without the non-appearing party. If the appearance of a party such as a parent, is deemed essential, he can be brought in by subpoena under section 18 or by order on the summons under section 22.

1   SECTION 22. [*Summons.*]
2   (a) After the petition has been filed the court shall fix a time
3   for hearing thereon, which, if the child is in detention, shall not be
4   later than 10 days after the filing of the petition. The court shall
5   direct the issuance of a summons to the parents, guardian, or other
6   custodian, a guardian ad litem, and any other persons as appear
7   to the court to be proper or necessary parties to the proceeding,
8   requiring them to appear before the court at the time fixed to an-
9   swer the allegations of the petition. The summons shall also be
10 directed to the child if he is 14 or more years of age or is alleged
11 to be a delinquent or unruly child. A copy of the petition shall
12 accompany the summons unless the summons is served by publi-
13 cation in which case the published summons shall indicate the
14 general nature of the allegations and where a copy of the petition
15 can be obtained.
16 (b) The court may endorse upon the summons an order direct-
17 ing the parents, guardian or other custodian of the child to appear
18 personally at the hearing and directing the person having the
19 physical custody or control of the child to bring the child to the
20 hearing.
21 (c) If it appears from affidavit filed or from sworn testimony
22 before the court that the conduct, condition, or surroundings of
23 the child are endangering his health or welfare or those of others,
24 or that he may abscond or be removed from the jurisdiction of the
25 court or will not be brought before the court, notwithstanding the
26 service of the summons, the court may endorse upon the summons
27 an order that a law enforcement officer shall serve the summons
28 and take the child into immediate custody and bring him forth-
29 with before the court.
30 (d) The summons shall state that a party is entitled to counsel
31 in the proceedings and that the court will appoint counsel if the
32 party is unable without undue financial hardship to employ
33 counsel.
34 (e) A party, other than the child, may waive service of sum-
35 mons by written stipulation or by voluntary appearance at the
36 hearing. If the child is present at the hearing, his counsel, with

37 the consent of the parent, guardian or other custodian, or guardian
38 ad litem, may waive service of summons in his behalf.

COMMENT

Service of the summons upon the child is required in cases where the child
is alleged to be delinquent or unruly and in deprivation cases where the child
is 14 or more years of age. A guardian ad litem will always be appointed for
the child in deprivation cases in which event the summons will be served upon
such guardian. See Section 51. It should be noted that the child is not permitted
to waive service of the summons. This has been the direction of judicial decisions.

1   SECTION 23. [*Service of Summons.*]
2   (a) If a party to be served with a summons is within this State
3   and can be found, the summons shall be served upon him per-
4   sonally at least 24 hours before the hearing. If he is within this
5   State and cannot be found, but his address is known or can with
6   reasonable diligence be ascertained, the summons may be served
7   upon him by mailing a copy by registered or certified mail at least
8   5 days before the hearing. If he is without this State but he can be
9   found or his address is known, or his whereabouts or address can
10 with reasonable diligence be ascertained, service of the summons
11 may be made either by delivering a copy to him personally or
12 mailing a copy to him by registered or certified mail at least 5
13 days before the hearing.
14 (b) If after reasonable effort he cannot be found or his post
15 office address ascertained, whether he is within or without this
16 State, the court may order service of the summons upon him by
17 publication in accordance with [Rule] [Section] _____
18 [the general service by publication statutes]. The hearing shall
19 not be earlier than 5 days after the date of the last publication.
20 (c) Service of the summons may be made by any suitable per-
21 son under the direction of the court.
22 (d) The court may authorize the payment from [county funds]
23 of the costs of service and of necessary travel expenses incurred
24 by persons summoned or otherwise required to appear at the
25 hearing.

COMMENT

The summons and the service thereof give notice of the proceedings to the
parties affected and warn them that action may be taken as stated in the petition
unless they appear. Persons required to be present but who are not intended to
be participants as parties can be brought into court by subpoena.

In the interest of consistency of procedures for the publication of the summons,
reference is made to the general publication statute.

Judicial decisions indicate that service by publication is not constitutionally
permissible unless a substantial showing is made that alternative and better modes
of notice are not available.

1   SECTION 24. [*Conduct of Hearings.*]
2   (a) Hearings under this Act shall be conducted by the court
3 without a jury, in an informal but orderly manner, and separate
4 from other proceedings not included in section 3.
5   (b) The [prosecuting attorney] upon request of the court shall
6 present the evidence in support of the petition and otherwise con-
7 duct the proceedings on behalf of the state.
8   (c) If requested by a party or ordered by the court the pro-
9 ceedings shall be recorded by stenographic notes or by electronic,
10 mechanical, or other appropriate means. If not so recorded full
11 minutes of the proceedings shall be kept by the court.
12   (d) Except in hearings to declare a person in contempt of court,
13 [and in hearings under section 44,] the general public shall be ex-
14 cluded from hearings under this Act. Only the parties, their coun-
15 sel, witnesses, and other persons accompanying a party for his
16 assistance, and any other persons as the court finds have a proper
17 interest in the proceeding or in the work of the court may be ad-
18 mitted by the court. The court may temporarily exclude the child
19 from the hearing except while allegations of his delinquency or
20 unruly conduct are being heard.

COMMENT

Most juvenile court acts do not contain provisions for recording of the proceedings. This has been the product largely of the fact that appeals are allowed
to the court of general jurisdiction for trial *de novo*.

Section 59 permits appeals only for review on the record of the action of the
juvenile court. Hence, the necessity of an adequate record. Since appeals are
seldom taken, provision is made for the recording of testimony only if a party
asks for it or it is ordered by the court. The court may find it desirable to record
the testimony, even though a party does not ask for it, e. g., a hearing leading
to transfer for criminal prosecution. The need for an adequate record was pointed
out in the *Gault* case.

There has been some recent tendency to permit publicity to juvenile court
proceedings, on the theory that this will act as a curb to juvenile delinquency.
There is little evidence to support this theory and considerable indication that
it affords the hard core delinquent the kind of recognition he wants. On the
other hand, the harm it causes may be great in the case of the repentant offender.

The section as drawn permits the court in its discretion to admit news reporters.
This is frequently done with the understanding that the identity of the cases
observed will not be published, a procedure generally satisfactory to the
news media.

The exception in contempt cases is probably required in *In re Oliver,* 333
U.S. 257, 68 S. Ct. 499, 92 L.Ed. 682.

1   SECTION 25. [*Service by Publication—Interlocutory Order of*
2 *Disposition.*]
3   (a) If service of summons upon a party is made by publication
4 the court may conduct a provisional hearing upon the allegations

5 of the petition and enter an interlocutory order of disposition if:
6 (1) the petition alleges delinquency, unruly conduct, or de-
7 privation of the child;
8 (2) the summons served upon any party (i) states that prior to
9 the final hearing on the petition designated in the summons a
10 provisional hearing thereon will be held at a specified time and
11 place, (ii) requires the party who is served other than by pub-
12 lication to appear and answer the allegations of the petition at
13 the provisional hearing, (iii) states further that findings of fact
14 and orders of disposition made pursuant to the provisional hear-
15 ing will become final at the final hearing unless the party served
16 by publication appears at the final hearing, and (iv) otherwise
17 conforms to section 22; and
18 (3) the child is personally before the court at the provisional
19 hearing.
20 (b) All provisions of this Act applicable to a hearing on a peti-
21 tion, to orders of disposition, and to other proceedings dependent
22 thereon shall apply under this section, but findings of fact and
23 orders of disposition have only interlocutory effect pending the
24 final hearing on the petition. The rights and duties of the party
25 served by publication are not affected except as provided in sub-
26 section (c).
27 (c) If the party served by publication fails to appear at the
28 final hearing on the petition the findings of fact and interlocutory
29 orders made become final without further evidence and are gov-
30 erned by this Act as if made at the final hearing. If the party ap-
31 pears at the final hearing the findings and orders shall be vacated
32 and disregarded and the hearing shall proceed upon the allega-
33 tions of the petition without regard to this section.

COMMENT

When service of summons is made by publication the length of time between
the initiation of the proceedings and the hearing on the petition is substantially
increased. In the large majority of these cases, the prospect that the party so
served will appear at the hearing fixed by the summons is remote. There is need,
in the meantime, that the court be empowered to take necessary action in appropriate cases, for example, when the child is being held in detention. However,
any hearing on the petition and disposition before the final hearing fixed by the
summons must be temporary only and without prejudice to the party being
served by publication, should he appear. See *Armstrong v. Manzo*, 380 U.S. 545,
85 S. Ct. 1187, 14 L.Ed. 2d 62.

1 SECTION 26. [*Right to Counsel.*]
2 (a) Except as otherwise provided under this Act a party is en-
3 titled to representation by legal counsel at all stages of any pro-
4 ceedings under this Act and if as a needy person he is unable to

5 employ counsel, to have the court provide counsel for him. If a
6 party appears without counsel the court shall ascertain whether
7 he knows of his right thereto and to be provided with counsel by
8 the court if he is a needy person. The court may continue the
9 proceeding to enable a party to obtain counsel and shall provide
10 counsel for an unrepresented needy person upon his request.
11 Counsel must be provided for a child not represented by his
12 parent, guardian, or custodian. If the interests of 2 or more parties
13 conflict separate counsel shall be provided for each of them.
14   (b) A needy person is one who at the time of requesting counsel
15 is unable without undue financial hardship to provide for full pay-
16 ment of legal counsel and all other necessary expenses for repre-
17 sentation.

COMMENT

Subsection (b) is derived from the Model Defense of Needy Persons Act.
Due process requires the appointment of counsel for a needy child charged
with delinquency. See *Kent* and *Gault*.

1 SECTION 27. [*Other Basic Rights.*]
2   (a) A party is entitled to the opportunity to introduce evidence
3 and otherwise be heard in his own behalf and to cross-examine
4 adverse witnesses.
5   (b) A child charged with a delinquent act need not be a witness
6 against or otherwise incriminate himself. An extra-judicial state-
7 ment, if obtained in the course of violation of this Act or which
8 would be constitutionally inadmissible in a criminal proceeding,
9 shall not be used against him. Evidence illegally seized or obtained
10 shall not be received over objection to establish the allegations
11 made against him. A confession validly made by child out of court
12 is insufficient to support an adjudication of delinquency unless it
13 is corroborated in whole or in part by other evidence.

COMMENT

The provision against self-incrimination and the use of invalid confessions
appears to be required by *Gault*.
The phrase, "to establish the charge against him" is consistent with the qualification in *Walder v. U.S.*, 347 U.S. 62, 74 S. Ct. 354, 98 L. Ed. 503, holding
that illegally seized evidence may be used to impeach a defendant who "went
beyond a mere denial . . ." The exact scope of the qualification is not clear.

1 SECTION 28. [*Investigation and Report.*]
2   (a) If the allegations of a petition are admitted by a party or
3 notice of a hearing under section 34 has been given the court, prior
4 to the hearing on need for treatment or rehabilitation and disposi-
5 tion, may direct that a social study and report in writing to the

6 court be made by the [probation officer] of the court, [Commis-
7 sioner of the Court or other like officer] or other person designated
8 by the court, concerning the child, his family, his environment,
9 and other matters relevant to disposition of the case. If the allega-
10 tions of the petition are not admitted and notice of a hearing
11 under section 34 has not been given the court shall not direct the
12 making of the study and report until after the court has heard the
13 petition upon notice of hearing given pursuant to this Act and the
14 court has found that the child committed a delinquent act or is an
15 unruly or deprived child.
16   (b) During the pendency of any proceeding the court may order
17 the child to be examined at a suitable place by a physician or psy-
18 chologist and may also order medical or surgical treatment of a
19 child who is suffering from a serious physical condition or illness
20 which in the opinion of a [licensed physician] requires prompt
21 treatment, even if the parent, guardian, or other custodian has not
22 been given notice of a hearing, is not available, or without good
23 cause informs the court of his refusal to consent to the treatment.

COMMENT

These reports are for purposes of disposition. Their use during the hearing
on the petition would violate the hearsay rule and the due process clause, since
cross-examination of the sources of the information contained in the report
would not be available. This section protects the privacy of a party denying
the petition until adjudication or notice of hearing to transfer for criminal prosecution is given. A statute similar to subsection (b) was sustained in In re Clark,
21 Oh. Op. (2d) 86, 90 L. Abst. 21, 185 N.E. 2d 128 (1962). See also Comment
to Section 2 (3).

1   SECTION 29. [Hearing—Findings—Dismissal.]
2   (a) After hearing the evidence on the petition the court shall
3 make and file its findings as to whether the child is a deprived
4 child, or if the petition alleges that the child is delinquent or
5 unruly, whether the acts ascribed to the child were committed
6 by him. If the court finds that the child is not a deprived child
7 or that the allegations of delinquency or unruly conduct have
8 not been established it shall dismiss the petition and order the
9 child discharged from any detention or other restriction thereto-
10 fore ordered in the proceeding.
11   (b) If the court finds on proof beyond a reasonable doubt that
12 the child committed the acts by reason of which he is alleged
13 to be delinquent or unruly it shall proceed immediately or at a
14 postponed hearing to hear evidence as to whether the child is
15 in need of treatment or rehabilitation and to make and file its
16 findings thereon. In the absence of evidence to the contrary

17 evidence of the commission of acts which constitute a felony is
18 sufficient to sustain a finding that the child is in need of treat-
19 ment or rehabilitation. If the court finds that the child is not in
20 need of treatment or rehabilitation it shall dismiss the proceeding
21 and discharge the child from any detention or other restriction
22 theretofore ordered.

23 (c) If the court finds from clear and convincing evidence that
24 the child is deprived or that he is in need of treatment or rehabili-
25 tation as a delinquent or unruly child, the court shall proceed
26 immediately or at a postponed hearing to make a proper disposi-
27 tion of the case.

28 (d) In hearings under subsections (b) and (c) all evidence
29 helpful in determining the questions presented, including oral
30 and written reports, may be received by the court and relied upon
31 to the extent of its probative value even though not otherwise
32 competent in the hearing on the petition. The parties or their
33 counsel shall be afforded an opportunity to examine and con-
34 trovert written reports so received and to cross-examine individu-
35 als making the reports. Sources of confidential information need
36 not be disclosed.

37 (e) On its motion or that of a party the court may continue
38 the hearings under this section for a reasonable period to receive
39 reports and other evidence bearing on the disposition or the need
40 for treatment or rehabilitation. In this event the court shall make
41 an appropriate order for detention of the child or his release
42 from detention subject to supervision of the court during the
43 period of the continuance. In scheduling investigations and hear-
44 ings the court shall give priority to proceedings in which a child
45 is in detention or has otherwise been removed from his home
46 before an order of disposition has been made.

COMMENT

Under this section, when delinquency or unruly conduct is alleged, the court must find further that the child is in need of treatment or rehabilitation before the dispositions authorized by the Act can be resorted to. Otherwise the case must be dismissed. If the need for treatment or rehabilitation does not exist, the primary thrust of *Gault* is that the departure from criminal proceedings is no longer justified.

Findings by the court are required. Both *Kent* and *Gault* stress the importance of adequate findings.

More is required to sustain a finding of delinquency, unruly conduct or deprivation than a preponderance of evidence. Since the child's liberty or the parent's right to his custody is involved, at least "clear and convincing evidence" should be required. The Illinois Supreme Court has recently held that implications of the *Gault* case require that proof must be beyond a reasonable doubt to support a finding of delinquency. *In re Urbasek*, 38 Ill. 2d 535, 232 N.E. 2d 716

(1967). This section follows the Illinois view in delinquency and unruly cases, but adopts the "clear and convincing evidence" rule in deprivation cases and in determining the need for treatment or rehabilitation.

This section gives to the parties and their counsel access to the predispositional reports and the right to question their content. This is deemed required by *Kent*.

1   SECTION 30. [*Disposition of Deprived Child.*]
2   (a) If the child is found to be a deprived child the court may
3 make any of the following orders of disposition best suited to
4 the protection and physical, mental, and moral welfare of the
5 child:
6   (1) permit the child to remain with his parents, guardian,
7   or other custodian, subject to conditions and limitations as the
8   court prescribes, including supervision as directed by the court
9   for the protection of the child;
10   (2) subject to conditions and limitations as the court pre-
11 scribes transfer temporary legal custody to any of the following:
12   (i) any individual who, after study by the probation officer
13   or other person or agency designated by the court, is found
14   by the court to be qualified to receive and care for the child;
15   (ii) an agency or other private organization licensed or
16   otherwise authorized by law to receive and provide care for
17   the child; or
18   (iii) the Child Welfare Department of the [county] [state,]
19   [or other public agency authorized by law to receive and pro-
20   vide care for the child;]
21   (iv) an individual in another state with or without super-
22   vision by an appropriate officer under section 40; or
23   (3) without making any of the foregoing orders transfer
24 custody of the child to the juvenile court of another state if
25 authorized by and in accordance with section 39 if the child
26 is or is about to become a resident of that state.
27   (b) Unless a child found to be deprived is found also to be
28 delinquent he shall not be committed to or confined in an institu-
29 tion or other facility designed or operated for the benefit of de-
30 linquent children.

COMMENT

Since child welfare departments vary in their organization between state departments on the one hand and county departments on the other, the bracketed alternatives have been included.

1   SECTION 31. [*Disposition of Delinquent Child.*] If the child is
2 found to be a delinquent child the court may make any of the
3 following orders of disposition best suited to his treatment, re-
4 habilitation, and welfare:

5   (1) any order authorized by section 30 for the disposition
6   of a deprived child;
7   (2) placing the child on probation under the supervision of
8   the probation officer of the court or the court of another state
9   as provided in section 41, or [the Child Welfare Department
10   operating within the county,] under conditions and limitations
11   the court prescribes;
12   (3) placing the child in an institution, camp, or other facility
13   for delinquent children operated under the direction of the
14   court [or other local public authority;] or
15   (4) committing the child to [designate the state department
16   to which commitments of delinquent children are made or, if
17   there is no department, the appropriate state institution for
18   delinquent children].

COMMENT

Under subsection (2) of this section, the court may restrict the use of an automobile and impound the license plates as one of the conditions of restraint which the court may prescribe. It is considered unnecessary to set out this or other conditions of probation which may also include conditions applicable to the parents, guardian, or other custodian.

1   SECTION 32. [*Disposition of Unruly Child.*] If the child is found
2   to be unruly the court may make any disposition authorized for
3   a delinquent child except commitment to [the state department
4   or state institution to which commitment of delinquent children
5   may be made]. [If after making the disposition the court finds
6   upon a further hearing that the child is not amenable to treatment
7   or rehabilitation under the disposition made it may make a dis-
8   position otherwise authorized by section 31.]

COMMENT

This section does not permit commitment of an unruly child to a state institution for delinquent children except under the bracketed provisions after efforts have been made by other dispositions to treat or rehabilitate the child and these have failed. The court would also have to find that commitment to the institution will facilitate his treatment of rehabilitation.

The second sentence is bracketed because some states may not want to give this authority in cases of unruly children.

1   SECTION 33. [*Order of Adjudication—Non-Criminal.*]
2   (a) An order of disposition or other adjudication in a proceed-
3   ing under this Act is not a conviction of crime and does not im-
4   pose any civil disability ordinarily resulting from a conviction or
5   operate to disqualify the child in any civil service application
6   or appointment. A child shall not be committed or transferred

7 to a penal institution or other facility used primarily for the execu-
8 tion of sentences of persons convicted of a crime.
9 (b) The disposition of a child and evidence adduced in a hear-
10 ing in juvenile court may not be used against him in any proceed-
11 ing in any court other than a juvenile court, whether before or
12 after reaching majority, except in dispositional proceedings after
13 conviction of a felony for the purposes of a pre-sentence investiga-
14 tion and report.

COMMENT

Although several states permit commitment or transfer of a delinquent child
to a penal institution, its constitutionality is in serious doubt since it permits
confinement in a penal institution as a product of a non-criminal proceeding.
Such legislation has been held invalid in a number of states. See *In re Rich*, 125
Vt. 373, 216 A. 2d 266 (1966). A few decisions have held to the contrary. See
Wilson v. Coughlin, (Ia.) 147 N.W. 2d 175 (1966).

1 SECTION 34. [*Transfer to Other Courts.*]
2 (a) After a petition has been filed alleging delinquency based
3 on conduct which is designated a crime or public offense under
4 the laws, including local ordinances, [or resolutions] of this state,
5 the court before hearing the petition on its merits may transfer
6 the offense for prosecution to the appropriate court having juris-
7 diction of the offense if:
8 (1) the child was 16 or more years of age at the time of
9 the alleged conduct;
10 (2) a hearing on whether the transfer should be made is
11 held in conformity with sections 24, 26, and 27;
12 (3) notice in writing of the time, place, and purpose of the
13 hearing is given to the child and his parents, guardian, or other
14 custodian at least 3 days before the hearing;
15 (4) the court finds that there are reasonable grounds to
16 believe that
17 (i) the child committed the delinquent act alleged;
18 (ii) the child is not amenable to treatment or rehabilita-
19 tion as a juvenile through available facilities;
20 (iii) the child is not committable to an institution for the
21 mentally retarded or mentally ill; and
22 (iv) the interests of the community require that the child
23 be placed under legal restraint or discipline.
24 (b) The transfer terminates the jurisdiction of the juvenile
25 court over the child with respect to the delinquent acts alleged
26 in the petition.
27 (c) No child, either before or after reaching 18 years of age,
28 shall be prosecuted for an offense previously committed unless

29 the case has been transferred as provided in this section.
30 (d) Statements made by the child after being taken into
31 custody and prior to the service of notice under subsection (a)
32 or at the hearing under this section are not admissible against
33 him over objection in the criminal proceedings following the
34 transfer.
35 (e) If the case is not transferred the judge who conducted the
36 hearing shall not over objection of an interested party preside at
37 the hearing on the petition. If the case is transferred to a court
38 of which the judge who conducted the hearing is also a judge
39 he likewise is disqualified from presiding in the prosecution.

COMMENT

Subsection (a), it is believed, meets the requirements laid down in Kent.

Some states leave to the prosecuting attorney of the county whether the child should be brought into juvenile court or prosecuted for a criminal offense. Under the principles stated in Kent, this may be unconstitutional as denying equal protection of the laws.

A number of state decisions have held that failure to observe the essential procedural requirements for transfer results in want of jurisdiction of the criminal court to try the case.

Subsection (d) deals with two problems. First, a child may make statements unaware that he may be transferred for criminal prosecution. Fairness requires that these not be used against him in a criminal prosecution. See Harling v. United States, 295 F. 2d, 161 (1961), stating, ". . . if admissions obtained in juvenile proceedings before waiver of jurisdiction may be introduced in an adult proceeding after waiver, the juvenile proceedings are made to serve as an adjunct to and part of the adult criminal process. This would destroy the Juvenile Court's parens patriae relation to the child and would violate the non-criminal philosophy which underlies the Juvenile Court Act."

Second, a child should not be handicapped in presenting his case against transfer by the prospect that what is presented may be used against him in the criminal prosecution. Otherwise, the proceeding becomes in effect a discovery procedure for the state. Since whether or not to transfer is one of the most important decisions the juvenile court makes, the hearing should be a full and unrestricted one. See Kent.

Subsection (e). On a hearing to transfer, the judge of necessity must hear and consider matters relating adversely to the child which would be inadmissible in a hearing on the merits of the petition. Hence, the need of avoiding their prejudicial effect by requiring over objection that another judge hear the charges made in the petition or in the criminal court if the case is transferred.

1 SECTION 35. [Disposition of Mentally Ill or Mentally Retarded
2 Child.]
3 (a) If, at a dispositional hearing of a child found to be a de-
4 linquent or unruly child or at a hearing to transfer a child to
5 another court under section 34, the evidence indicates that the
6 child may be suffering from mental retardation or mental illness

7   the court before making a disposition shall commit the child for
8   a period not exceeding 60 days to an appropriate institution,
9   agency, or individual for study and report on the child's mental
10 condition.
11   (b) If it appears from the study and report that the child is
12 committable under the laws of this state as a mentally retarded
13 or mentally ill child the court shall order the child detained and
14 direct that within 10 days after the order is made the appropriate
15 authority initiate proceedings for the child's commitment.
16   (c) If it does not so appear, or proceedings are not promptly
17 initiated, or the child is found not to be committable, the court
18 shall proceed to the disposition or transfer of the child as other-
19 wise provided by this Act.

1   SECTION 36. [*Limitations of Time on Orders of Disposition.*]
2   (a) An order terminating parental rights is without limit as
3 to duration.
4   (b) An order of disposition committing a delinquent or unruly
5 child to the [State Department of Corrections or designated in-
6 stitution for delinquent children,] continues in force for 2 years
7 or until the child is sooner discharged by the [department or in-
8 stitution to which the child was committed]. The court which
9 made the order may extend its duration for an additional 2 years,
10 subject to like discharge, if:
11   (1) a hearing is held upon motion of the [department or in-
12 stitution to which the child was committed] prior to the expira-
13 tion of the order;
14   (2) reasonable notice of the hearing and an opportunity to
15 be heard is given to the child and the parent, guardian, or
16 other custodian; and
17   (3) the court finds that the extension is necessary for the
18 treatment or rehabilitation of the child.
19   (c) Any other order of disposition continues in force for not
20 more than 2 years. The court may sooner terminate its order or
21 extend its duration for further periods. An order of extension
22 may be made if:
23   (1) a hearing is held prior to the expiration of the order upon
24 motion of a party or on the court's own motion;
25   (2) reasonable notice of the hearing and opportunity to be
26 heard are given to the parties affected;
27   (3) the court finds that the extension is necessary to ac-
28 complish the purposes of the order extended; and
29   (4) the extension does not exceed 2 years from the expiration
30 of prior order.

31 (d) Except as provided in subsection (b) the court may
32 terminate an order of disposition or extension prior to its expira-
33 tion, on or without an application of a party, if it appears to the
34 court that the purposes of the order have been accomplished. If
35 a party may be adversely affected by the order of termination the
36 order may be made only after reasonable notice and opportunity
37 to be heard have been given to him.
38 (e) Except as provided in subsection (a) when the child
39 reaches 21 years of age all orders affecting him then in force
40 terminate and he is discharged from further obligation or control.

1   SECTION 37. [Modification or Vacation of Orders.]
2   (a) An order of the court shall be set aside if (1) it appears
3   that it was obtained by fraud or mistake sufficient therefor in a
4   civil action, or (2) the court lacked jurisdiction over a necessary
5   party or of the subject matter, or (3) newly discovered evidence
6   so requires.
7   (b) Except an order committing a delinquent child to the
8   [State Department of Corrections or an institution for delinquent
9   children,] an order terminating parental rights, or an order of
10 dismissal, an order of the court may also be changed, modified,
11 or vacated on the ground that changed circumstances so require
12 in the best interest of the child. An order granting probation to
13 a child found to be delinquent or unruly may be revoked on the
14 ground that the conditions of probation have not been observed.
15 (c) Any party to the proceeding, the probation officer or other
16 person having supervision or legal custody of or an interest in
17 the child may petition the court for the relief provided in this
18 section. The petition shall set forth in concise language the
19 grounds upon which the relief is requested.
20 (d) After the petition is filed the court shall fix a time for
21 hearing and cause notice to be served (as a summons is served
22 under section 23) on the parties to the proceeding or affected
23 by the relief sought. After the hearing, which may be informal,
24 the court shall deny or grant relief as the evidence warrants.

1   SECTION 38. [Rights and Duties of Legal Custodian.] A custo-
2   dian to whom legal custody has been given by the court under
3   this Act has the right to the physical custody of the child, the
4   right to determine the nature of the care and treatment of the
5   child, including ordinary medical care and the right and duty
6   to provide for the care, protection, training, and education, and
7   the physical, mental, and moral welfare of the child, subject to
8   the conditions and limitations of the order and to the remaining
9   rights and duties of the child's parents or guardian.

1   SECTION 39. [*Disposition of Non-Resident Child.*]
2   (a) If the court finds that a child who has been adjudged to
3 have committed a delinquent act or to be unruly or deprived is
4 or is about to become a resident of another state which has
5 adopted the Uniform Juvenile Court Act, or a substantially similar
6 Act which includes provisions corresponding to sections 39 and
7 40, the court may defer hearing on need for treatment or re-
8 habilitation and disposition and request by any appropriate means
9 the juvenile court of the [county] of the child's residence or
10 prospective residence to accept jurisdiction of the child.
11   (b) If the child becomes a resident of another state while on
12 probation or under protective supervision under order of a
13 juvenile court of this State, the court may request the juvenile
14 court of the [county] of the state in which the child has become
15 a resident to accept jurisdiction of the child and to continue his
16 probation or protective supervision.
17   (c) Upon receipt and filing of an acceptance the court of this
18 State shall transfer custody of the child to the accepting court
19 and cause him to be delivered to the person designated by that
20 court to receive his custody. It also shall provide that court with
21 certified copies of the order adjudging the child to be a de-
22 linquent, unruly, or deprived child, of the order of transfer, and
23 if the child is on probation or under protective supervision under
24 order of the court, of the order of disposition. It also shall provide
25 that court with a statement of the facts found by the court of
26 this State and any recommendations and other information it
27 considers of assistance to the accepting court in making a disposi-
28 tion of the case or in supervising the child on probation or
29 otherwise.
30   (d) Upon compliance with subsection (c) the jurisdiction of
31 the court of this State over the child is terminated.

COMMENT

See comment to section 40.

1   SECTION 40. [*Disposition of Resident Child Received from An-*
2 *other State.*]
3   (a) If a juvenile court of another state which has adopted the
4 Uniform Juvenile Court Act, or a substantially similar Act which
5 includes provisions corresponding to sections 39 and 40, requests
6 a juvenile court of this State to accept jurisdiction of a child
7 found by the requesting court to have committeed a delinquent
8 act or to be an unruly or deprived child, and the court of this State
9 finds, after investigation that the child is, or is about to become,

10   a resident of the [county] in which the court presides, it shall
11   promptly and not later than 14 days after receiving the request
12   issue its acceptance in writing to the requesting court and direct
13   its probation officer or other person designated by it to take
14   physical custody of the child from the requesting court and bring
15   him before the court of this State or make other appropriate
16   provisions for his appearance before the court.
17   (b) Upon the filing of certified copies of the orders of the request-
18   ing court (1) determining that the child committed a delinquent
19   act or is an unruly or deprived child, and (2) committing the
20   child to the jurisdiction of the juvenile court of this State, the
21   court of this State shall immediately fix a time for a hearing on
22   the need for treatment or rehabilitation and disposition of the
23   child or on the continuance of any probation or protective super-
24   vision.
25   (c) The hearing and notice thereof and all subsequent pro-
26   ceedings are governed by this Act. The court may make any
27   order of disposition permitted by the facts and this Act. The
28   orders of the requesting court are conclusive that the child com-
29   mitted the delinquent act or is an unruly or deprived child and
30   of the facts found by the court in making the orders, subject
31   only to section 37. If the requesting court has made an order
32   placing the child on probation or under protective supervision,
33   a like order shall be entered by the court of this State. The court
34   may modify or vacate the order in accordance with section 37.

COMMENT

Sections 39 and 40 deal with the increasingly frequent problem of the delinquent, unruly or deprived child who is a resident of another state. On the one
hand, the obligation to provide the necessary treatment or care should lie with
the resident state. On the other hand, the fact of delinquency, unruly conduct
or deprivation can usually best be determined by the court situated where the
facts occurred and the witnesses are available. These sections permit these respective functions to be carried out by direct cooperative action between the courts
of the two states.

To avoid controversy where the question of residence is in dispute, the court
making the request retains the case if the court to which the request is directed
denies that the child is or is about to become a resident of its state.

No particular form of request is necessary, the written acceptance being sufficient for the order of transfer. The cost of obtaining the child will be assumed
by the receiving court.

These sections supplement the Interstate Compact on Juveniles, adopted by
most states, and are not in conflict with it. They do not, for example, deal with
children committed to institutions, escapees, run-aways, or parolees. There is
some overlap between these sections and the Compact where the residence of
a delinquent child changes to another state while he is on probation. The Compact permits transfer of supervision to the court of the new residence. However,

unlike the above sections, the Compact provides that the court which adjudicates the child delinquent retains jurisdiction. The Compact does not permit the receiving court to determine the need for treatment or rehabilitation.

These sections become operative only as between states which have adopted this Act or a similar act containing these sections. It is necessary that each state have these reciprocal sections before the procedure can operate. Substantial similarity between the acts of the two states is also deemed necessary to assure that the law governing the case being transferred will have the same meaning in the two states.

1   SECTION 41. [*Ordering Out-of-State Supervision.*]
2   (a) Subject to the provisions of this Act governing dispositions
3   and to the extent that funds of the [county] are available the
4   court may place a child in the custody of a suitable person in
5   another state. On obtaining the written consent of a juvenile court
6   of another state which has adopted the Uniform Juvenile Court
7   Act or a substantially similar Act which includes provisions cor-
8   responding to sections 41 and 42 the court of this State may order
9   that the child be placed under the supervision of a probation
10 officer or other appropriate official designated by the accepting
11 court. One certified copy of the order shall be sent to the accept-
12 ing court and another filed with the clerk of the [Board of County
13 Commissioners] of the [county] of the requesting court of this
14 State.
15   (b) The reasonable cost of the supervision including the expenses
16 of necessary travel shall be borne by the [county] of the request-
17 ing court of this State. Upon receiving a certified statement signed
18 by the judge of the accepting court of the cost incurred by the
19 supervision the court of this State shall certify if it so appears
20 that the sum so stated was reasonably incurred and file it with
21 [the appropriate officials] of the [county] [state] for payment.
22 The [appropriate officials] shall thereupon issue a warrant for the
23 sum stated payable to the [appropriate officials] of the [county]
24 of the accepting court.

COMMENT

See comment following section 42.

1   SECTION 42. [*Supervision Under Out-of-State Order.*]
2   (a) Upon receiving a request of a juvenile court of another
3   state which has adopted the Uniform Juvenile Court Act, or a
4   substantially similar act which includes provisions corresponding
5   to sections 41 and 42 to provide supervision of a child under the
6   jurisdiction of that court, a court of this State may issue its
7   written acceptance to the requesting court and designate its pro-
8   bation or other appropriate officer who is to provide supervision,

9   stating the probable cost per day therefor.

10   (b) Upon the receipt and filing of a certified copy of the order
11 of the requesting court placing the child under the supervision of
12 the officer so designated the officer shall arrange for the recep-
13 tion of the child from the requesting court, provide supervision
14 pursuant to the order and this Act, and report thereon from time
15 to time together with any recommendations he may have to the
16 requesting court.

17   (c) The court in this state from time to time shall certify to
18 the requesting court the cost of supervision that has been incurred
19 and request payment therefor from the appropriate officials of
20 the [county] of the requesting court to the appropriate officials
21 of the [county] of the accepting court.

22   (d) The court of this State at any time may terminate super-
23 vision by notifying the requesting court. In that case, or if the
24 supervision is terminated by the requesting court, the probation
25 officer supervising the child shall return the child to a repre-
26 sentative of the requesting court authorized to receive him.

COMMENT

Sections 41 and 42 permit the direct placement of a child by the court of one state under the supervision of a probation officer of a court of another state. The situation is not uncommon where the court wishes to place a child with friends or relatives located in another state but does not wish to do so without some control and supervision. Under these sections the court retains jurisdiction and the probation and supervision are by virtue of its order operating under the laws of another state. The court of the receiving state would have no jurisdiction other than to provide the supervision.

The cost is to be borne by the court which sends the child.

Resort to these sections in such cases requires the cooperation of the courts of both states. If, however, the court of the sending state wishes to place the child with relatives or friends without supervision by the court of the receiving state, the sections will permit it to do so without obtaining the consent of a court of the other state. Section 43 can be resorted to in such situations if the court so desired.

It will be noted that the sections permit supervision by the court of the receiving state only in those states which have adopted the Uniform Act or a similar act containing these sections.

Article VII (a) of the Interstate Compact on Juveniles provides an alternative but is limited to "delinquent juveniles." A sending state "may permit" such juveniles "to reside" in the receiving state if his parent, etc., "is residing or undertakes to reside" in the receiving state. A receiving state "may agree to accept supervision" where the parent, etc., is a non-resident of the receiving state and "the sending state may transfer supervision accordingly."

1   SECTION 43. [*Powers of Out-of-State Probation Officers.*] If a
2 child has been placed on probation or protective supervision by a
3 juvenile court of another state which has adopted the Uniform

4 Juvenile Court Act or a substantially similar act which includes
5 provisions corresponding to this section, and the child is in this
6 State with or without the permission of that court, the probation
7 officer of that court or other person designated by that court to
8 supervise or take custody of the child has all the powers and
9 privileges in this State with respect to the child as given by this
10 Act to like officers or persons of this State including the right of
11 visitation, counseling, control, and direction, taking into custody,
12 and returning to that state.

COMMENT

The section will have its principal application between adjoining states. The aim is to reduce to a minimum the barrier of state lines in the supervision of children. When more distant states are involved, the juvenile court can, under section 41, ask the state to which the child goes to provide the necessary supervision.

Article VII (c) of the Interstate Compact on Juveniles may also be used to secure the return of a child from another state.

1 [SECTION 44. [Juvenile Traffic Offenses.]
2 (a) Definition. Except as provided in subsection (b), a juvenile
3 traffic offense consists of a violation by a child of:
4 (1) a law or local ordinance [or resolution] governing the
5 operation of a moving motor vehicle upon the streets, highways
6 of this State, or the waterways within or adjoining this State; or
7 (2) any other motor vehicle traffic law or local ordinance
8 [or resolution] of this State if the child is taken into custody
9 and detained for the violation or is transferred to the juvenile
10 court by the court hearing the charge.
11 (b) A juvenile traffic offense is not an act of delinquency
12 unless the case is transferred to the delinquency calendar as pro-
13 vided in subsection (g).
14 (c) Exceptions. A juvenile traffic offense does not include a
15 violation of: [Set forth the sections of state statutes violations of
16 which are not to be included as traffic offenses, such as the so-
17 called negligent homicide statute sometimes appearing in traffic
18 codes, driving while intoxicated, driving without, or during
19 suspension of, a driver's license, and the like].

COMMENT

This section is based on the division of traffic offenses into three categories:
(1) The most serious traffic violations of the character indicated. Their exclusion as traffic offenses leaves them under the definition of delinquent acts in section 2 (2). The scope of the exclusions is left to the individual states adopting this Act.
(2) The moving traffic violations. The intent here is to provide a group of

traffic offenses which the juvenile court will handle but will do so more like a well-run traffic court than as a case of delinquency.

(3) The remaining traffic offenses. These will consist largely of double and over-time parking, etc. These, it is believed, should be left to the usual courts except in two instances: (a) when the child is taken into custody and, in that event, he should have the protections we give any child taken into custody; (b) where the traffic court judge thinks there is a more serious problem manifested by the traffic offense, he is given authority to refer the case to the juvenile court by subsection (d). Most of these non-moving traffic offenses are taken care of simply by paying a fine in some cash register office and never show up in court. It is not thought that they warrant the intervention of a juvenile court hearing.

The above is a mid-way position. Some observers believe that all traffic cases should be dealt with by the juvenile court. This is the position taken in the Standard Juvenile Court Act. Others would exclude all traffic cases on the ground that a child old enough and responsible enough to drive a car should be treated like any other driver.

The position taken by the proposed sections is that traffic offenses, primarily the moving type frequently evidence a genuine delinquency pattern particularly, when repeatedly occurring. By keeping these cases in the juvenile court, the court will be able to recognize these situations and deal with them accordingly. Also a juvenile court may be able to do a more constructive job with youngsters entrusted with the dangerous business of driving on our highways than the ordinary traffic court. See Children's Bureau, Standards for Juvenile and Family Courts, 1966, p. 35.

20   (d) *Procedure.* The [summons] [notice to appear] [or other
21   designation of a ticket] accusing a child of committing a juvenile
22   traffic offense constitutes the commencement of the proceedings
23   in the juvenile court of the [county] in which the alleged violation
24   occurred and serves in place of a summons and petition under
25   this Act. These cases shall be filed and heard separately from
26   other proceedings of the court. If the child is taken into custody
27   on the charge, sections 14 to 17 apply. If the child is, or after
28   commencement of the proceedings becomes, a resident of another
29   [county] of this State, section 12 applies.
30   (e) *Hearing.* The court shall fix a time for hearing and give
31   reasonable notice thereof to the child, and if their address is
32   known to the parents, guardian, or custodian. If the accusation
33   made in the [summons] [notice to appear] [or other designation
34   of a ticket] is denied an informal hearing shall be held at which
35   the parties have the right to subpoena witnesses, present evidence,
36   cross-examine witnesses, and appear by counsel. The hearing is
37   open to the public.
38   (f) *Disposition.* If the court finds on the admission of the child
39   or upon the evidence that he committed the offense charged it
40   may make one or more of the following orders:
41   (1) reprimand or counsel with the child and his parents;
42   (2) [suspend] [recommend to the [appropriate official having

43 the authority] that he suspend] the child's privilege to drive
44 under stated conditions and limitations for a period not to
45 exceed that authorized for a like suspension of an adult's
46 license for a like offense;
47   (3) require the child to attend a traffic school conducted by
48 public authority for a reasonable period of time; or
49   (4) order the child to remit to the general fund of the [state]
50 [county] [city] [municipality] a sum not exceeding the lesser
51 of $50 or the maximum applicable to an adult for a like offense.
52   (g) In lieu of the preceding orders, if the evidence indicates
53 the advisability thereof, the court may transfer the case to the
54 delinquency calendar of the court and direct the filing and service
55 of a summons and petition in accordance with this Act. The judge
56 so ordering is disqualified upon objection from acting further in
57 the case prior to an adjudication that the child committed a de-
58 linquent act.]

COMMENT

Probation has not been included on the ground that if the matter is of sufficient seriousness to warrant probation, it should be under the regular procedures of the juvenile court, and transfer to the delinquency calendar should be made.

The portion of subsection (2) providing suspension of driver's license under conditions is a form of probation.

1 [SECTION 45. [*Traffic Referee.*]
2   (a) The court may appoint one or more traffic referees who
3 shall serve at the pleasure of the court. The referee's salary shall
4 be fixed by the court [subject to the approval of the [Board of
5 County Commissioners]].
6   (b) The court may direct that any case or class of cases arising
7 under section 44 shall be heard in the first instance by a traffic
8 referee who shall conduct the hearing in accordance with section
9 44. Upon the conclusion of the hearing the traffic referee shall
10 transmit written findings of fact and recommendations for dis-
11 position to the judge with a copy thereof to the child and other
12 parties to the proceedings.
13   (c) Within 3 days after receiving the copy the child may file a
14 request for a rehearing before the judge of the court who shall
15 thereupon rehear the case at a time fixed by him. Otherwise, the
16 judge may confirm the findings and recommendations for dis-
17 position which then become the findings and order of disposition
18 of the court.]

1 [SECTION 46. [*Juvenile Traffic Offenses—Suspension of Juris-*
2 *diction.*]

3   (a) The [Supreme] court, by order filed in the office of the
4 [   ] of the [county,] may suspend the jurisdiction
5 of the juvenile courts over juvenile traffic offenses or one or more
6 classes thereof. The order shall designate the time the suspension
7 becomes effective and offenses committed thereafter shall be tried
8 by the appropriate court in accordance with law without regard
9 to this Act. The child shall not be detained or imprisoned in a
10 jail or other facility for the detention of adults unless the facility
11 conforms to subsection (a) of section 16.
12   (b) The [Supreme] court at any time may restore the jurisdiction
13 of the juvenile courts over these offenses or any portion thereof by
14 like filing of its order of restoration. Offenses committed thereafter
15 are governed by this Act.]

COMMENT

This section permits the highest rule making court of each state to determine the extent to which the juvenile courts should assume jurisdiction over juvenile traffic offenses. In states where lay judges generally hear traffic offenses on a fee basis, the highest rule making court may wish to retain jurisdiction of such offenses in the juvenile courts to avoid exposing juveniles to the evils of such a system.

1   SECTION 47. [*Termination of Parental Rights.*]
2   (a) The court by order may terminate the parental rights of a
3 parent with respect to his child if:
4   (1) the parent has abandoned the child;
5   (2) the child is a deprived child and the court finds that the
6 conditions and causes of the deprivation are likely to continue
7 or will not be remedied and that by reason thereof the child
8 is suffering or will probably suffer serious physical, mental,
9 moral, or emotional harm; or
10   (3) the written consent of the parent acknowledged before
11 the court has been given.
12   (b) If the court does not make an order of termination of
13 parental rights it may grant an order under section 30 if the court
14 finds from clear and convincing evidence that the child is a
15 deprived child.

COMMENT

The second ground goes beyond many statutes in requiring the irremediable character of the deprivation and a serious harm to the child. If these conditions are not found to exist, the last sentence permits the court to make the usual order in deprivation cases.

Acknowledgment of consent before the court is designed to assure that consent will not be given in a climate of emotional stress or under undue pressure.

Many adoption statutes authorize adoption based on the written consent of the parents without resorting to a separate termination proceeding. The above proposed section would not require these to be changed unless those interested in adoption so desire. This section merely provides an additional procedure by which the adoption proceedings are completely divorced from those ending the rights of the parents. This will be desirable in many instances. Thus, the question whether the consent is valid can be judicially foreclosed before adoption arrangements have proceeded to the point where a petition for adoption has been made. Cases are not infrequent where an adoption has been granted based on a written consent, only to have it attacked by the natural parents on the ground that the consent was wrongfully obtained for one reason or another. A termination proceeding would end this kind of attack.

A state which adopts this Act should examine its adoption statutes and such amendments as may be necessary to integrate the two acts.

1   SECTION 48. [*Proceeding for Termination of Parental Rights.*]
2   (a) The petition shall comply with section 21 and state clearly
3   that an order for termination of parental rights is requested and
4   that the effect thereof will be as stated in the first sentence of
5   section 49.
6   (b) If the paternity of a child born out of wedlock has been
7   established prior to the filing of the petition the father shall be
8   served with summons as provided by this Act. He has the right
9   to be heard unless he has relinquished all parental rights with
10   reference to the child. The putative father of the child whose
11   paternity has not been established, upon proof of his paternity
12   of the child, may appear in the proceedings and be heard. He is
13   not entitled to notice of hearing on the petition unless he has
14   custody of the child.

COMMENT

Statutes frequently set up separate procedures for these proceedings. This is considered unnecessary. It is important however that the petition clearly indicate that the parties recognize that the rights of the parents to their child may be lost.

The second paragraph accords with the increasing recognition being given to the rights of the father of a child born out of wedlock.

1   SECTION 49. [*Effect of Order Terminating Parental Rights.*]
2   An order terminating the parental rights of a parent terminates
3   all his rights and obligations with respect to the child and of the
4   child to him arising from the parental relationship. The parent is
5   not thereafter entitled to notice of proceedings for the adoption
6   of the child by another nor has he any right to object to the
7   adoption or otherwise to participate in the proceedings.

1   SECTION 50. [*Commitment to Agency.*]
2   (a) If, upon entering an order terminating the parental rights
3   of a parent, there is no parent having parental rights, the court
4   shall commit the child to the custody of [the State (County)

5   Child Welfare Department] or a licensed child-placing agency,
6   willing to accept custody for the purpose of placing the child for
7   adoption, or in the absence thereof in a foster home or take other
8   suitable measures for the care and welfare of the child. The
9   custodian has authority to consent to the adoption of the child,
10 his marriage, his enlistment in the armed forces of the United
11 States, and surgical and other medical treatment for the child.
12   (b) If the child is not adopted within 2 years after the date of
13 the order and a general guardian of the child has not been ap-
14 pointed by the [_____] court, the child shall be returned
15 to the court for entry of further orders for the care, custody, and
16 control of the child.

COMMENT

This section emphasizes that the ultimate purpose of the termination proceedings is the adoption of the child. It is undesirable to terminate a parental relationship except in contemplation of establishing another. But the inability to secure the adoption of the child will not result in a revocation of the termination. The child then remains the responsibility of the state.

In practice, the court will not order termination unless the prospect of adoption appears, or in the exceptional case where the welfare of the child otherwise requires.

The section does not apply when the rights of one parent only are terminated and the child is in the custody of the other parent. For example, a divorced parent, having custody of the child, remarries and brings termination proceedings against the former spouse to enable the present spouse to adopt the child.

The section does not speak in terms of guardianship. In many states, the appointment of a guardian of a minor, whether of the person or of the estate, resides in a constitutionally designated court. Another court may be given juvenile court jurisdiction. The commitment here is for a more limited purpose. If the broader powers of a guardian are considered needed, application to the court having such jurisdiction can be made. See Comment to Section 2 (5) (iv).

1   SECTION 51. [*Guardian ad litem.*] The court at any stage of a
2 proceeding under this Act, on application of a party or on its own
3 motion, shall appoint a guardian ad litem for a child who is a
4 party to the proceeding if he has no parent, guardian, or custo-
5 dian appearing on his behalf or their interests conflict with his
6 or in any other case in which the interests of the child require a
7 guardian. A party to the proceeding or his employee or repre-
8 sentative shall not be appointed.

1   SECTION 52. [*Costs and Expenses for Care of Child.*]
2   (a) The following expenses shall be a charge upon the funds
3 of the county upon certification thereof by the court:
4   (1) the cost of medical and other examinations and treatment
5 of a child ordered by the court;
6   (2) the cost of care and support of a child committed by the

7   court to the legal custody of a public agency other than an
8   institution for delinquent children, or to a private agency or
9   individual other than a parent;
10   (3) reasonable compensation for services and related ex-
11 penses of counsel appointed by the court for a party;
12   (4) reasonable compensation for a guardian ad litem;
13   (5) the expense of service of summons, notices, subpoenas,
14 travel expense of witnesses, transportation of the child, and
15 other like expenses incurred in the proceedings under this Act.
16   (b) If, after due notice to the parents or other persons legally
17 obligated to care for and support the child, and after affording
18 them an opportunity to be heard, the court finds that they are
19 financially able to pay all or part of the costs and expenses stated
20 in paragraphs (1), (2), (3), and (4) of subsection (a), the
21 court may order them to pay the same and prescribe the manner
22 of payment. Unless otherwise ordered payment shall be made to
23 the clerk of the juvenile court for remittance to the person to
24 whom compensation is due, or if the costs and expenses have
25 been paid by the [county] to the [appropriate officer] of the
26 [county].

1   SECTION 53. [*Protective Order.*] On application of a party or on
2   the court's own motion the court may make an order restraining
3   or otherwise controlling the conduct of a person if:
4   (1) an order of disposition of a delinquent, unruly, or de-
5   prived child has been or is about to be made in a proceeding
6   under this Act;
7   (2) the court finds that the conduct (1) is or may be detri-
8   mental or harmful to the child and (2) will tend to defeat the
9   execution of the order of disposition; and
10   (3) due notice of the application or motion and the grounds
11 therefor and an opportunity to be heard thereon have been
12 given to the person against whom the order is directed.

1   SECTION 54. [*Inspection of Court Files and Records.*] [Except
2   in cases arising under section 44] all files and records of the court
3   in a proceeding under this Act are open to inspection only by:
4   (1) the judge, officers, and professional staff of the court;
5   (2) the parties to the proceeding and their counsel and
6   representatives;
7   (3) a public or private agency or institution providing su-
8   pervision or having custody of the child under order of the
9   court;
10   (4) a court and its probation and other officials or profes-

11 sional staff and the attorney for the defendant for use in pre-
12 paring a presentence report in a criminal case in which the de-
13 fendant is convicted and who prior thereto had been a party
14 to the proceeding in juvenile court;
15   (5) with leave of court any other person or agency or in-
16 stitution having a legitimate interest in the proceeding or in
17 the work of the court.

COMMENT

These provisions are consistent with the privacy of hearings provided in section 24.

1 SECTION 55. [*Law Enforcement Records.*] Law enforcement
2 records and files concerning a child shall be kept separate from
3 the records and files of arrests of adults. Unless a charge of de-
4 linquency is transferred for criminal prosecution under section 34,
5 the interest of national security requires, or the court otherwise
6 orders in the interest of the child, the records and files shall not
7 be open to public inspection or their contents disclosed to the
8 public; but inspection of the records and files is permitted by:
9   (1) a juvenile court having the child before it in any pro-
10 ceeding;
11   (2) counsel for a party to the proceeding;
12   (3) the officers of public institutions or agencies to whom
13 the child is committed;
14   (4) law enforcement officers of other jurisdictions when
15 necessary for the discharge of their official duties; and
16   (5) a court in which he is convicted of a criminal offense
17 for the purpose of a pre-sentence report or other dispositional
18 proceeding, or by officials of penal institutions and other penal
19 facilities to which he is committed, or by a [parole board] in
20 considering his parole or discharge or in exercising supervision
21 over him.

COMMENT

This and the next section are consistent with the non-criminal character of juvenile court proceedings involving a delinquent child. At the same time, they do not prevent inspection of law enforcement records by appropriate authorities concerned with the child.

See also section 24.

1 SECTION 56. [*Children's Fingerprints, Photographs.*]
2   (a) No child under 14 years of age shall be fingerprinted in the
3 investigation of a crime except as provided in this section. Finger-
4 prints of a child 14 or more years of age who is referred to the
5 court may be taken and filed by law enforcement officers in in-
6 vestigating the commission of the following crimes: [specify such

7 crimes as murder, non-negligent manslaughter, forcible rape,
8 robbery, aggravated assault, burglary, housebreaking, purse
9 snatching, and automobile theft].

10 (b) Fingerprint files of children shall be kept separate from
11 those of adults. Copies of fingerprints known to be those of a
12 child shall be maintained on a local basis only and not sent to a
13 central state or federal depository unless needed in the interest
14 of national security.

15 (c) Fingerprint files of children may be inspected by law en-
16 forcement officers when necessary for the discharge of their
17 official duties. Other inspections may be authorized by the court
18 in individual cases upon a showing that it is necessary in the
19 public interest.

20 (d) Fingerprints of a child shall be removed from the file and
21 destroyed if:

22 (1) a petition alleging delinquency is not filed, or the pro-
23 ceedings are dismissed after either a petition is filed or the
24 case is transferred to the juvenile court as provided in section
25 9, or the child is adjudicated not to be a delinquent child; or

26 (2) the child reaches 21 years of age and there is no record
27 that he committed a criminal offense after reaching 16 years
28 of age.

29 (e) If latent fingerprints are found during the investigation of
30 an offense and a law enforcement officer has probable cause to
31 believe that they are those of a particular child he may finger-
32 print the child regardless of age or offense for purposes of im-
33 mediate comparison with the latent fingerprints. If the comparison
34 is negative the fingerprint card and other copies of the finger-
35 prints taken shall be immediately destroyed. If the comparison is
36 positive and the child is referred to the court, the fingerprint card
37 and other copies of the fingerprints taken shall be delivered to
38 the court for disposition. If the child is not referred to the court,
39 the fingerprints shall be immediately destroyed.

40 (f) Without the consent of the judge, a child shall not be
41 photographed after he is taken into custody unless the case is
42 transferred to another court for prosecution.

COMMENT

A number of states prohibit the taking of fingerprints of children subject to the jurisdiction of the juvenile court, but the opinion of qualified observers is receding from this absolute position. Thus, in the Children's Bureau Standards for Juvenile and Family Courts, 1966, p. 50, it is said:

"Fingerprints are an important police tool in identification. The fingerprinting of children has been the subject of much controversy. It should be remembered that the use of fingerprints also protects the innocent and the general public.

"Also to be considered is the fact that in 1963 persons under 18 years of age accounted for about half of all arrests for crime index offenses (murder and non-negligent manslaughter, forcible rape, robbery, aggravated assault, burglary, larceny-theft, and auto-theft) in cities and the suburbs.

"In view of the seriousness of the situation and the fact that many of the offenses in these categories can be and are solved through the use of fingerprints, procedures governing this activity must be developed.

"Whether provided for by statute, regulation, or rules of court, these regulations need to be designed so as to attain maximum community protection. They also must be designed to prevent indiscriminate, unnecessary fingerprinting and abuse of the prints which might have a detrimental effect upon the individual later in life."

See also Police Work with Children, published by the Children's Bureau, pp. 87, et seq.

The above Section incorporates the conditions which, it is believed, should be embodied in the statute on the subject.

1   Section 57. [*Sealing of Records.*]
2   (a) On application of a person who has been adjudicated de-
3   linquent or unruly or on the court's own motion, and after a
4   hearing, the court shall order the sealing of the files and records
5   in the proceeding, including those specified in sections 55 and 56,
6   if the court finds:
7   (1) 2 years have elapsed since the final discharge of the
8   person;
9   (2) since the final discharge he has not been convicted of
10   a felony, or of a misdemeanor involving moral turpitude, or
11   adjudicated a delinquent or unruly child and no proceeding is
12   pending seeking conviction or adjudication; and
13   (3) he has been rehabilitated.
14   (b) Reasonable notice of the hearing shall be given to:
15   (1) the [prosecuting attorney of the county];
16   (2) the authority granting the discharge if the final dis-
17   charge was from an institution or from parole; and
18   (3) the law enforcement officers or department having cus-
19   tody of the files and records if the files and records specified
20   in sections 55 and 56 are included in the application or motion.
21   (c) Upon the entry of the order the proceeding shall be
22   treated as if it never occurred. All index references shall be de-
23   leted and the person, the court, and law enforcement officers and
24   departments shall properly reply that no record exists with respect
25   to the person upon inquiry in any matter. Copies of the order
26   shall be sent to each agency or official therein named. Inspection
27   of the sealed files and records thereafter may be permitted by an
28   order of the court upon petition by the person who is the subject
29   of the records and only by those persons named in the order.

COMMENT

This section is designed to protect a rehabilitated youth from the harmful effects of a continuing record of the adjudication of delinquency. See Gough, The Expungement of Adjudication Records of Juvenile and Adult Offenders: A Problem of Status, 1966 Wash. U. L. Quart. 147, 174.

1 [SECTION 58. [*Contempt Powers.*] The court may punish a
2 person for contempt of court for disobeying an order of the court
3 or for obstructing or interfering with the proceedings of the court
4 or the enforcement of its orders subject to the laws relating to
5 the procedures therefor and the limitations thereon.]

COMMENT

This section may not be needed where the juvenile court is a branch of a court of general jurisdiction. Its inclusion removes any question as to the existence of the power to punish for contempt.

1 SECTION 59. [*Appeals.*]
2 (a) An aggrieved party, including the state or a subdivision of
3 the state, may appeal from a final order, judgment, or decree of
4 the juvenile court to the [Supreme Court] [court of general juris-
5 diction] by filing written notice of appeal within 30 days after
6 entry of the order, judgment, or decree, or within any further
7 time the [Supreme Court] [court of general jurisdiction] grants,
8 after entry of the order, judgment, or decree. [The appeal shall
9 be heard by the [court of general jurisdiction] upon the files,
10 records, and minutes or transcript of the evidence of the juvenile
11 court, giving appreciable weight to the findings of the juvenile
12 court.] The name of the child shall not appear on the record on
13 appeal.
14 (b) The appeal does not stay the order, judgment, or decree
15 appealed from, but the [Supreme Court] [court of general juris-
16 diction] may otherwise order on application and hearing con-
17 sistent with this Act if suitable provision is made for the care and
18 custody of the child. If the order, judgment or decree appealed
19 from grants the custody of the child to, or withholds it from, one
20 or more of the parties to the appeal it shall be heard at the
21 earliest practicable time.

COMMENT

The appeals provisions of the several states present the greatest variety and have little in common. See Bowman, Appeals From Juvenile Court, 11 Crime & Delinquency 63, 1965.

Two alternatives are provided. One, appeal to the court of general jurisdiction for trial de novo. This is probably the most common present day method where the juvenile court is not a branch of the court of general jurisdiction. However,

232/ RIGHTS OF JUVENILES

the above section would not permit the presentation of new evidence and weight must be given to the juvenile court's findings. This, it is believed, is to be preferred, since the juvenile court is the experienced court and its decisions should not be lightly overturned.

The other alternative, direct appeal to an appellate court, is common where the court of general jurisdiction constitutes the juvenile court.

Either form of appeal necessitates a record being kept of the proceedings in juvenile court. The trend toward judicial insistance on certain basic procedures and constitutional rights in juvenile court will necessitate the keeping of more complete records. See *Gault*. A provision for the recording of testimony appears in Section 24 subsection (b).

1   SECTION 60. [*Rules of Court.*] The [Supreme] Court of this
2   State may adopt rules of procedure not in conflict with this Act
3   governing proceedings under it.

When deemed desirable, the procedural provisions of this Act may be supplemented by rules of courts. For examples, see the Rules of Court of the States of Alaska and New York.

1   SECTION 61. [*Uniformity of Interpretation.*] This Act shall be so
2   interpreted and construed as to effectuate its general purpose to
3   make uniform the law of those states which enact it.

1   SECTION 62. [*Short Title.*] This Act may be cited as the Uniform
2   Juvenile Court Act.

1   SECTION 63. [*Repeal.*] The following Acts and parts of Acts are
2   repealed:
3   (1)
4   (2)
5   (3)

1   SECTION 64. [*Time of Taking Effect.*] This Act shall take effect
2   ....

APPENDIX B

Chart of Selected State Statutes

ALABAMA

jurisdictional age: 16
waiver age: 14
type of jurisdiction: Exclusive; in addition, criminal court has discretion to transfer children 16 or older but under 18 to juvenile court. Ala. Code tit. 13, § 363 (1959).
offenses excluded: None

ALASKA

jurisdictional age: 18
waiver age: None given
type of jurisdiction: Apparently exclusive
offenses excluded: None

ARIZONA

jurisdictional age: 18
waiver age: No provision made for waiver
type of jurisdiction: Apparently exclusive. *Eyman v. Superior Court*, 9 Ariz. App. 6, 448 P.2d 878 (1968).
offenses excluded: None

ARKANSAS

jurisdictional age: 18
waiver age: None given
type of jurisdiction: Concurrent. Ark. Stat. Ann. § 45-224, 45-241 (1964); *Monts v. State*, 233 Ark 816, 349 S.W.2d 350 (1961).
offenses excluded: None

233

CALIFORNIA

jurisdictional age:	18
waiver age:	None given; however, juvenile court may not transfer child under 18 to criminal court on a misdemeanor charge and may not transfer in any event a child under 15. 40 Ops. Atty. Gen. 83.
type of jurisdiction:	Exclusive
offenses excluded:	None

COLORADO

jurisdictional age:	18
waiver age:	14 (waiver permitted only where child charged with felony). Colo. Rev. Stat. Ann. § 22-1-4(4) (a) - (b) (Supp. 1969).
type of jurisdiction:	Exclusive
offenses excluded:	Excludes crimes of violence punishable by death or life imprisonment when committed by child 14 or older. Colo. Rev. Stat. Ann. § 22-1-3 (17) (b) (Supp. 1969).

CONNECTICUT

jurisdictional age:	16
waiver age:	Waiver allowed where child is charged with murder allegedly committed after child becomes 14. Conn. Gen. Stat. Ann. § 17-60a (Supp. 1973).
type of jurisdiction:	Exclusive
offenses excluded:	None

DELAWARE

jurisdictional age: 18

waiver age: No waiver process as such; however, any child 14 or older who otherwise would be treated as juvenile may be tried as an adult if court before whom he appears determines he is not amenable to rehabilitation. Del. Code Ann. tit. 11, 2711 (Supp. 1970).

type of jurisdiction: Exclusive

offenses excluded: Excludes capital felonies. Del. Code Ann. tit. 10, § 1159 (1953).

DISTRICT OF COLUMBIA

jurisdictional age: 18

waiver age: 15 where child is charged with felony; 16 where child is already under commitment as delinquent child, without regard to offense; and 18 where person is 18 or older and charged with any offense allegedly committed before reaching 18. D.C. Code Ann. § 16-2307(a) (1973).

type of jurisdiction: Exclusive

offenses excluded: Excludes persons 16 or older charged with murder, forcible rape, burglary in the first degree, robbery while armed, or assault with intent to commit any such offense. D.C. Code Ann. § 16-2301 (3) (A) (1973).

FLORIDA

jurisdictional age:	17
waiver age:	14 where child is charged with felony; however, waiver mandatory upon demand of child, without regard to offense. Fla. Stat. Ann. § 39.02(6) (a)-(b) (Supp. 1973).
type of jurisdiction:	Exclusive, except with regard to child charged by indictment with offense punishable by death or life imprisonment. Fla. Stat. Ann. § 39.02(1) (a) (Supp. 1973).
offenses excluded:	Excludes child of any age charged by indictment with an offense punishable by death or life imprisonment. Fla. Stat. Ann. § 39.02(6) (c) (Supp. 1973).

GEORGIA

jurisdictional age:	17
waiver age:	15 generally; in case of a child charged with offense punishable by death or life imprisonment, waiver age is 13. Ga. Code Ann. § 24A-2501(a) (4) (Supp. 1973).
type of jurisdiction:	Concurrent jurisdiction over children charged with offense punishable by death or life imprisonment; otherwise exclusive. Ga. Code Ann. § 24A-301(b) (Supp. 1973).
offenses excluded:	None

HAWAII

jurisdictional age:	18
waiver age:	16 in case of child alleged to have committed a felony, and 18 in case of child alleged to have committed any offense before reaching 18. Hawaii Rev. Stat. § 571-22(a)(1), (2) (Supp. 1972).
type of jurisdiction:	Exclusive
offenses excluded:	None

IDAHO

jurisdictional age:	18
waiver age:	16 where child charged with felony; 18 where person charged with committing any offense prior to becoming 18; waiver mandatory where person is over 18 and already under supervision of court. Idaho Code § 16-1806(1)(a)-(b), (2) (Supp. 1973).
type of jurisdiction:	Concurrent jurisdiction over felony offenses. Idaho Code § 16-1806(1)(a) (Supp. 1973); *State v. Lindsey,* 78 Idaho 241, 300 P.2d 491 (1956).
offenses excluded:	None

ILLINOIS

jurisdictional age:	17
waiver age:	13
type of jurisdiction:	Exclusive
offenses excluded:	None

INDIANA

jurisdictional age:	18
waiver age:	15
type of jurisdiction:	Concurrent jurisdiction over children 16 or older charged with capital offense. Ind. Ann. Stat. § 9-3213 (1956).
offenses excluded:	None

IOWA

jurisdictional age:	18
waiver age:	None given
type of jurisdiction:	Exclusive. *Mallory v. Paradise,* 173 N.W.2d 264 (Iowa 1969).
offenses excluded:	None

KANSAS

jurisdictional age:	18
waiver age:	16
type of jurisdiction:	Exclusive
offenses excluded:	None

KENTUCKY

jurisdictional age:	18
waiver age:	16 in case of child charged with felony; also permitted in case of any child charged with murder, rape, or being accessory to either offense. Ky. Rev. Stat. Ann. § 208.170(1) (1972).
type of jurisdiction:	Exclusive
offenses excluded:	None

LOUISIANA

jurisdictional age:	17

LOUISIANA (Cont'd)

waiver age:	No provision for waiver
type of jurisdiction:	Exclusive
offenses excluded:	Excludes capital offenses and attempted aggravated rape where child is 15 or older. La. Rev. Stat. Ann. § 13:1570(A)(5) (1968).

MAINE

jurisdictional age:	17
waiver age:	None given
type of jurisdiction:	Exclusive
offense excluded:	None

MARYLAND

jurisdictional age:	18
waiver age:	14, except jurisdiction may be waived over any child charged with offense punishable by death or life imprisonment. Md. Ann. Code, Cts. & Jud. Proc. § 3-816(b) (1974).
type of jurisdiction:	Exclusive
offenses excluded:	Excludes offenses punishable by death or life imprisonment committed by child 14 or older, and the offense of robbery with a deadly weapon when committed by child 16 or older, unless the case is transferred to juvenile court from criminal court. Md. Ann. Code, Cts. & Jud. Proc. § 3-808(1), (4) (1974).

MASSACHUSETTS

jurisdictional age:	17

MASSACHUSETTS (Cont'd)
waiver age: 14
type of jurisdiction: Exclusive
offenses excluded: None

MICHIGAN
jurisdictional age: 17
waiver age: 15 (waiver permitted only where child charged with felony). Mich. Compiled Laws Ann. § 712A.4 (Supp. 1974).
type of jurisdiction: Exclusive; in addition, juvenile court has concurrent jurisdiction over persons between 17 and 18 charged with certain enumerated offenses or conduct. Mich. Compiled Laws Ann. § 712A.2(d) (Supp. 1974).
offenses excluded: None

MINNESOTA
jurisdictional age: 18
waiver age: 14
type of jurisdiction: Exclusive
offenses excluded: None

MISSISSIPPI
jurisdictional age: 18
waiver age: 13 (waiver permitted only where child charged with felony). Miss. Code Ann. § 43-21-31 (1972).
type of jurisdiction: Exclusive
offenses excluded: Excludes offenses punishable by death or life imprisonment when committed by child 13 or older. Miss. Code Ann. § 43-21-31 (1972).

MISSOURI

jurisdictional age:	17
waiver age:	14, in case of child charged with felony; also permitted in case of person over 17 but under 21 charged with any offense allegedly committed before becoming 17. Mo. Ann. Stat. § 211.071 (1962).
type of jurisdiction:	Exclusive
offenses excluded:	None

MONTANA

jurisdictional age:	18
waiver age:	16 (waiver permitted only in case of child charged with murder, attempted murder, manslaughter, arson in first or second degree, assault in first or second degree, robbery, burglary, carrying a deadly weapon with intent to assault, and forcible rape). Mont. Rev. Codes Ann. § 10-603(c) (Supp. 1973).
type of jurisdiction:	Exclusive
offenses excluded:	None

NEBRASKA

jurisdictional age:	18
waiver age:	No provision for waiver
type of jurisdiction:	Concurrent jurisdiction over

NEBRASKA (Cont'd)

criminal offenses. *State v. McCoy*, 145 Neb. 750, 18 N.W.2d 101 (1945).

offenses excluded: None

NEVADA

jurisdictional age: 18

waiver age: 16 (waiver permitted only where child charged with felony). Nev. Rev. Stat. § 62.080 (1973).

type of jurisdiction: Concurrent jurisdiction over capital offenses. Nev. Rev. Stat. § 62.050 (1973).

offenses excluded: None

NEW HAMPSHIRE

jurisdictional age: 17 in case of child alleged to be delinquent on the basis of a violation of law; 18 in case of child alleged to be neglected or delinquent on basis of incorrigible behavior or wayward status. N.H. Rev. Stat. Ann. § 169:2 (III) (Supp. 1971).

waiver age: No age given (waiver permitted only where child charged with felony). N.H. Rev. Stat. Ann. § 169:21 (1964).

type of jurisdiction: Exclusive

offenses excluded: None

NEW JERSEY

jurisdictional age: 18

waiver age: 16

NEW JERSEY (Cont'd)
type of jurisdiction: Exclusive
offenses excluded: None

NEW MEXICO
jurisdictional age: 18
waiver age: 16 (waiver permitted only where child charged with felony). N.M. Stat. Ann. § 13-14-27(A)(1) (Supp. 1973).
type of jurisdiction: Exclusive
offenses excluded: None

NEW YORK
jurisdictional age: 16 in case of child charged with delinquent act; in case of child alleged to be a person in need of supervision, jurisdictional age is 16 for males and 18 for females. N.Y. Fam. Ct. Act § 712(a)-(b) (McKinney Supp. 1973). Section 712(b) was held unconstitutional on equal protection grounds in *Patricia A. v. City of New York*, 31 N.Y.2d 83, 286 N.E.2d 432, 335 N.Y.S.2d 33 (1972).
waiver age: No provisions for waiver
type of jurisdiction: Exclusive
offenses excluded: None

NORTH CAROLINA
jurisdictional age: 16
waiver age: 14 (waiver permitted only where child charged with felony; however, waiver is

NORTH CAROLINA (Cont'd)

mandatory if felony charged is a capital offense). N.C. Gen. Stat. § 7A-280 (1969).

type of jurisdiction: Exclusive

offenses excluded: In effect, excludes capital offenses from juvenile court's jurisdiction where child is 14 or older. N.C. Gen. Stat. § 7A-280 (1969).

NORTH DAKOTA

jurisdictional age: 18
waiver age: 16
type of jurisdiction: Exclusive
offenses excluded: None

OHIO

jurisdictional age: 18
waiver age: 15 (waiver permitted only where child charged with felony). Ohio Rev. Code Ann. § 2151.26(A), (C) (1971).
type of jurisdiction: Exclusive
offenses excluded: None

OKLAHOMA

jurisdictional age: 18
waiver age: No age given (waiver permitted only where child charged with felony). Okla. Stat. Ann. tit. 10, § 1112(b) (Supp. 1974).
type of jurisdiction: Exclusive
offenses excluded: None

OREGON

jurisdictional age: 18
waiver age: 16
type of jurisdiction: Exclusive
offenses excluded: None

PENNSYLVANIA

jurisdictional age: 18
waiver age: 14 (waiver mandatory where child is charged with murder). Pa. Stat. Ann. tit. 11, § 50-325(a)(1), (e) (Supp. 1974).
type of jurisdiction: Concurrent jurisdiction over all children charged with murder. Pa. Stat. Ann. tit. 11, § 50-303 (Supp. 1974).
offenses excluded: None; however, juvenile court has jurisdiction in a case where child is charged with murder, only if the case is transferred to juvenile court from criminal court. Pa. Stat. Ann. tit. 11, §§ 50-102(2), 50-303, 50-325(e) (Supp. 1974).

RHODE ISLAND

jurisdictional age: 18
waiver age: 16 (waiver permitted only where child charged with indictable offense). R.I. Gen. Laws Ann. §14-1-7 (Supp. 1973).
type of jurisdiction: Exclusive

RHODE ISLAND (Cont'd)

offenses excluded: None; however, in case of child 16 or older who has been found delinquent for having committed two indictable offenses after reaching the age of 16, any subsequent felony offenses are prosecuted as in the case of an adult. R.I. Gen. Laws Ann. § 14-1-7.1 (Supp. 1973).

SOUTH CAROLINA

jurisdictional age: 16 in Domestic Relations Court; 17 in Juvenile Domestic Relations Court. S.C. Code Ann. § 15-1103(1), (7) (1962).

waiver age: No age given

type of jurisdiction: Exclusive

offenses excluded: Excludes offenses punishable by death or life imprisonment. S.C. Code Ann. § 15-1103(9)(a) (1962).

SOUTH DAKOTA

jurisdictional age: 18

waiver age: No age given

type of jurisdiction: Concurrent jurisdiction in felony cases. S.D. Compiled Laws § 26-11-3 (1967).

offenses excluded: None

TENNESSEE

jurisdictional age: 18

waiver age: 16 generally, except that jurisdiction may also be waived in any case in which th

TENNESSEE (Cont'd)

15 or older at the time the offense allegedly occurred and the offense charged is murder, rape, robbery with a deadly weapon, or kidnapping. Tenn. Code Ann. § 37-234(a)(1) (Supp. 1973).

type of jurisdiction: Exclusive

offenses excluded: None

TEXAS

jurisdictional age: 17

waiver age: 15 (waiver permitted only where child charged with felony). Tex. Fam. Code Ann. § 54.02(a)(1)-(2) (1973).

type of jurisdiction: Exclusive

offenses excluded: None

UTAH

jurisdictional age: 18

waiver age: 14 (waiver permitted only where child charged with felony). Utah Code Ann. § 55-10-86 (Supp. 1973).

type of jurisdiction: Exclusive

offenses excluded: None

VERMONT

jurisdictional age: 16 in case of delinquent child; 18 in case of neglected or unmanageable child. Vt. Stat. Ann. tit. 33, § 632(a)(1) (Supp. 1973).

waiver age: No provision for waiver

VERMONT (Cont'd)

type of jurisdiction: Exclusive; however, criminal court has discretion to transfer to juvenile court a person who was over 16 but under 18 at time offense was allegedly committed. Vt. Stat. Ann. tit. 33, § 635(b) (Supp. 1973).

offenses excluded: None

VIRGINIA

jurisdictional age: 18

waiver age: 15 (waiver permitted only where child charged with felony). Va. Code Ann. § 16.1-176(a) (Supp. 1973).

type of jurisdiction: Concurrent jurisdiction in certain cases. Va. Code Ann. §16.1-175 (1960).

offenses excluded: None

WASHINGTON

jurisdictional age: 18

waiver age: No age given

type of jurisdiction: Exclusive

offenses excluded: None

WEST VIRGINIA

jurisdictional age: 18

waiver age: 16

type of jurisdiction: Exclusive

offenses excluded: Excludes capital offenses. W. Va. Code Ann. § 49-1-4 (2) (1966).

WISCONSIN

jurisdictional age: 18
waiver age: 16
type of jurisdiction: Exclusive
offenses excluded: None

WYOMING

jurisdictional age: 18
waiver age: No age given
type of jurisdiction: Concurrent jurisdiction. Wyo. Stat. Ann. §§ 14-115.4(c), 14-115.12 (Supp. 1973).
offenses excluded: None

BIBLIOGRAPHY

[References are to sections]

Alexander, Paul, Constitutional Rights in the Juvenile Court, in M. Rosenheim, ed., Justice for the Child. New York, Free Press (1962)................1.02; 1.03

Baum, Martha, and Wheeler, Stanton, Becoming an Inmate, in S. Wheeler, ed., Controlling Delinquents. New York, John Wiley (1968).......................3.05

Birnbaum, Morton, The Right to Treatment, 46 A.B.A.J. 499 (1960)..6.07

Breckinridge, Sophanisba P., and Abbott, Edith, The Delinquent Child and the Home. New York, Arno Press (1970) (reprinted from 1912 ed.)...........1.02

Cardozo, Benjamin, The Nature of the Judicial Process. New Haven, Yale University Press (1921)......3.06

Chevigny, Paul, Police Power: Abuses in New York City. New York, Random House (1969)................3.05

Davis, Samuel M., The Jurisdictional Dilemma of the Juvenile Court, 51 N.C. L. Rev. 195 (1972).....2.02

——————, and Charies, Susan C., Equal Protection for Juveniles: The Present Status of Sex-Based Discrimination in Juvenile Court Laws, 7 Ga. L. Rev. 494 (1973) 2.01

Donoghoe, Diane C., Emerging First and Fourth Amendment Rights of the Student, 1 J. Law & Educ. 449 (1972)..3.07

Dorsen, Norman, and Rezneck, Daniel, In Re Gault and the Future of Juvenile Law, 1 Fam. L.Q. 1 (Dec. 1967)..2.07

Empey, La Mar T., and Rabow, Jerome, The Provo Experiment in Delinquency Rehabilitation, 26 Am. Soc. Rev. 679 (1961) 6.03

Ferster, Elyce, and Courtless, Thomas, The Beginning of

Juvenile Justice, Police Practices, and the Juvenile
Offender, 22 Van. L. Rev. 567 (1969) ....
....3.01; 3.02; 3.04

Ferguson, A. Bruce, and Douglas, Alan C., A Study of
Juvenile Waiver, 7 San Diego L. Rev. 39 (1970)....
....3.13

Fox, Sanford, The Reform of Juvenile Justice: An Historical
Perspective, 22 Stan. L. Rev. 1187 (1970) 1.03

Gill, Thomas D., The Legal Nature of Neglect, 6 N.P.P.A.J.
1 (1960)...6.05

Gough, Aidan R., The Beyond Control Child and the Right
to Treatment: An Exercise in the Synthesis of
Paradox, 16 St. Louis U.L.J. 182 (1971)..........6.07

Kenny, John P., and Pursuit, Dan G., Police Work With
Juveniles and the Administration of Juvenile Justice. Springfield, Ill., Charles C. Thomas Publish-
ing Co. (3d ed. 1965).................................3.02

Ketcham, Orman W., Guidelines from Gault: Revolutionary Requirements and Reappraisal, 53 Va. L.
Rev. 1700 (1967)......................................2.08

———————————, Legal Renaissance in the Juvenile
Court, 60 Nw. U.L. Rev. 585 (1965) 3.05

———————————, The Unfulfilled Promise of the
American Juvenile Court, in M. Rosenheim, ed.,
Justice for the Child. New York, Free Press
(1962)...6.07

Keve, Paul W., Imaginative Programming in Probation
and Parole. Minneapolis, Univ. of Minnesota Press
(1967)...6.03

Kittrie, Nicholas N., Can the Right to Treatment Remedy
the Ills of the Juvenile Process? 57 Geo. L.J. 848
(1969)...6.07

Lou, Herbert H., Juvenile Courts in the United States.
New York, Arno Press (1972) (reprinted from 1927
ed.) 1.01; 1.02

Luger, Milton, The Youthful Offender, in The President's Commission on Law Enforcement and the Administration of Justice, Task Force Report: Juvenile Delinquency and Youth Crime (1967).............3.01

MacIver, Robert M., The Prevention and Control of Delinquency. Chicago, Aldine (1966).............3.04; 3.05

Mack, Julian W., The Juvenile Court, 23 Harv. L. Rev. 104 (1909)...1.02

Maher, Brendan, The Delinquent's Perception of the Law and the Community, in S. Wheeler, ed., Controlling Delinquents. New York, John Wiley (1968) ...
....3.05

Mennel, Robert M., Origins of the Juvenile Court: Changing Perspectives on the Legal Rights of Juvenile Delinquents, 18 Crime & Delinq. 68 (1972)....1.01

National Council on Crime and Delinquency, Standards and Guides for the Detention of Children and Youth (1961) 3.05; 3.09

Paulsen, Monrad G., The Delinquency, Neglect, and Dependency Jurisdiction of the Juvenile Court, in M. Rosenheim, ed., Justice for the Child. New York, Free Press (1962)..................2.03; 2.07; 2.08; 6.05

——————————, The Expanding Horizons of Legal Services—II, 67 W. Va. L. Rev. 267 (1965)......3.02

——————————–, Fairness to the Juvenile Offender, 41 Minn. L. Rev. 547 (1957)..........3.05; 3.09; 3.10

Pilnick, S., Elias, A., and Clapp, N., The Essexfield Concept: A New Approach to the Social Treatment of Juvenile Delinquents, 2 J. Applied Behav. Sci. 109 (1966) 6.03

The President's Commission on Law Enforcement and the Administration of Justice, The Challenge of Crime in a Free Society (1967)...................3.04; 3.05

——————————, Task Force Report: Corrections (1967)......
....6.03

—————————, Task Force Report: Juvenile Delinquency and Youth Crime (1967).............3.01; 3.02; 4.03

—————————, Task Force Report: The Police (1967) ....
....3.01; 3.04

Remington, Frank J., and others, Criminal Justice Administration. New York, Bobbs-Merrill (1969)......
....3.01; 3.05

A Right to Treatment for Juveniles? Note, 1973 Wash. U.L.Q. 157...6.07

Rudstein, David S., Double Jeopardy in Juvenile Proceedings, 14 Wm. & Mary L. Rev. 266 (1972)........5.08

Scarpitti, Frank R., and Stephenson, Richard M., The Use of the Small Group in the Rehabilitation of Delinquents, 30 Fed. Prob., Sept. 1966 ....6.03

Schaefer, Walter V., The Suspect and Society. Evanston, Northwestern Univ. Press (1967)...................3.06

Socio-Legal Aspects of Racially Motivated Police Misconduct, Comment, 1971 Duke L.J. 751.............3.04

Stephens, Sir James F., A History of the Criminal Law of England. London, Macmillan and Co. (1883)..2.08

Studt, Elliot, The Client's Image of the Juvenile Court, in M. Rosenheim, ed., Justice for the Child. New York, Free Press (1962)..............................3.09

Sussman, Frederick B., and Baum, F.S., Law of Juvenile Delinquency. Dobbs Ferry, N.Y., Oceana (3d ed. 1968)...3.03

Swanson, Lynn, Police and Children, in R.S. Cavan, ed., Readings in Juvenile Delinquency. Philadelphia, Lippincott (1969) 3.04; 3.05

Tappan, Paul W., Unofficial Delinquency, 29 Neb. L. Rev. 547 (1950)...3.05

Warren, Marguerite, The Community Treatment Project: History and Prospects, in S. Yefsky, ed., Law Enforcement Science and Technology. Thompson Book Co. (1967) 6.03

Weeks, H. Ashley, Youthful Offenders at Highfields: An Evaluation of the Effects of the Short-Term Treatment of Delinquent Boys. Ann Arbor, Univ. of Michigan Press (1958) 6.03

Wheeler, Stanton, and Cottrell, Leonard S., Juvenile Delinquency. New York, Russell Sage Foundation (1966) 3.05

Wigmore, John H., Juvenile Court vs. Criminal Court, 21 Ill. L. Rev. 375 (1926) 1.03

Wilson, James Q., The Police and the Delinquent in Two Cities, in S. Wheeler, ed., Controlling Delinquents. New York, John Wiley (1968) 3.01; 3.04

_____, Varieties of Police Behavior: The Management of Law and Order in Eight Communities. Cambridge, Harvard Univ. Press (1968) 3.04; 3.05

TABLE OF CASES

[References are to sections]

— A —

— B —

— D —

— E —

— F —

— G —

— I —

— J —

— K —

— M —

— R —

— T —

GENERAL INDEX

[References are to pages]

A

[References are to pages].

[References are to pages]

[References are to pages]

[References are to pages]

[References are to pages]

[References are to pages]

[References are to pages]

J

[References are to pages]

M

N

[References are to pages]

[References are to pages]

R

[References are to pages]

[References are to pages]